AMERICA AND THE WORLD POLITICAL ECONOMY

ATLANTIC DREAMS AND NATIONAL REALITIES

David P. Calleo
Benjamin M. Rowland

AMERICA
AND THE
WORLD
POLITICAL
ECONOMY
ATLANTIC DREAMS AND
NATIONAL REALITIES

INDIANA UNIVERSITY PRESS
Bloomington and London

TO ROBERT E. OSGOOD
AND ROBERT W. TUCKER

PUBLISHED IN CANADA BY FITZHENRY & WHITESIDE LIMITED,
DON MILLS, ONTARIO
LIBRARY OF CONGRESS CATALOG CARD NUMBER: 72–88911
ISBN: 0–253–30574–8 CL.; 0–253–20160–8 PA.

MANUFACTURED IN THE UNITED STATES OF AMERICA

CONTENTS

Tables • vii
Abbreviations • ix
Preface • xi

PART I General Considerations
  Chapter One: The American Economic Vision
    in a Plural World • 3

PART II The Idea of the Atlantic Community:
    Rise and Decline
  Introduction • 16
  Chapter Two: Free Trade • 20
  Chapter Three: Geopolitics • 44
  Chapter Four: Federalism • 67

PART III Main Issues within the Atlantic
    Political Economy
  Introduction • 85
  Chapter Five: The Monetary System • 87
  Chapter Six: Atlantic Community Trade • 118
  Chapter Seven: International Corporations • 162

PART IV The Atlantic Community and
the World Outside

Introduction • 193
Chapter Eight: Japan and the Atlantic Community • 196
Chapter Nine: The Atlantic Community
and the Third World • 220

PART V Conclusion
Chapter Ten: The True Bases of a
Liberal World Economic System • 250

Notes • 260
Bibliography • 346
Index • 361

TABLES

CHAPTER FIVE

5–1. Elements of the U.S. Balance of Payments, 1970 • 97

5–2. U.S. Government Transactions and Their Effects on the Basic Balance of Payments, 1970 • 98

5–3. U.S. Basic Balance and Net Military Transactions Compared, 1960–1970 • 98

5–4. GNP, Exports and Imports as Percent of GNP • 113

CHAPTER SIX

6–1. U.S. Merchandise Trade Balance with Major Trading Partners, 1967–1971 • 144, 145

6–2.A. World Exports (f.o.b.), by Major Regions, Countries and Country Groups • 146

6–2.B. Exports as Percent of "Free World" Total • 147

6–3.A. World Imports (q.i.f.), by Major Regions, Countries and Country Groups • 148

6–3.B. Imports as Percent of "Free World" Total • 149

6–4.A. Trade within the "Atlantic Trading Community," 1958 • 150

6–4.B. Trade within the "Atlantic Trading Community," 1970 • 151

6–4.C. Intra-"ATC" Trade as Percent of Total "ATC" Trade, 1958 & 1970 • 151

6–5.A. U.S. Merchandise Exports, by Area • 152

6–5.B. U.S. Merchandise Imports, by Area • 153

6–6.A. Indices of U.S. Merchandise Exports to Major Areas • 154

6–6.B. Indices of U.S. Merchandise Imports by Areas • 155

6–7. U.S. Merchandise Exports to Western Europe and

Western Hemisphere, 1948–1971 • 156

6–8 Foreign Trade of the EFTA, 1959 and 1969 • 158

6–9 Foreign Trade of the FEC, 1958 and 1970 • 159, 160

6–10. Trade between the U.S. and EEC—Agricultural and Nonagricultural Goods • 161

6–11. Employment in Agriculture as Percent of Total Employment, and Percentage of Gross Domestic Product at Factor Cost Originating in Agriculture • 162

CHAPTER SEVEN

7–1. U.S. Direct Investments Abroad: Book Value at Yearend, by Geographic Area and Sector of Activity • 168, 169

7–2. Public Income and Expenditure (Central Government, Local Authorities and Social Security) in Western Europe's Economies • 179

7–3. Annual Expenditure for New Plant and Equipment by U.S. Business and by Foreign Affiliates of U.S. Corporations • 181

CHAPTER EIGHT

8–1. U.S.-Japanese Trade • 209

8–2. Japanese-European Trade • 211

See Notes for additional tables

ABBREVIATIONS

CAP	The Common Market's Common Agricultural Policy
EEC	The European Economic Community [now EC–the European Communities]
EFTA	European Free Trade Association
EPU	European Payments Union
GATT	General Agreement on Tariffs and Trade
GNP	Gross National Product
IMF	International Monetary Fund
ITO	International Trade Organization
MFN	Most Favored Nation
NATO	North Atlantic Treaty Organization
OECD	Organization for Economic Cooperation and Development
OEEC	Organization for European Economic Cooperation
SACEUR	Supreme Allied Commander for Europe
SCAP	Supreme Commander for the Allied Powers (Japan)
UN	United Nations
Unctad	United Nations Conference on Trade and Development

PREFACE

America and the World Political Economy continues and carries into a new dimension a series of books by David Calleo on postwar Europe and its relations with America. The most recent volume before this, *The Atlantic Fantasy*, focused on the political weaknesses and dangers of the present Atlantic military arrangements and suggested gradual but decisive change. Previous volumes, in particular *Britain's Future* and *The Atlantic Fantasy*, have also dealt at some length with the economic aspect of European and transatlantic relations.

In recent years, these economic issues, important enough in themselves, have increasingly become metaphors for a gathering political confrontation between the United States and Europe. Thus, such issues must be understood in their larger political and historical dimension. In this task, historians, political scientists and economists all have much to learn from each other. We have tried to absorb and fuse the insights of all three. At the very least we hope our study will provoke greater attentiveness to their close interdependence.

The book's co-author, Benjamin Rowland, has for the past few years been a doctoral candidate and research assistant at the Johns Hopkins School of Advanced International Studies (S.A.I.S.) in Washington. He was closely involved in the research and discussion which led to *The Atlantic Fantasy*. His own studies in economics, European and Latin American politics, as well as his experiences as a Peace Corps volunteer, have made him a full contributor to the authors' joint capital.

The book has been greatly helped by a number of other doctoral students at S.A.I.S. In particular, Götz Schreiber, and Judith Kooker have been invaluable research assistants and critics. And the authors owe much to Marjorie Rosenthal, who has patiently guided the manuscript through its many drafts, and to George Reigeluth and David Litt, who prepared the index.

Something should also be said of the series of meetings, organized around various chapters, which took place at the Johns Hopkins Washington Center of Foreign Policy Research. Colleagues, doctoral students and outside experts attended a number of lively sessions which greatly contributed to sharpening the arguments in the text. We should like, in particular, to thank Robert Osgood, Director of the Washington Center, as well as Kendall Myers, Charles Pearson, Robert Skidelsky, Robert W. Tucker from S.A.I.S.; John Hulley from the World Bank; Michel Montenay, who was our Ford European Fellow at the School and Center in the fall of 1971; and Professor Richard Ullman, at the Center on leave from Princeton.

Needless to say, these scholars bear no responsibilities for the results, except perhaps for the stimulation and encouragement their interest gave to the authors.

Much of this particular activity and the general concentration of talent and interest in European economic affairs has been made possible by Ford Foundation grants for research and writing to the Washington Center of Foreign Policy Research and, for European studies, to the School of Advanced International Studies. Our book is part of the Center's continuing project on the environment of American foreign policy. The School itself—with its international faculty and student body, its interdisciplinary approach and its policy discussions at the Washington Center—has provided a most appropriate and encouraging setting for our study.

1 JUNE 1972   DAVID P. CALLEO

WASHINGTON, D.C.   BENJAMIN M. ROWLAND

AMERICA AND THE WORLD POLITICAL ECONOMY

ATLANTIC DREAMS AND NATIONAL REALITIES

PART I

GENERAL CONSIDERATIONS

CHAPTER ONE

The American Economic Vision in a Plural World

Interdependence and American Hegemony

Ever since Woodrow Wilson's presidency, and certainly since 1932, the notion of an ideal international order has hovered over American foreign policy. From the beginning, this vision has had an important economic dimension. Economically as well as politically, we have been the champions of a "liberal" world order, that is to say, we have favored an international capitalist system where money is easily convertible and countries welcome each other's trade and investment. Our experiences in the 1930's, as we have usually interpreted them, only reinforced our devotion to this liberal ideal. The prewar breakdown of economic liberalism into "mercantilist" blocs, we commonly believe, contributed heavily to the Darwinian struggle that followed. Thus, we say, if the capitalist countries are not to destroy themselves in periodic internecine warfare, they must agree to accept the benign discipline of a liberal world economic order.

Since World War II, we have been in a strong position to impose our vision upon the other capitalist powers. And the institutions and practices fostered by us have indeed encouraged a more stable and prosperous world economy. The events of the past few years, however, suggest the rapid deterioration of this postwar system. Monetary crises have become endemic. Free trade seems everywhere on the defensive. International investments meet increasing resentment and control.

This deterioration in the liberal world economic system has paralleled a general decline in America's political and military position. That the parallel is merely fortuitous seems unlikely. During the era of postwar duopoly, when the two superpowers and their blocs have appeared to dominate the world scene, fashionable writers have noted how small the world has become and how interdependent its peoples. Nationalism therefore has been seen as a retrograde and spent political force, especially among the advanced and integrating states of the Atlantic world.

Nowadays, however, observers increasingly note the relative decline of the old superpowers and envisage, in consequence, a more plural international order. Such an evolution is likely to be accompanied by a growing intolerance for external interference with domestic affairs, a new "nationalism" which will run counter to the prevalent clichés about inexorable economic and cultural integration.

Of course, the new technologies of travel and communication are real enough: growing interdependence obviously does characterize certain important aspects of economic and political relations, among advanced capitalist countries especially. Nevertheless, even among these countries, nationalism remains a powerful if protean force, and a diminishing will to maintain the core of national sovereignty is not obvious.

Nationalism is hardly a new phenomenon. Few ideas have been studied more. It is fashionable to explain nationalism in psychological terms: in a world of rapid change, people seek their personal identities by grouping themselves together in distinction to heterogeneous external forces. To define itself, the ego needs both to identify and to discriminate. It needs both a community and a world of outsiders beyond that community. Before industrialization, it is said, the relevant community was generally much smaller—the village or the province. Today it is the nation-state. Perhaps tomorrow it will be larger units or the entire world together.

Such a view, sound as far as it goes, underestimates nationalism's general significance and current revival. For nationalism feeds not only on the psychological hunger for collective identity in a bewildering world, but also on the powerful urge to assert collective human control over a chaotic environment.

Domestic unrest and dissatisfaction in most countries reflect widespread resentment against a general economic and social environment which appears out of control. To many people, the supposed means of human advancement seem the masters rather than the servants of human purposes. In the United States, radical students and hippies, blacks, conservationists and those thirsty for law and order all share a similar sense of angry helplessness at a world which looks to be drifting out of control.

The same feelings are often shared by those Saint-Simonian priests at the vanguard of the new technocratic order, the planners and systems analysts. They themselves commonly cry out for a broad philosophy to affirm humane priorities and regain control over the economic and social environment. But technocracy in itself is unlikely to perform this task. Value-free science cannot provide the rules to govern itself; that is the function inevitably reserved to philosophy, to the science of ends. Politics is, or should be, philosophy in action. Only an effective political will can bridle technology, and only an effective political community can arouse and articulate that will.

Many observers, sympathetic with the need for political control, nevertheless retain a deep antipathy to "nationalism." In our modern technological era, it is said, any merely national political authority is doomed to fail. The problems of modern society can no longer be resolved within a purely national

context, nor indeed by traditional forms of interstate cooperation. Thus nationalism and the nation-state are the great
evils of the modern world. Serious progress waits for their
demise.

Such a view ignores some of the more important facts of
modern political life. Human communities have their own
dimensions, imposed not solely by the possibilities of economics and technology but also by the limitations of man's
nature and history. In the modern age, peoples have generally been able to form democratic political communities
only within the shared cultural community of an historic
nation. The cultural ties of language and shared historical
memory have proved necessary to sustain that "consensus,"
or system of shared symbols and intensive communication
which is the essential foundation for a common democratic
political authority.

Such nation-states cannot easily be fabricated. It generally
takes a long time and considerable blood to nourish them to
maturity. When in health they resist outside intrusions which
disrupt their inner equilibrium and threaten their sense of
self-determination. Thus, when a powerful state presses "interdependence" and "openness" upon its enfeebled neighbors,
they are inclined to see imperialism and resist it if they can.
Hence, as the predominance of the superpowers recedes and
the world becomes more plural, nation-states are likely to dis-
port themselves in a new independence. Collective international institutions which depend primarily on hegemony will
have trouble surviving once hegemony is gone.

These nationalist principles relate to an international economic system no less than to a security system. Economic
self-determination is no less precious than political self-determination. Unless, in short, the institutions of the postwar
economic system can adapt to a pluralist rather than a
hegemonic order, that system will break down. Along with
it will go the beneficial international economic cooperation

which has been the fruit of America's leadership.

To argue this point is not to deny that America's postwar leadership, economic as well as political, was for its time, both inevitable and benevolent. It is difficult to believe, on balance, that America's hegemony has worked to the disadvantage of the Europeans. Quite the contrary. But now Europe is growing too powerful for the old hegemonial relationship to persist. The liberal order must either adapt itself to pluralism or break up into protectionist blocs.

American policy has not, in our view, much helped the adaptation. Instead it has often been a principal obstacle to it. An essentially imperialist view, frequently unconscious, often dominates American international economic policy. In many respects, our ideals have been considerably worse than our practices. For we have become addicted to the rhetoric of a specious internationalism which uses "interdependence" as a euphemism for imperialism. Given our postwar position of hegemony, an ideology stressing "outward-looking" transatlantic "interdependence" and denigrating "inward-looking nationalism" is transparently convenient for imperialist purposes.

It is probably fair to say that the persistence of imperial perspectives among Americans is not so much a failure of good will as of imagination. The internationalist ideals popular in the United States have so intertwined the notions of international cooperation and our hegemony that it is difficult for Americans to conceive of the one without automatically assuming the other.

Our book explores these imperial perspectives and some of their consequences. Part II traces the origins of these perspectives by a historical study of the ideal of the Atlantic Community. Part III analyzes the shortcomings of recent American views and policies toward international money, trade and investment—in particular as these policies have led us to an increasingly serious confrontation with Western Europe. Part IV is a similar discussion of our views and policies toward both Japan and the Third World.

Finally, in Part V, we gather together the various themes developed throughout the book to propose a perhaps more appropriate view of international economic relations in a plural community of national states.

Interstate Political Systems

Before proceeding further, a brief definition of terms and a discussion of a few alternate types of international political and economic systems seem to be in order. Such discussions are invariably both too abstract and too imprecise. The kinds of systems defined here are put forward merely as ideal types, useful perhaps in clarifying the definitions and alternatives which our study emphasizes. Such models cannot pretend to offer fixed accommodations for all the great variety of relations that pass through history.

Imperial Systems

By a *system* we mean a group of closely interrelated or interdependent states. We characterize as *imperial* an international political system with one dominant power and with the other states in some considerable degree of dependence and constraint. Such a pattern may characterize a formal empire, such as the Roman Empire, or an alliance bloc with one hegemonic power, like the Warsaw Pact countries today. Such imperial systems often seek a centralizing ideology designed to legitimize the overlordship of the hegemonic power. Two or more imperial systems may divide the world between them, as many believe was happening in the heyday of Soviet-American "duopoly" and the Cold War.

Plural Systems

In contrast to an imperial system, a *plural* interstate system is composed of closely related powers, sufficiently equal in resources and pretensions so that none is able or perhaps even willing to exercise overlordship over the others. Such a system normally organizes its relations around conceptions of a balance of power and rules of the game—models and precepts designed to moderate competition and prevent hegemony. Ideologies in plural systems frequently seek to buttress these restraining concepts by showing their general usefulness to all participants. Hence the post-Napoleonic Concert of Europe stressed the common interest in "legitimacy," meaning by it the legal property rights of monarchs to their thrones and territories. With the concept of national self-determination, the League of Nations sought a new principle of legitimacy acceptable to nation-states in a liberal democratic age. The balance which prevents aggressions within a plural system is often precarious and requires considerable agility and intelligence to prevent its breakdown. A plural balance-of-power system is especially difficult to sustain if there are powerful peripheral neighbors, as the quarreling Italian cities of the Renaissance eventually discovered. It was partly to avoid such a fate that the Founding Fathers urged a federal union of the thirteen American states.

Federal Systems

Federalism introduces several variations in these interstate models and their governing ideologies. A federal system seeks the unifying order and certainty of an imperial system, but without the hegemonic domination by a single state. Unity is sustained either by placing over the constituent states a *supranational* "federal" authority, designed to represent the federation as a whole rather than any of its units in particular, or else by establishing a *confederal* arrangement among the constituent states, designed to engage them in an organized procedure for making and carrying out certain decisions collectively. The United States after 1789 gives an example of the first kind of attempted federal system; the Common Market today gives an example of the second.

Federations often fail. They seem difficult to sustain, short of becoming empires or unified national states. Lack of consensus often means an eventual civil war within the federation. One part then crushes the other—as in the United States in the nineteenth century or Nigeria in the twentieth—or the federation dissolves into separate parts—as happened to Pakistan in 1971. Often, of course, the trappings of federalism are used to soften, legitimize and thus consolidate an imperial hegemony that continues.

Each of those kinds of systems—imperial, plural or federal—can itself be a unit within a larger system. Two or three empires or hegemonic blocs grouped together can be part of a larger plural system. The same larger system may also include federations and confederations.

Interstate systems are seldom static. An imperial hegemonic system, for example, can go through a federal stage before breaking up completely—as seems to have happened with the British Commonwealth.

Interstate Economic Systems

These patterns of political relations have their economic equivalents. While economic relations are perhaps easier to measure, the notion of an economic system is no less elusive than that of a political system. Each represents a pattern, abstracted from the fullness of events, which the analyst believes is significant.

In modern times, industrial development has been the *sine qua non* not only for economic power but also for political and military power. Hence, imperial systems have been built around major industrialized nations.

Imperial Economic Systems: Colonialism and Liberal Imperialism

In an *imperial* economic system, tributary economies depend upon a metropole for both imports and exports, and are themselves discouraged from self-sufficiency. At least since the industrial revolution, imperial economic relationships generally mean that raw materials go to the metropole in return for manufactures to the tributaries. The relations may, but need not, be exploitative. Such a system can be openly *colonial*, meaning that the metropole exercises direct political control, as in the mercantilist British Empire of the eighteenth century against which the Americans revolted. In more recent times, *liberal* or *free-trade imperialism* has also been common: a dominant economic power penetrates and controls important aspects of foreign economies, but without formal political control. Such a pattern was typical, for example, of relations in the last century between the British and various Latin American states. In this free-trade imperialism, no less than in colonial imperialism, the imperial metropole generally provides the tributary with the capital for developing the export products which the metropole requires. The invested capital, besides returning interest to investors, also stimulates purchasing power in the tributaries for the manufactures of the metropole. Hence British capital developed Latin America's mines, railways, ports and plantations. The British generally financed and equipped and often ran these enterprises, even if they were careful to share some profits with the local elites.

The elaborate economic interdependence of free-trade imperialism is obviously not without its political implications. It often promotes *minimal nation-states,* political units lacking political or economic viability except as tributaries of the imperial power. Where there is no direct political control from the metropole, the imperial economic system may seem extremely unstable. The commercial reciprocity upon which the system is based can be destroyed when a tributary state begins expropriating capital invested by the metropole or pursues autarchic policies encouraging domestic production to replace imports. But the imperial economic relation may be more stable than it appears. In the last century, for example, despite frequent political turbulence in many independent parts of her liberal empire, Britain's navy generally provided the necessary security for her bondholders, and expatriate businessmen, and foreign property. While local political leaders who threatened the existing economic arrangements were sometimes forcibly discouraged, formal annexations were seldom required. The system worked well enough while Britain was, in effect, the only modern industrial economy and had the only world navy. As other Western nations rose to challenge her position, Britain felt constrained to annex what she could. In short, economic imperialism tends to require political imperialism. It is, in fact, difficult to sustain any free-trade system without a concomitant political hegemony.

Plural Economic Systems: Protectionism and Free Trade

By the same token, an international political order that is plural has a tendency toward economic protectionism among its parts. Nations seeking to maintain national political self-determination also wish to avoid economic dependency. Thus, they often pursue autarchic policies of "import substitution." Such was the policy of the United States and Germany in the nineteenth century while an industrially overweening Britain promoted free trade. Import substitution has also been the policy of many of the developing countries in the twentieth century, particularly Russia and China, whenever they have been strong enough to resist outside incursions of military and economic power.

Where the nation-states in a plural system are roughly equal, both economically and politically, and none feels seriously threatened by political or economic hegemony from within their number, they can possibly sustain an open economic system among themselves. Such a system is then liberal and plural as opposed to liberal and imperial. In the classic conditions of domestic laissez-faire, such a liberal system required only low tariffs and the Gold Standard—conditions that existed occasionally among the European states in the last century. Domestic laissez-faire, in other words, meshed easily with international liberalism.

Federal Economic Systems: Mercantilist States and Customs Unions

In the contemporary world, however, few states are liberal domestically. On the contrary, they are all mercantilist in the sense that government takes an active role in shaping the domestic economic environment according to some idea of the general national welfare. Governments participate heavily in domestic economies. A liberal economic system among nations nowadays thus can no longer base itself on free trade and convertibility alone, but demands as well considerable sustained and organized cooperation among governments. International economic systems where the relations among the members are both liberal and plural therefore incline to some degree of political federalism among the participating states. Hence the Common Market, a customs union which sustains a liberal plural economic relationship among domestically mercantilist states, has required increasingly elaborate intergovernmental machinery, including a separate bureaucracy with independent powers. Even EFTA, which was only a free trade area and not a full customs union, required an intergovernmental organization and bureaucracy.

Much the same could be said of the postwar "Atlantic Community"—where the intergovernmental machinery and staffs of the GATT, the IMF and the OECD have been necessary to sustain liberal transatlantic economic relations. But whereas no clearly hegemonic power emerges from among the states of the European Communities, the predominating economic and political role of the United States has often made the liberal Atlantic system seem more imperial than plural. The United States has often seemed to be using Atlantic federalist institutions essentially to sustain and legitimize a hegemonic position.

Economic systems, like political systems, can be units or subsystems within still larger systems. An imperial system or a customs union can carry on a regulated trade with others beyond its own orbit. A customs union can conceivably exist as an element within a larger free-trade system, especially if free trade is limited to certain products and not extended completely to capital movements. Insofar as the customs union is also a coherent political federation, it doubtless becomes increasingly difficult to fit easily within a free-trade system which is essentially imperial. If the weaker members of an imperial system federate successfully, they are likely to resist a continuing hegemony. The imperial system will either break up or become more plural.

Economic and Political Interdependence

This last point only further illustrates what should by now be obvious: the difficulty in sustaining a separation between political and economic systems. To be sure, an imperial free-trade system, by definition, encompasses no direct political control. Economic and political-military hegemony tend, however, to go hand in hand. Where one stumbles, the other often falls. An imperial economic system seems to call for some sort of political hegemony, however informal.

None of these tendencies is, however, inevitable in every situation. Today, of course, both Europe and Japan have become economic giants, but still lack corresponding military power. The United States, which still protects them militarily, increasingly seems to lack the economic power to sustain its commitments.

At the end, in Part V, we shall return to this rather abstract discussion of systems, after our generalizations have been given some content by the intervening analysis.

PART II
THE IDEA OF THE ATLANTIC COMMUNITY: RISE AND DECLINE

Introduction

No one can comprehend America's postwar foreign policy without knowing something of what might be called the American political imagination. We, therefore, begin our discussion of America's international economic policy with three chapters on various aspects of that imagination, each analyzing ideas and experiences which have contributed to the vision of an Atlantic Community.

Few ideals can be more typical and revealing of the American political imagination. For older generations of Americans, Atlanticism evokes the proud moment when the United States turned from provincial isolation and began at last to take up its world responsibilities. But when a somewhat cynical outsider, like General de Gaulle, looked at these characteristic American visions, he saw a will to power cloaked in idealism. De Gaulle's view, even if ungrateful and incomplete, was not without insight. For us the Atlantic ideal, essentially a mixture of free trade and federalism, was inextricably joined with a heady sense of America's maturing power and beckoning destiny. As we shall see in due course, the power and destiny had long been anticipated and relished.

To give any precise definition to the Atlantic Community or Atlanticism is not an easy task. For Atlanticism is a dynamic and fertile ideal, rather than a precise set of concepts, arguments and institutions. It represents an extraordinary amalgam of disparate ideas, held together with only a limping coherence.

Therein lies its vagueness and its strength. It is a vision which lies deep in the American political psyche, an ideal which shapes the perspectives of the public and its leaders and hence constantly informs policies and pronouncements. The significance of Atlanticism lies not so much in its particular momentary expressions as in the particular thrust and energy it gives to the American imagination. Not unlike Marxism, Atlanticism is a sort of political religion—although perhaps befitting its Anglo-Saxon origins, the Atlantic catechism appears less systematized and less doctrinaire.

As with many an idea in history, the influence of Atlanticism is so pervasive that few can see it. Many people would certainly deny being anything as ideological or naive as an "Atlanticist." They are all the more enthralled. Now that Atlanticist assumptions underlie so many existing international institutions and relationships, the lack of philosophical self-consciousness among policy makers and their apologists only reinforces their natural conservatism.

How can an ideal that is indeterminate, dynamic, and unconscious be a useful concept in analyzing foreign affairs? The problem is old. Tocqueville wrestled with Democracy and Equality; Henry Adams with the Virgin and St. Michael. Many people in this century have sought to capture the essence of totalitarianism or fascism or communism. It would be tidier if these great idea-forces did not exist in history. To ignore them, however, is to hide from reality. There is no escape from the necessity for that fusion of fact, sympathy, and intuition which is the foundation of any serious knowledge about the forces that move history.

To grasp an idea-force, it is often helpful to observe it in its duration—to see how the protean energy has expressed itself in shifting conditions, to see how its past is in its present and its present is in its past, and to see also how various marriages of love and convenience have taken place between one element and another, and the tensions that result.

Three main streams have fed the Atlantic ideal. As de Gaulle observed, America's historic drive for world power was certainly one of them. From the end of the last century, an American "geopolitical" school of writers and politicians had eagerly anticipated America's leading role in consolidating the Western nations. Many were avid partisans of an Anglo-American special relationship, by which they generally meant that the United States would inherit Britain's empire and assume the leadership of the western powers. Besides power in this world-political sense, two other important sources of contemporary Atlanticism emerge—the liberal economic notion of free trade, which Britain first promoted and then abandoned, and that federalist political theory which Americans have always hankered to extend throughout the globe. The Cold War blended these elements into the postwar ideal and institutions of an Atlantic Community. The mixture has proved surprisingly stable. For, as we shall see, neither free trade nor federalism is uncongenial to hegemony.

The three historical essays that follow cannot, of course, be said to exhaust or capture all the elements in "Atlanticism." They attempt rather to illuminate a few significant relationships between persisting ideas and the general thrust toward an American economic and political hegemony over the West. It is our hope that by demonstrating how these ideas have become so entangled, we may suggest how they might regain their creative functions in a new more plural era.

CHAPTER TWO

Free Trade

The Classic British Formula

At the very core of today's Atlanticist ideology lies the venerable liberal ideal of free trade. Strongly Anglo-Saxon in its origins, free trade has been one of the most powerful idea-forces of modern times. Indeed, it has provided a formula for organizing modern international life which has long rivalled the nation-state itself. Free trade's classic formulation, Adam Smith's *Wealth of Nations*, appeared the same year as the Declaration of Independence. It would be difficult to decide which has had greater influence on modern times.

Because of numerous suggestive parallels with the contemporary American situation, it is worth a lengthy digression to note how the ideal of free trade fitted in with British circumstances in the last century, as well as how it came to be adopted so fervently by our own policymakers in the postwar era.

Greatest of the free-trade theorists was probably David Ricardo (1772–1823). Even more than Smith, Ricardo set the frame for modern economic theory—not only of liberal-capitalist persuasion, but of Marxist as well. Ricardo built his economic system on the concepts of comparative advantage and the free market. In an economically ideal world, as Ricardo saw it, both producing and buying would take place at the lowest possible cost. This ideal condition would occur naturally, Ricardo believed, if the free market—man's rational desire to buy cheap and sell dear—was left unhindered.

Ricardo's writings are filled with a sense of urgency. Achieving his ideal was not a matter of abstract convenience. Along with his friend David Malthus (1766–1834), Ricardo concluded that population expanded inexorably until it pressed the margin of survival. Economic growth was the only alternative to mass starvation. Hence, hindering capital's most efficient allocation and maximum saving was wicked. It only hastened the day when demand would outstrip supply and starvation would come to restore the balance.[1]

Ricardo's desperation stemmed not only from Malthus' studies on population, but also from his own principle of diminishing returns. The ever-rising demand for goods, Ricardo believed, led to heavier and heavier investment. But each new wave of investment would be closer and closer to the margin of profitability. For as production rose beyond a certain level, costs would begin to accelerate. Land and raw materials would become increasingly scarce and thus increasingly dear. Wages, on the other hand, could not fall below the level necessary for survival. Hence, as an economy matured, the entrepreneur and his capital were more and more squeezed between fixed wages and rising rents—between the workers and the landlords.[2] In the long run, Ricardo saw no real solution other than famine, catastrophe, or perhaps birth control. Economics was inescapably the dismal science. But in the immediate future, a free market would at least squeeze the maximum out of existing resources.

Competition, however, had to be free not only within the national economy, but among nations as well. Hence, the free market ought to govern international commerce as well as domestic. To advance international free trade on scientific principles, Ricardo offered his famous proof, illustrated with English cloth and Portuguese wine. He began by assuming that the factors of production—land, labor and capital—although domestically mobile, were internationally immovable. With his two-country, two-commodity model, he demonstrated that

even if one country could produce both commodities more cheaply, it would be better economically for that country, and the world, to produce only its best commodity and buy the other from its neighbor.[3]

Free Trade and the Supremacy of British Industry

Ricardo's ideas had a rather special application to Britain's politics in the early and middle nineteenth century. The British had gained a formidable lead over other nations in industry and commerce; British manufacturers were more than capable of competing favorably in any open market. British industrialists naturally hoped to extend and consolidate their position as the "workshop of the world." Other countries would provide raw materials and markets. Britain would provide the manufactured goods.

To maintain their position, British manufacturers needed, first of all, cheap and abundant labor. Thus, in the manufacturer's view, the faster British labor left the country's relatively uneconomic farms, the better. For if Britain was hoping to remain the world's manufacturing center, domestic agriculture was unnecessary. Cheaper food could be purchased abroad and allowed to enter duty-free. With low food prices, British wages and hence prices could be kept down. Moreover, with the money earned from selling their raw products in Britain, foreigners could pay for British manufactures. Britain, by buying so much from foreigners, could insist in return that foreign markets be open to British goods. If, on the other hand, Britain refused to buy their food and raw materials, foreigners would be encouraged to seek other trading partners. Even worse, they might be tempted to try manufacturing for themselves.

Among large sections of Britain's middle class—indeed, among educated classes generally—the doctrine of free trade grew with a religious intensity. The *Economist* wrote in 1843:

Free trade is itself a good, like virtue, holiness and right-
eousness, to be loved, admired, honoured and steadfastly
adopted, for its own sake, though all the rest of the world
should love restrictions and prohibitions, which are of themselves evils, like vice and crime, to be hated and abhorred
under all circumstances and at all times.[4]

Throughout the middle portion of the century, Britain gradually dismantled her tariffs and sought wherever possible to
persuade others to do the same. To a remarkable extent, Britain
transformed herself after Ricardo's model. The old mercantilist
idea of a balanced, self-contained economy was abandoned.
After rail and steam brought cheap food from North America,
British farming languished. Britain built up a vast industrial
complex, highly dependent on trade and, of course, highly
vulnerable to blockade or any other development which threatened the ceaseless flow of that trade.

Domestic Opposition to Free Trade

The consequences of Britain's conversion to free trade
were far-reaching, if not always happy. The country grew
infinitely richer and more populous, but many people—on both
Left and Right—deplored the social and political costs. Among
Ricardo's contemporaries, humanist conservatives like Coleridge
or Cobbett found it outrageous that the nation's social relations
and political choices should be viewed so exclusively through
"the medium of the market." For Coleridge, the blind application of economic dogma was destroying the natural balance
of society and deranging its culture. The ruin of agriculture
would rob the state of its best leaders and most loyal servants.
The cyclical thrashings of an unregulated free-market economy,
however efficient in economic terms, brutalized labor and encouraged profiteers and speculators. National equilibrium and
health would return, Coleridge believed, only after the "Spirit
of the State" arose to counterbalance the rampaging "Spirit of

Commerce." Coleridge, of course, denied Ricardo's central premise of scarcity. The economy would be abundant enough, he believed, were it not for the mad, insatiable greed which Ricardo's capitalism enshrined as a virtue.[5]

The humanist critique fed reform movements on both Left and Right. Disraeli, eyeing "the top of the greasy pole,"[6] broke with his Tory leader, Sir Robert Peel, over the abolition of agricultural protection. Disraeli's speeches in 1846 suggest not only opportunism, but the broad vision of his Tory Democracy. Repeal of the Corn Laws, he argued, by destroying British agriculture would bring disruption and suffering to the poor, crush the gentry, unbalance the society generally, and make the nation dangerously vulnerable in wartime. All was to be done, Disraeli believed, for the sake of an abstract ideology which masked class greed:

> It may be vain now, in the midnight of their intoxication, to tell them that there will be an awakening of bitterness. It may be idle now, in the springtime of their economic frenzy, to warn them that there will be an ebb of trouble. But the dark and inevitable hour will arrive. Then, when their spirits are soft-ened by misfortune, they will recur to those principles which have made England great and which, in our belief, will only keep England great.[7]

Marx and Engels also borrowed and developed from the humanist critique. But whereas Coleridge believed laissez-faire a false religion intoxicating a sickened culture, Marx believed it the inevitable "ideological superstructure" of a bourgeois society. "Constant revolutionizing of production, un-interrupted disturbance of all social conditions, everlasting uncertainty and agitation," were all, according to Marx, the inevitable hall marks of bourgeois domination: "All fixed, fast-frozen relations, with their train of ancient and venerable prejudices and opinions, are swept away, all new-formed ones become antiquated before they can ossify."[8]

The liberals, however, had a powerful hold, not only among

the middle classes, but among the workers and their spokesmen. In the "hungry 'forties," trade was successfully promoted
as the best answer to proletarian misery. Cheap food, it was
said, would bring prosperity to British labor and capital alike.
It was not the bourgeois enterpreneur who stood between the
worker and prosperity, but the protected feudal landlord, with
his high-priced food.[9]

Free Trade and Imperialism, First Stage

The ascendancy of free trade had great consequences not
only for Britain but for the Empire. Many Ricardian liberals
hoped to destroy it. Empires, they believed, were the mis-
begotten offspring of mercantilism. Unenlightened governments, not content with the natural economic order of the free
market, had used their colonial power to shape patterns of
trade and production. Insofar as these patterns were contrary
to what would occur in a free market, everyone—the controlling
nation not least—suffered from a misuse of precious capital and
energy.[10]

Liberal opposition to empire reflected class antagonism as
well. Empire seemed the plaything of aristocratic buccaneers,
their political and economic position at home sustained through
wasteful military and political conquests abroad. The aristo-
crats and their empire were parasites on the capitalist economy
—difficult to remove because of their skill in appealing to the
jingoist passions of the populace. Cobden, the greatest of the
free-trade publicists, wrote in 1842:

> The colonial system, with all its dazzling appeal to the pas-
> sions of the people, can never be got rid of except by the indirect
> process of free trade which will gradually and imperceptibly
> loose the bonds which unite our colonies to us by a mistaken
> notion of self-interest.[11]

To be sure, the nineteenth-century British never did give up
their empire, although they did not extend it further until late

in the century. Mercantilist schemes for an imperial system continued to present themselves and to enjoy strong support.[12] Nevertheless, free trade continued to dominate the minds and policies of successive governments. Free-trade policies gradually eroded the old mercantilist preferences and monopolies which had sought to link the colonies into a single imperial economy. In colonial arrangements as in domestic, nothing was supposed to survive which could not meet the test of the market.

For the colonies, it should be said, the consequences were often catastrophic. Withdrawing the West Indian sugar quota in 1854 completed the ruin of the British Caribbean. Withdrawing the timber quota in 1860 brought grave consequences to Canadian development. Indian industrial development, exposed to the full force of British competition, was supposedly set back by a century.[13] Comforted by the best liberal principles, Ireland starved in 1848.[14]

Foreign Opposition to Free Trade

For a time, the British managed to promote free trade in Western Europe generally. The American economy, however, remained protected not only by geography and high tariffs, but by an unregenerate nationalist mercantilism. America's leading economist at mid-century, Henry Carey, denounced free trade as Britain's policy to perpetuate her supremacy and reduce all agricultural states to permanent tributaries.[15] European resistance, too, began to stiffen as the century wore on.[16]

Among the major continental nations, Italy was the first to abandon free trade in 1878, followed by Germany in 1879 and France in 1881.[17] At mid-century, the Swabian-American economist, Friedrich List, presented a popular rationale for a return to mercantilism. Free trade, he argued, was the natural view of a powerful developed nation, especially a dominant economy seeking to prevent the rise of competitors abroad. Britain's

daring attempt to become the world's permanent workshop—
"to become to other nations what a vast city is to a country"—
dwarfed all previous attempts at universal domination. Free
trade, List admitted, was also the best policy for a primitive
nation raising itself from barbarism. But for a nation still developing into a modern economy, free trade was a chimerical and
short-sighted policy which sacrificed long-range national interests and productive power. Significantly, List's analysis
emphasized productive power rather than increased consumption. The "power of producing wealth is therefore infinitely
more important than wealth itself. . . ."[18] Following the American mercantilist tradition of Alexander Hamilton and Daniel
Raymond, List believed long-range interest called for a balanced national economy to avoid external domination and
vulnerability in wartime.[19] The world was not "one indivisible
republic of merchants."[20] Hence it followed that infant industries
should be protected and fostered. The interests of manufacturing and agriculture should not be sacrificed to the pretensions
of commerce. Nor should the interests of workers and ordinary
people be sacrificed to short-range increases in production.[21] An
intelligent policy of social planning guided by the state should
soothe the trauma of social adjustment that inevitably accompanied industrialization.

Bismarck translated many such ideas into policy. High German tariffs and a mercantilist customs union shut out overweening competition. Income from the tariff helped finance an
extensive welfare program for workers. Heavy official encouragement fostered a powerful German industrial structure.[22]

German mercantilism eventually went on the offensive.
German goods began to challenge British goods in markets
throughout the world. The Germans began to dream both of
a colonial empire for themselves and of a continental economic
bloc in *Mitteleuropa.*

Along with German competition in Europe came the massive
industrial growth of America. By 1890, the United States had

the world's largest economy. American manufactures, protected at home, began to challenge Britain throughout the globe.[23]

Free Trade and Imperialism, Second Stage

The rise of foreign mercantilist blocs and the relative decline of her own industry obviously posed major problems for Britain. How did the British adapt?

As the nineteenth century progressed, two broad trends became apparent in the British economy and its world relations. The British trade deficit in visible goods grew larger and larger and British trade and even investments focused increasingly on the nonindustrial world.[24]

In spite of the huge proportion of her production that went into exports, Britain ran a visible trade deficit almost every year throughout the nineteenth century. The deficit accelerated after 1860. The growing deficit corresponded with and was sometimes reinforced by a number of long-range trends in Britain's economy: a growing domestic market, a favorable change in the terms of trade, capital investment abroad on a scale nearly equal to net investment at home,[25] and a shift away from textiles toward iron, steel, coal, ship-building and machinery.[26] Despite her visible trade deficit and heavy foreign investment, Britain continued to run a comfortable surplus in the overall balance of payments. The surplus depended on a large income from "invisibles"—shipping, services to trade, brokerage and insurance fees and, increasingly, the return on foreign investment. Britain, in short, moved increasingly toward becoming a service and rentier economy, less and less the world's workshop, and more and more its commercial brain and banker.[27]

At the same time as Britain was developing her commercial services and investments, her manufacturers were diverting exports away from the competitive and resistant markets of Europe and the United States and toward the industrially undeveloped areas of the world. India, of course, was a crucial

military as well as economic. India was a colony, administered as a mercantilist possession.[29] Canada and Australia, on the other hand, were dominions with relatively loose political ties. In some of the imperial economy's most crucial parts, in Latin America especially, no formal political hegemony existed at all. As the Cobdenites had always maintained, it seemed possible to have the advantages of empire with none of the costs. Free commerce and investment could bind peoples together far more effectively and cheaply than colonial empires. Liberal free trade made colonies obsolete.

Behind the easy assurance of many Cobdenites, of course, lay the unconscious or tacit assumption that Britain's industrial and naval superiority would continue. And indeed, with the major exception of India, the liberal system worked well enough without colonial overlordship as long as Britain was, in effect, the world's only developed industrial economy. Even after others were surpassing Britain industrially, it was difficult to dislodge her from overseas markets as long as she had a virtual monopoly of force on the high seas. As long as these circumstances prevailed, British political control over the actual territories was superfluous. But as more recently industrialized economies began to turn outward, build navies and seek spheres of their own, the British system seemed more and more precarious. European colonialism threatened Britain's traditional access to much of the underdeveloped world. As a result, Britain found herself reverting rather unwillingly from free trade to political imperialism. A new spate of preventive annexations and protectorates seemed prudent to keep others from pre-empting broad areas and vast resources. Enthusiasm for a formal empire revived as the new economic arguments reinforced the usual imperialist appeals to grandeur. As Germany and the United States built navies, many suspected the days of England's free-trade imperialism were numbered. Britain, so unbalanced and vulnerable in her economy, had better consolidate her external inheritance. The fullest development of these ideas came with Chamberlain's grand scheme for a new mercantilist empire. In effect, Chamberlain presented Britain with a major option in national strategy.

Joseph Chamberlain (1836–1914), although never Prime Minister, is a towering figure in modern British politics.[30] His plan called for a system of imperial preferences aimed to build the white parts of the Empire into a single multinational economy, linked by political and cultural ties and cheap water transport.[31] Geographic diversity, he argued, would offer broad opportunities for mutually profitable specialization within a balanced and protected system.

Chamberlain's mercantilist program had wide support, but never enough for success during his lifetime. There were many reasons. The Boer War (1899–1902) discouraged extension of British commitments abroad. It reminded the British of how expensive, divisive and unpleasant it could be to sustain a formal colonial empire. Canada and the nascent dominions also had many reservations. And free-trade dogma was not easily put aside. Ricardo's ideas had thoroughly soaked into educated British public opinion. The dogmas represented real interests, chiefly those of the City of London. For the City had become the financial center for the world, its magnetism attracting capital for reinvestment from everywhere, and its services earning an increasingly important part of the nation's overall income.

The City's pre-eminence worked powerfully against Chamberlain's plans for a neomercantilist empire. Why should British capital, his opponents argued, channel itself "artificially" within the particular countries composing the Empire? Greater return might be earned elsewhere.[32] In 1911, in fact, the United States and Latin America held roughly half of Britain's foreign investment.[33]

The clash between Chamberlain and his opponents was between two kinds of imperialism. Chamberlain's imperial bloc was to be a kind of superstate, mercantilist in its economic system and federalist in its political structure. Hence Chamberlain's main concern was Canada and the other white countries that were to become dominions. India was an embarrassment for him. It was too exotic to integrate either economically or politically. In many respects, as we shall see, Chamberlain's blending of power, federalism and trade was not so unlike the later ideal of an Atlantic Community.

In contrast to Chamberlain, the liberal imperialists of his day wanted to continue economic hegemony without direct political responsibility. Britain's empire was to remain essentially economic rather than political—a privileged position in the world's developing economies, built on the early penetration of British capital. Moreover, it was to depend essentially on capital and services rather than trade in goods. All these arguments were strong enough to thwart Chamberlain until he finally grew ill and retired from politics in 1903.

The Collapse of Britain's Liberal Empire

The First World War, however, dealt a heavy blow to the liberal empire. Britain had to borrow heavily from the United States and liquidate much of her capital abroad. It was difficult for London to re-establish the old position. Postwar disruptions everywhere meant that foreigners had relatively little money to bring to London for reinvestment. British manufacturing, long undernourished with capital and increasingly obsolescent, was hard pressed to earn export surpluses to finance new external investments. The 1920's witnessed a desperate attempt to restore the old position, at the cost of fearsome domestic deflation and unemployment.[34] The liberal order finally fell in 1931. Britain abandoned the gold standard, devalued the pound, and turned, at last, to Chamberlain's mercantilist bloc. An imperial preferential tariff and a sterling zone marked Britain's apostasy from the ideal that had dominated her politics for a century.

The Free Trade Ideal in America

Free trade was not dead. It had simply moved to America. There it found a new champion, the American Secretary of State, Cordell Hull. His untiring efforts were to make free trade the dominant economic dogma for a rejuvenated Atlantic economy.

A late convert to free trade, America had begun its history firmly in the mercantilist camp. The Federalist policy of high tariffs and government bounties deliberately fostered industrial growth in the interest of national power and self-sufficiency. And even after laissez-faire overpowered domestic mercantilism, protectionism, fostered by both geography and legislation, continued to prevail.[35] There was, to be sure, an American free-trade movement, encompassing at various times Southern planters, Western farmers, labor interests and antimonopolists. But protectionism was the rule.

By the late nineteenth century, as our industry began to surpass Britain's, the United States began to promote a rather special form of free trade—the Open Door Policy. The doctrine was framed for China, but its basic principles informed American policy toward Latin America and much of the rest of Asia as well. Markets for exports and investments, we believed, should be open equally to all comers. We opposed European protectorates and "spheres of influence."

The policy fitted our image as the patron of international freedom and suited well our own economic position. Our products would be increasingly competitive as long as European political imperialism did not block their way. Despite the booty we seized in the Spanish-American War and our occasional forays into the Caribbean, we had little interest in colonial empire. By the twentieth century, moreover, European colonial powers had already annexed much of the globe. The problem was to keep them from shutting out our products. Like the British liberals, we saw no need for a formal empire as long as the world was open to our goods and our money.

Keeping the world open to us, however, increasingly pre-occupied American industrial, political and intellectual leaders. In the harsh deflationary conditions of the world slump throughout most of the 1870's, eighties and early nineties, many American businesses failed, and many small manufacturers were eaten by the big trusts. The American scene seemed to bear out Marx's predictions about the inexorable concentration of capital. Hard times produced a feverish agitation for cheap money—agitation which seemed to reveal a certain fragility in the social as well as the economic order. Thoughtful leaders began to ponder whether American capitalism was not entering some fundamental crisis.[36]

At heart, capitalist theory had been uneasy since Ricardo's day. For the very Ricardian laws of comparative advantage and diminishing returns, which justified the whole system, also predicted its ultimate stagnation and breakdown.

Not until the great postwar boom in the two decades after World War II did American capitalism seem to have weathered its crises. In that cheerful age, now perhaps closing, it seemed clear that Ricardo had erred in underestimating the beneficial effects for the system of technology, foreign investment and advertising. The opportunity for new and profitable investment, either in new countries or new processes, seemed endless; the induced demand for new products infinitely elastic. Expansion, in short, could apparently postpone indefinitely the gloomy fate Ricardo had foreseen.

Such views seem especially congenial with America's own historical experience. From Madison's day onward, expansion had been the cure prescribed for America's internal tensions. In the late nineteenth century it therefore seemed more than coincidental that the end of the frontier and an American economic and social crisis were occurring together. To the American imperialists, the cure seemed obvious. Where but overseas could America turn for new markets, new supplies and new opportunities for enterprise? As the force of these ideas worked on the American mind, important elements of American business gradually came to look outward to foreign markets. As American industry grew increasingly confident of its competitive prowess, protectionism diminished and free trade gained increasing adherence. The conversion, to be sure, was lengthy, selective and highly volatile. It may well have reached its zenith in the post World War II era, when American industrial and commercial superiority over Europe seemed firmly established. It now appears declining as that superiority is increasingly challenged.

Cordell Hull and America's Liberal Vision

The great era of the American government's free-trade policy began in the 1930's, when Cordell Hull began his long tenure as Roosevelt's Secretary of State. Hull's vision of a new liberal world order dominated his policy. Indeed, his career strikingly illustrates what Halévy wrote of Bentham, the power of a man with one idea.[37] Hull's free-trade convictions were, for the most part, based on traditional arguments. Specialization would maximize economic welfare, and hence promote that general world prosperity which was a precondition for peace. Universal access to foreign supplies, markets and investments would neutralize that competitive territorial imperative which lay at the base of the modern imperial scramble.

To the classic arguments, Hull added two with a particular American slant. Free trade would check domestic monopolies. And it would create a strong mutual interest between industrial and backward countries, the former afraid of overproduction and the latter starved for goods.

Throughout his long tenure, Hull had constantly to struggle not only against protectionist opposition, but against Roosevelt's ambiguous support. In the early New Deal, favored economists like Raymond Moley and George Peek advised Roosevelt

toward a mercantilist policy of isolation, protection and preference.[38] Thus Hull, his views ignored by Roosevelt, was power-
less to act at the London Economic Conference of 1933, the
conclave which confirmed the breakdown of the old liberal
world system.

Nevertheless, in the fall of 1933, Hull scored a great success
at the Montevideo Conference of American Nations. The Conference faithfully proclaimed the essentials of Hull's world
vision: nonintervention, peaceful settlement of disputes and
nondiscriminatory commerce. Thus fortified, Hull was able the
following year to push through his masterstroke, the Trade
Agreements Act. According to its provisions, the foundation
of most American trade legislation ever since, all nonagricultural trade agreements were to be based on a reciprocal most-
favored-nation principle.[39]

The Montevideo Treaty, in effect, established an American
regional bloc. But Hull also held it up as the prototype for a
liberal system throughout the world. As he wrote in his
Memoirs:

> Throughout 1934 and into 1935 I seldom lost an opportu-
> nity, in my conversations with the ambassadors of the major
> countries in Europe and Asia, to point to the example of Pan
> America. I assured them that the principles we were laying
> down and the agreements we were reaching were not exclusive.
> We should be more than delighted to share them with the
> nations of the rest of the world.[40]

Exclusive regional economic blocs, Hull believed, were dangerous. As he wrote after the War:

> In the United States' relationship with the American Repub-
> lics in the Pan American system we, at least under the Roose-
> velt Administration, had exercised economic and other self-
> restraint; we had not sought to set up preferential arrange-
> ments in the Western Hemisphere or to dominate the econo-
> mies of the other Republics. But such self-restraint might not
> be exercised by a great power in another region, and there

might develop, in consequence, closed trade areas or discriminatory systems. These would . . . . induce the creation of similar systems in other regions, and produce serious interregional economic conflicts with dangerous political repercussions.[41]

Once the War was under way, Hull saw his great chance to build a liberal order throughout the world. But the attempt, he realized, would bring him into direct conflict with those recent liberal apostates, the British. With his usual patient determination, Hull set out to destroy the British imperial preference system. Although Roosevelt gave him scant support in the beginning, Hull found the leverage he needed in Lend-Lease. In the agreement of 1942, the reluctant but desperate British "promised the elimination of all forms of discriminatory treatment in international commerce."[42] Before he finished, Hull used the same Lend-Lease Agreement to commit eleven other countries to his grand postwar vision.[43]

Hull's vision, as it unfolded, encompassed far more than liberal free trade. With his allies in the Treasury, Morgenthau and White, Hull promoted a world-wide liberal financial order, to be based on free convertibility and free movement of capital. Closed currency blocs, like closed trading blocs, were declared anathema.

These principles, free trade and convertibility, were to be embodied in something more durable than agreements among sovereign nations. True to his federalist American heritage, Hull believed no principle or agreement was safe without an organization to embody and police it. Hence free trade called for an International Trade Organization and free convertibility called for an International Monetary Fund. To cap off the whole multilateral liberal edifice there was to be the old liberal dream of a Parliament of Man; hence the United Nations.

Britain and America in Economic Conflict

As the War drew to a close, the tensions between Hull's

American universalism and the interests of Britain and Russia grew more and more acute. Both Churchill and Stalin had quite different ideas about organizing the postwar world. Both shied away from the universal institutions where America's overwhelming power would predominate. Instead of American universalism, they preferred dividing the world into regional blocs.

Popular memory dwells upon the Cold War. But for a time, the financial struggle with Britain loomed as large in our policy. Churchill was determined to resist Hull's new order, which he, like de Gaulle, saw as a sign of a growing American taste for dominance. Churchill instructed Eden in 1944:

> As I see it, the Big Three or Big Four will be the trustees or steering committee of the whole body in respect of the use of force to prevent war; but I think much larger bodies, and possibly functional bodies, would deal with the economic side. You should make it clear that we have no idea of three or four Great Powers ruling the world. On the contrary, their victory will entitle them to serve the world in the supreme respect of preventing the outbreak of more wars. We should certainly not be prepared ourselves to submit to an economic, financial, and monetary system laid down, by, say, Russia, or the United States with her fagot-vote China.[44]

Under the Socialists, the Anglo-American quarrel soon encompassed not only Britain's external economic relations, but the policies for domestic reconstruction in Britain and Europe generally. The new Labour Government was determined to achieve a domestic economy based on full employment and the welfare state. Above all, it was determined not to return to the deflationary policies and massive unemployment of the interwar years. The British workingman, it was said, was no longer to be sacrificed to the interests of the City and the liberal international system. To maintain full employment, Labour was prepared to protect and control the British economy. Labour, moreover, was determined to preserve the imperial preference system as the device to stabilize British exports and currency.[45] A modern form of mercantilism, by way of Keynesian economics, had come back into fashion.[46]

There were, of course, urgently practical reasons for the Labour Government's view. To balance her payments, a Britain shorn of foreign assets and income had to increase prewar exports by some 50 percent, even if imports were kept stationary at the prewar level. It was difficult to imagine how the British might perform such a feat without strong import and financial controls. Britain, moreover, needed all the external support she could find—both from her traditional preferential trading system to help her exports and from a sterling bloc to tie up her huge wartime debts.

Such arrangements, however, were anathema to the votaries of multilateral free trade in the American State Department and Treasury. According to the prevalent State Department view, Europe's economic reconstruction depended essentially on a return to a liberal trading system as soon as possible. Doubtless some aid was necessary, but trade was to be Europe's chief restorative. Many Americans, moreover, feared a depression if no outlet were found for their country's greatly expanded productive capacity. The solution was to create as rapidly as possible an open liberal world, with sound convertible money and markets for our goods.[47]

Europeans, too, feared a breakdown in the American economy. But the chief danger, they believed, came from American policies which were either naive and doctrinaire or short-sighted and greedy. If there was a slump, they believed, it would come from the mounting American trade and payments surplus and the accompanying dollar shortage in Europe. Without dollars, Europeans could not buy the goods to rebuild. Europe, therefore, needed a huge transfer of American funds, not lectures on the virtues of liberal free trade and convertibility. Europeans desperately wanted their old preferential markets while they were struggling to rebuild.[48] Hull's liberal system seemed designed to consolidate a temporary American pre-dominance into a permanent fact. It was a view Henry Carey would have understood.

The conflict between American plans and British interests was reflected in a series of strenuous negotiations—starting in 1944 with Bretton Woods, which established the IMF, and ending with the Geneva and Havana negotiations of 1947 and 1948, which finally failed to establish an International Trade Organization.

The Bretton Woods Conference was called to lay down the new international financial order. Commanding figures at the Conference were Britain's Lord Keynes and America's Harry Dexter White. At issue was the rigor and immediacy of the Fund's disciplinary action against a country in a balance-of-payments deficit. White, true to his liberal principles, insisted that countries in deficit be permitted only a minimum of restrictions on convertibility. To encourage monetary discipline, he also insisted on relatively limited credit to debtors. Keynes, concerned about full employment, insisted on a more forgiving system—with credits sufficiently ample to permit deficit countries to reach equilibrium without the traditional recourse to deflation and unemployment. The result was a compromise, heavily loaded toward the American position.

In any event, Bretton Woods proved only a declaration of principles, fated to remain mostly theoretical. No European currency was convertible at the time. The Americans, however, were determined to make the system operate as they wanted it.

Paradoxically, British weakness made it difficult either to meet or to resist American demands. The war had exhausted British economic power. To a considerable extent, the United States was responsible. Throughout the War, Hull, determined to break up the British bloc, had used the leverage of Lend-Lease skillfully and systematically to reduce Britain to a financial satellite.[49] By 1945, British reserves and foreign investments were gone and Britain was begging a reluctant Congress for a massive American loan. Keynes arrived asking for a $6.6 billion grant. Aside from the U.S. Treasury's more sophisticated reservations, many in the Congress opposed aiding a socialist welfare state that seemed so busy assaulting the rights of private property. Keynes finally negotiated an offer of $3.75 billion. We used the opportunity to insist on various liberal conditions—chiefly, convertibility of the pound by 1947.[50]

Meeting the requirement proved a disaster. Up to 1947, the British economy had done surprisingly well. In the second half of 1946, British exports were running at 111 percent of prewar, and imports had been reduced to 72.2 percent. Only one quarter of the American loan had actually been used up.[51] But with convertibility came collapse. The trade account deteriorated rapidly—partly, it was felt, because foreign traders hoarded sterling to convert it into dollars. Since Britain had the only convertible currency in a Europe starved for dollars, the pressure on sterling proved immense. The whole operation, moreover, was not handled very well. Britain had not managed to fund her wartime indebtedness to the rest of the sterling bloc, and regulations to limit convertibility to transactions on current account proved ineffective. In any event, once the run on sterling began, the rest of the American loan quickly disappeared. The experiment in liberal economics was abandoned. Sterling was devalued and convertibility was not re-established until 1958.

The British henceforth took a tougher line. In the 1947 and 1948 negotiations to establish an International Trade Organization, Britain flatly refused to abandon imperial preferences.[52] Hard bargaining ensued, with the British demanding genuine concessions that would help their trade, rather than specious declarations of principle. In the end, broad mutual reductions were negotiated, but the ITO that emerged was never put before Congress for a vote.[53]

In any event, by the late forties, the whole climate was becoming more favorable to British and European interests and policies. To begin with, the principal American actors had changed. Hull and Morgenthau were gone and White was soon to be destroyed.[54] Their immediate successors were mostly transitional figures, certainly less visionary. The new President had not yet completely found himself or his men. Through 1948, liberal initiatives were hobbled by a Republican Congress with strong protectionist and isolationist leanings.

By late 1947, moreover, even the most stubborn proponents of liberal multilateralism saw that America's postwar policy was failing to promote European recovery. Both America's trade surpluses and Europe's deficits had mounted higher each year.[55] American policy, counting on free trade and convertibility, had grossly underestimated the task of European recovery. The existing institutions, policies and subventions were manifestly insufficient. The year 1948 saw a new American policy based on massive aid, and a discriminatory European bloc. Temporarily, Hull's universal vision was abandoned.

Over time, perhaps, the deflation and austerity envisaged in the IMF Charter might have brought recovery to Europe. But the new political climate did not seem to warrant the experiment. For 1947 was dominated by a new factor of surpassing significance, the Cold War with Russian communism.

The Cold War Resolution

America's euphoric sense of omnipotence and vast visions of a new international order had confronted, in Stalin's Russia and later Mao's China, obstacles infinitely more contrary than Attlee's Britain. The family quarrels over money were overtaken by the Cold War. The American liberal universe, discovering communism, became finite. The universalism of the UN and the IMF shrank to the Atlanticism of NATO and the OEEC. To be sure, the new anticommunist policy had something of the same tendency toward universalism that characterized the visions of Hull and Morgenthau. The Truman Doctrine was to defend "free peoples" everywhere. But the visions were nevertheless greatly scaled down from Hull's day. As the Third World proved increasingly intractable to any integrating order, the liberal system evolved more and more into an Atlantic bloc of the world's developed capitalist economies—a bloc justified not so much by the economic ideals of Cobden, Hull and Morgenthau as by the geopolitical visions of Mahan, Acheson and Dulles. For free trade was not the link which actually brought together postwar America and Europe. On the contrary, it was the issue that divided them. As we shall see in the next chapter, the postwar Atlantic Community came into being only after the United States, prompted by its fear of Russian and domestic European communism, suppressed its liberal economic scruples in the interest of "mutual security" and Europe's rapid recovery. America's operating vision switched from Cobden to something that Chamberlain would have at least understood. Economics was subordinated to politics. Trade took directions from the flag. And America's hegemony over Europe took a more visible form than free-trade imperialism, and also a form more useful and acceptable to the Europeans.

To be sure, Hull's liberal lamp never went out, even if for some time it was obscured by the NATO shield. While the early 1950's were dominated by the politics of security, economic liberalism moved back to the center as the Cold War ebbed, Europe recovered, and the hegemonic Atlantic system, which was the Cold War's offspring, demanded a new pedigree.

Meanwhile, however, the American political imagination drew on another stream of ideas—a geopolitical tradition which had, for many decades, confidently anticipated America's hegemony over a Western world united in its fear of the East. Harry Dexter White made way for General Eisenhower.

CHAPTER THREE

Geopolitics

Europe Welcomes the Atlantic Protectorate

Whereas Hull's scheme for a liberal economic order had met spirited resistance from European governments, establishing an American military protectorate through NATO provoked little official opposition. Security was far less divisive than economics. To many, the communist threat appeared quite real enough—if not from Russia then from domestic revolutionaries. Moreover, the American preoccupation with security brought lavish help for the urgent needs of European economic recovery.

With the Marshall Plan and the mutual security pacts millions in American funds began to flow. Demand created by the Korean War further boosted European recovery. Not only were Americans now extraordinarily generous, but the price for their aid was much lower. No longer were Europeans importuned with liberal trade and monetary policies, seemingly designed to capture their markets and leave their economies defenseless. Instead, the Marshall Plan pressured Europeans to resolve their monetary problems as a bloc.[1] The European Payments Union was allowed to discriminate against the dollar. Later European institutions received warm American support. And these discriminatory systems of trade and payments did appear to encourage European prosperity.[2] At the price of military independence, which most continental governments neither had nor sought, Europe gained the prospect of the economic recovery which was an immediate and desperate need.

To be sure, not everyone was pleased. From his retreat at Colombey, General de Gaulle criticized the NATO arrangements on both military and political grounds.[3] But he was out of power, with no immediate prospects for returning. France was already bogged down in the Indo-China War and in no position to resist American help.

The British, who had more reason to think of themselves as a great military power than the French, saw particular advantages in America's new concern with security. Britain would be much more comfortable in the role of principal ally than in that of principal economic rival. The Commonwealth could be presented as a bulwark against communism in the Third World. Its loss would enfeeble America's major military ally. British leaders thus quickly became avid partisans of collective security. Churchill contributed his famous "Iron Curtain" speech with its dramatic vision of worlds in conflict. And as we have already mentioned, in June 1946, Congress finally approved the British loan, clearly because of a rising American fear of Russia.[4] The British took up with alacrity the American suggestion of a European security pact. The Brussels Treaty of 1947 was the stalking horse for NATO, which followed closely upon its heels.

NATO, as it began, was very much an Anglo-Saxon affair. It was not difficult for the British to see it as a partnership rather than an American protectorate. Of the Alliance's thirteen principal commands, the Americans took seven, the British five. The French got one.[5] Britain's special nuclear relationship, while it led to considerable friction, was at least a symbolic check on American hegemony. British officers were often more sophisticated about geopolitics and world systems of peace than their American colleagues. All sorts of domestically redundant British soldiers, experts and ideas found a snug shelter under the American imperial mantle. For a fading British military elite, the Special Relationship extended the imperial function for one more generation and postponed a little longer the final reckoning with history. To be sure, as time went on, Britain's imperial pleasures would become increasingly vicarious rather than direct. Inexorably, she would seem more and more an American tributary. With her economy stagnant and France coming to lead Europe, Britain's claim to a special status would become ever more sentimental, precarious and irritating. Nevertheless, for a quarter century and beyond, she would cling to NATO with the passion she once reserved for free trade.

Whereas the British penchant for geopolitics was long-established, the American transformation seemed surprising in its suddenness and completeness. Why did a supposedly isolationist America assume, indeed create, a hegemonial military role so exposed, ambitious and elaborately institutionalized as the NATO protectorate over Western Europe? While American business had traditionally ventured far into the outside world, the United States had never been thought to nurse grand schemes for a world military empire. Hull's free-trade imperialism might have been expected, but not a new Roman Empire with an Atlantic *Mare Nostrum*. It was almost as if the United States, spurning Europe's colonies, had decided to annex the mother countries instead.

Early American Roots for the Atlantic Military Empire

America's Atlantic dreams, of course, were not new. The idea of a grand Atlantic alliance, with America presiding, was nourished in prominent recesses of the American political imagination for several generations. Indeed, since the 1880's, a geopolitical vision, preoccupied with America's destiny and Britain's decline, had generated a persisting stream of ideas into American thinking on world affairs.

The nucleus of this geopolitical tradition formed itself in the final quarter of the last century around a small circle of friends and relations drawn from the older American elites: Henry and Brooks Adams, Henry Cabot Lodge, Alfred Thayer Mahan, John Hay and Theodore Roosevelt. Significantly, perhaps, all of them moved from their bases to make their real homes in Washington. In many respects, they were the forebears of that imperialist intellectual, military and political complex which is so familiar a part of the contemporary American scene. The group not only pressed for overseas expansion, as did many other elements in American society, but developed what might properly be called an imperialist world view.

While American elites had always enjoyed a continual inter-change of ideas and people with Europe, it was nevertheless traditional to depreciate the significance of events beyond the Western Hemisphere for American security and welfare. The imperialists, on the contrary, believed our vital interests de-manded an active military and political role in the affairs of Europe and the Pacific. In their view, the United States, having filled its continental destiny, must press on to a commanding world role.

While this imperialism broke with American tradition in one sense, it seemed its logical completion in another. While the imperialists turned from traditional isolationism, they were also merely extending to overseas the traditional American faith in territorial expansion as the key to domestic harmony. And true also to the Federalist tradition, they looked to a new national elite at the center of affairs to manage the vast, out-ward-thrusting power which they saw in America's future.

Nearly all this group knew Europe well and had especially close connections with England. They looked admiringly at the British elites and noted with interest how imperial functions abroad gave new prestige and vigor to British aristocracy at home.[6] All tended, moreover, to see the United States as the eventual heir to Britain's world position. Their imperialism, however, had more substantial motives than a simple desire to emulate the British upper classes. They were, in fact, an impressively learned, able and influential group, who came to their views after deep and well-informed reflection.

While men like the Adamses, Mahan and Lodge were each highly individual, certain themes were common among them. To begin with, they were almost all burdened with an overwhelming pessimism, for which Henry and Brooks Adams provided an elaborate philosophical foundation. While the troubled economic climate of the time doubtless contributed, their gloom had a more general inspiration. Both Adamses shared in that vitalist world view to which the writings of Bergson and Nietzsche gave characteristic and distinguished expression. According to this view, nature is energy—vital thrusting force seeking to express itself in a crowded world, to flower and "exhibit its happiness."[7] But energy not only builds up, it also runs down. It was the running down which preoccupied the Adams brothers. Henry found in the second law of thermodynamics—entropy—the key to the broad shifts of history. Just as in physics inexorable laws fated matter to an inert mass at four degrees centigrade, so in politics inexorable laws fated democracy to a plebian society with no common will. When a society degenerated to democracy, it lost its sense of direction, its capacity to focus energy in response to challenge. In the end, it perished in chaos and torpor.[8]

Henry Adams' *Degradation of the Democratic Dogma* applied the general formula to American history. The original Federalist impulse had created the Union. It was held together by a strong national government serviced by a national elite. Power allied with scientific intelligence developed an economy geared to the national interest. With the arrival of Jackson and laissez-faire, the undisciplined energies of the country slipped their Federal leash. National policy was abandoned, the competent elites were flushed from office and the national institutions pillaged. The Union gradually disintegrated. Reunited in blood in the Civil War, the Union's disintegration had begun anew with Reconstruction. The society and its economy ran more and more out of control. No nationally-minded elite served the state. Chaos and disaster lay in the future. The Adams brothers hoped, rather forlornly to be sure, for grand world challenges that might restore vigor and direction to American life and reinstate a national elite.

While pessimism may have reached a relatively exorbitant state with the Adamses, the others often shared their mood. Lodge was skeptical about the chances for survival of the American political system.[9] He worried about the disintegrating cultural effects of ceaseless immigration, and during his years in Congress drove steadily to enact restrictions. At the same time, Lodge was nearly always in the front ranks of the imperialists: all for taking a hard line with the British in Venezuela, the Isthmus and Canada; eager for war with Spain; eager to annex Hawaii, Cuba, Puerto Rico and the Philippines; pushing hard for American penetration in China. Above all, Lodge was for a big navy and used his power in Congress to build it. Here he was in accord with his wife's family, the Davises, who were navy people, and with their friend and his, Alfred Thayer Mahan.[10]

Mahan articulated the imperial mood with admirable forthrightness and coherence. The world was a place full of danger —destructive forces without and within "threaten to submerge all the centuries have gained."[11] Western civilization was "an oasis set in the midst of a desert of barbarism, rent with many intestine problems," and surrounded by numerically superior "hosts of outsiders."[12] Western penetration had aroused the East, which would soon make a massive thrust to gain Western power and prosperity, while rejecting its spiritual values.[13] Explosive conflict was inevitable. By 1897, Mahan saw "the opening of a period when the question is to be settled decisively, though the issue may be long delayed, whether the Eastern or Western civilization is to dominate throughout the earth and to control its future."[14] To survive, the West must "express itself in a menacing and efficient attitude of physical force."[15]

Mahan thought the Eastern peoples would ultimately have their day. History had assigned the modern Western nations the Roman task of civilizing the barbarians before they came to power. Mahan recommended the Roman technique—a ring of peripheral defenses within barbarian territory. Hence his justification for a big navy.

In the face of their common peril, Mahan believed, the Western nations would draw together. While the major European states could guard the land with their great armies, America and Britain could patrol the seas with great navies. The Atlantic would become the Western lake, and the Pacific the forward outpost.

While they had impressive influence in their day, the early imperialists were, in many respects, far ahead of their time. Their immediate influence seemed paramount, of course, when one of their own, Theodore Roosevelt, unexpectedly became President. At the time, Brooks Adams wrote his old friend: "You have a greater place than Trajan, for you are the embodiment of a power not only vaster than the power of the empire, but vaster than men have ever known." Now, Adams announced, can begin the "contest for supremacy of America against the Eastern continent."[16]

The Adamses, Brooks in particular, also developed rather elaborate theories about the role of economics in history. Part of the group's general gloom doubtless arose from the depressed economic climate of the late nineteenth century. For the Adamses in particular, economic misfortune threatened to be personal as well as general.

Brooks Adams' *Law of Civilization and Decay* saw nations entering decline when their economies reached saturation and ceased to grow. For all the crankiness of some of his particular theories, his basic view is part of the established wisdom about American capitalism—that if it does not grow and grow, it will come crashing to the ground—a view espoused no less by Hoover than by Lenin.[17]

In general, however, economic considerations play a rather secondary role in the imperial apologies. Even for Brooks Adams, economic power was seen primarily as a function of political and cultural vitality. Certainly Mahan's imperialism was essentially geopolitical—military and cultural. Lodge's too. He was constantly irritated by what he saw as the pusillanimous timidity of Boston big business to any policy abroad that might temporarily interfere with trade—or cost money for armaments.[18]

Thus, while the geopolitical school had an important if secondary economic dimension to its imperialism, all business interests were by no means sympathetic to a political empire. The same was true, of course, in England. In both countries, the persisting influence of the liberal free-trade ideology continued to hold sway over large sections of the business community.

Not surprisingly, when the Great European War finally came, the imperialists were eager to engage American power on Britain's side. As Mahan had written, when America begins at last to take up its "duties to the world at large," "we shall stretch out our hands to Great Britain, realizing that in unity of heart among the English-speaking race lies the best hope of humanity in the doubtful days ahead."[19] The War seemed an excellent opportunity to build a world-embracing Western coalition led by the United States. As the U.S. entered the War in 1917, Henry Adams saw such an Atlantic Community at last becoming a reality:

> To my bewilderment, I find the great object of my life thus accomplished in the building up of a great community of Atlantic Powers which I hope will at least make a precedent that can never be forgotten. . . . Strange it is that we should have done it by means of inducing those blockheads of Germans to kick us into it. I think that I can now contemplate the total

ruin of our old world with more philosophy than I ever thought
possible . . . . it is really a joy to feel that we have established
one great idea even though we have pulled all the stars out of
their course in order to do it.[20]

Much as the group favored an Anglo-American Special Relationship as the first link in the Western system, their attitude
toward Britain was surprisingly unsentimental. The British
were creditors and commercial rivals as well as friends and
customers.[21] With Britain in distress, the American imperialists
were not so much dutiful children as impatient heirs. Men like
Adams and Lodge were little inclined to forget the thorny path
of Anglo-American diplomatic relations throughout the nineteenth century. The Adamses had not forgotten Britain's ambivalent policy while their father was the Union's ambassador
during the Civil War.[22] Lodge, for all his Anglophilia and close
English connections, was brutally tough in asserting American
interests at Britain's expense, as his role in the Venezuelan
Boundary Disputes, the revision of the Hay-Pauncefote Treaty
and the Alaskan Boundary Disputes clearly demonstrated. Indeed, American behavior was so outrageous that it is hard to
see how the British stood it. Lodge's attitude foreshadowed
the basic Anglo-American relationship. Britain is the junior
partner, sustained whenever it is in the American interest to
do so, but at the price America sees fit to charge. America takes
what she wants and brooks no interference.

Interestingly, when Andrew Carnegie urged a formal Anglo-
American partnership in 1893, Mahan felt any codification of
the relationship precipitate. America should wait for her immense power to mature. For America was rising and Britain
falling. In time, America would inherit the whole imperial
position. Meanwhile, there was no need for excessive deference
to British interests or sensibilities. Mahan hoped for a grand
federation when America was ready, but he could not imagine
why the British should welcome it:

Disunion, loss of national identity, changes of constitution more than radical, the exchange of a world-wide empire for a subordinate part in a great federation—such *may* be the destiny of Great Britain in the distant future. I know not; but sure I am, were I a citizen of Great Britain, the prospect would not allure me now to move an inch in such a direction.[23]

Britain's Dilemma and the Special Relationship

What, indeed, was the British interest in the Special Relationship? Nationalist *Realpolitik* might easily have dictated an opposite course. The United States, with surging commercial energies and immense resources, was by far the most formidable challenger to Britain's imperial position. Germany, with a much smaller base—boxed in by France and Russia and allied with an uncertain Austria-Hungary—was surely a lesser rival by far. Had Britain come to terms with Germany's ambitions, America's power might have been balanced and something of Britain's world position saved. Instead, Britain fought Germany and allied with America. After two great wars, Britain and Germany were ruined as great powers, and America took the imperial role.

Such an outcome was not impossible to foresee. Any number of people early in the nineteenth century speculated on what the consolidation of continent-sized industrial state would mean to world power-politics.[24]

After the Civil War, it was increasingly obvious that the United States would overshadow the nation-states of Europe and profoundly change the geography of world political and economic power.[25] While Russia, the other nascent "superpower," remained relatively backward, the United States in 1890 became the world's largest and most modern industrial economy. The significance was not obscure. In 1878 Gladstone wrote about the United States:

> It is she alone who, at a coming time, can, and probably will, wrest from us that commercial primacy. We have no title, I have no inclination to murmur at the prospect. If she acquires

it, she will make the acquisition by the right of the strongest; but, in this instance, the strongest means the best. She will probably become what we are now, the head servant in the great household of the world, the employer of all employed, because her service will be the most and ablest. We have no more title against her than Venice, or Genoa, or Holland, has had against us.[26]

Gladstone, with his old-fashioned free-trade liberalism, could foresee Britain's loss of empire and geopolitical pre-eminence with a certain complacency. Others, more attuned to the themes of an imperial age, foresaw disaster. Disraeli, in his famous *Crystal Palace Speech* of 1872, spelled out the imperial themes for Britain. England was either to be a dull, comfortable European state or a "great country, an Imperial country, a country where your sons, when they rise, rise to paramount positions, and obtain not merely the esteem of their countrymen, but command the respect of the world."[27]

Joseph Chamberlain's vision of an empire linked by water into a single political and economic system was, in part, an imperial Britain's answer to the rising superpowers. Germany's belated preoccupation with colonies had the same inspiration, as did the German idea of *Mitteleuropa*—a superpower within Europe itself.[28]

At Chamberlain's initiative, Britain and Germany flirted with an alliance—a bloc that would retain Europe's world supremacy on into the twentieth century. In the end, however, the two powers failed to accommodate each other's interests. Germany built a navy to rival Britain's position overseas. Britain joined the Franco-Russian *entente* to block Germany at every turn. Instead of seeking to contain America, Britain sought to appease her. The Special Relationship was the result.

From 1890 on, Britain seemed willing to pay almost any price for American friendship. The more outrageous the American demands, the more docile the British response. By 1900,

Americans began to see the advantages of so accommodating a Special Relationship. In 1917, the British got their reward. Germany was beaten, but at a terrible cost in British blood and treasure. America was the real winner. Economically, Britain lost her creditor status and became America's debtor. Politically and militarily, Britain's empire came to depend on American good will. At the time, Lloyd George remarked that if the British empire ever came to depend on American support, the empire was lost.[29] By 1920, the British were being told in the Washington Disarmament Conference that America was now the world's leading naval power, that any British attempt to reestablish their prewar naval predominance would not be tolerated, nor would a renewal of the British alliance with Japan.[30] The British acquiesced. What they had fought so fiercely to deny Germany, they handed over to America without a shot fired in anger. The Special Relationship was well on its way to becoming what Mahan had foreseen. But what is the reply to Mahan's question? Why did the English choose such a future for themselves?

One answer simply blames British statesmanship for an egregious lack of foresight. British policy, caught up in the short-run and the secondary, lacked the vision and energy to frame an adequate new policy to cope with America. British statesmen, preoccupied with the traditional threat from Europe, ignored the need for a balance in the world at large. The old formulas, in particular that of opposing automatically the strongest continental power, became, as it happened, suicidal for British imperial interests. The Special Relationship was sentimental nonsense, useful only to soften Britain's increasing subservience.

It is not difficult, however, to make plausible apologies for British statesmanship. In 1900, it can be argued, Germany was an immediate threat and infinitely and urgently expansive. No real accommodation was possible. Moreover, Franco-German antagonism made any scheme for a durable European bloc unrealistic. Then, as later, the Europeans, thinking of themselves as the cockpit of the world, found it easier to ally with outsiders than with each other. The same points, of course, could be made again about British policy in the 1930's.[31]

For many of the British, considerations of ideology reinforced considerations of power. Germany was ruled first by an authoritarian and then by a totalitarian regime, whereas the United States was a sister democracy. And America was, after all, Britain's child. America's blood was her blood. America's culture and political institutions were branches out of Britain's tree. Britain's natural place lay inside a great English-speaking Commonwealth, even if America was fated to become the dominant power within it. For Britain to resist this evolution, many British have believed, would be to renounce the grand destiny of the Anglo-Saxon people.

This notion of an Anglo-Saxon race and world mission flourished throughout the later nineteenth century. In 1868, for example, Sir Charles Dilke (1843–1911), the brilliant, ill-starred politician, published his popular *Greater Britain*, which spread the belief that Anglo-Saxons would conquer the globe. As Dilke saw it, the more powerful Saxon race was everywhere evicting weaker peoples while firmly resisting absorption by them. As the Saxon empire grew, Britain's relative role in it would inevitably decline. Still: "The ultimate future of any one section of our race . . . is of little moment by the side of its triumph as a whole, but the power of English laws and English principles of government is not merely an English question—its continuance is essential to the freedom of mankind."[32]

Another Anglo-Saxon racist, J. R. Seeley (1834–1895), the Cambridge historian, developed many of the themes current in today's Atlanticist ideology. For Seeley, the great drive of the English people was the key to their modern history—from Elizabeth's time to Victoria's. Their accomplishment was "The Expansion of England," the title of Seeley's famous essay of

1883. The English race had gone out to fill the world's empty spaces until the British nation stretched around the world, and an Englishman was at home in many places. Meanwhile, modern technology was making the world smaller, and world-wide states were becoming possible:

> In the eighteenth century Burke thought a federal state quite impossible across the Atlantic Ocean. In such times the metaphor of the grown-up son might well harden into a convincing demonstration. But since Burke's time the Atlantic Ocean has shrunk till it seems scarcely broader than the sea between Greece and Sicily. Why then do we not drop the metaphor?[33]

For Seeley, the modern problem was finding the appropriate political system for a vast interoceanic state. In the eighteenth century, the British had failed, but the British-Americans, by combining federalism with representative government, had succeeded. Their federal formula, Seeley believed, would be the foundation for the political system of the future.

Ironically, this notion of an Anglo-Saxon world empire and Chamberlain's vision of an imperial commonwealth were strongly reinforcing. But from the perspective of British national interest, the emphasis on Anglo-Saxon racial and cultural links meant that the Empire, while it could be mobilized against the Germans, was at a great disadvantage as a counterweight against the Americans. Culturally and institutionally, the dominions probably had as much if not more in common with America than with Britain. Hence, while the Anglo-Saxon Empire and the Special Relationship seemed natural complements, from the perspective of geopolitics Anglo-Saxon racism only further disabled England from meeting the American challenge.

Europe Pre-destined to America's Hegemony

By turning from an accommodation with the continent, Britain sealed her own and probably Europe's fate as America's

Atlantic dependency. None of these grand settlements, of course, took place immediately. The Atlantic drama took another quarter century to play itself out. With Woodrow Wilson, to be sure, the Europeans got more than a glimpse of the coming age of American hegemony. All the characteristic elements were there: free trade, federalism, and the assumption that our national power was sterilized by exceptional virtue. Hull changed only the details. Wilson envisaged an open and integrated liberal-capitalist world system in which America, with her maturing power and exceptional virtue, would naturally take the leading role. Indeed, American power would create this world. The world's suppressed nation-states were to be set free. Those nations corrupted by the atavistic right-wing imperialism of their feudal remnants, or by the new revolutionary socialism of the Bolsheviks, were to be purified by war and intervention. Once nation-states had been established and confirmed in liberal-capitalist democracy, they were to be admitted into a universal political and economic structure of peace—a system characterized by collective security and an open world economy. Power politics were to be eliminated. All nations were to be equal in their rights and security. America's great power, exceptional liberal stability and general moral prestige would naturally give her the leading role. For America would always "speak for liberals and friends of humanity in every nation."[34]

But America's hour had not yet come. Wilson's facile reconciliation of liberal universalism and American power caught him in too many foreign and domestic contradictions. Congress, dominated by a strange alliance, drew back from the scheme for American hegemony exercised through the League. While the isolationists hoped to avoid the imperial mantle, the imperialists feared the League might entangle rather than provide a legitimate channel for American power. Personal dislike of Wilson was itself a ruling passion, especially for Lodge and his friends.[35]

The common view that all would have been right with the world if only America had joined the League and guaranteed Versailles deserves serious qualification. Would Britain and France have been happy with an American protectorate? What would have been the commercial consequences? Perhaps there would have been a European Economic Community a quarter of a century earlier. In any event, the United States participating so actively in European politics would have constituted a major revolution in the map of world power. It is naive to assume that American power was somehow so politically sterile and non-abrasive that its introduction would not have provoked a corresponding reaction. As it was, sharp friction over economic policy between Europe and the United States marked the whole inter-war period. In the 1920's especially, the American government took a particularly vigorous role in promoting the country's business interests abroad.[36]

Throughout this period of commercial antagonism, the geopolitical vision of an armed Atlantic Alliance was, if dormant, not entirely extinguished. It found a resounding statement just before World War II in the popular writings of Clarence Streit, an American journalist who covered the League at Geneva. Streit's famous *Union Now* (1939) seems both remarkably unsophisticated in its assumptions, and also remarkably prescient about postwar American foreign policy.

According to Streit, the existing world disorder had become too dangerous to be tolerated any longer by the United States. Europe could not be left to herself. To preserve American security, American power would henceforth have to be engaged as far away from home as possible, before our potential enemies could consolidate themselves. Our security demanded not a balance of power, but an overwhelming imbalance in our favor.

Streit found nationalism the principal threat, both to the modern world in general and to American security in particular. Grouped around nationalism were all the other plagues of modern life—sovereignty, neutrality, balances of power, traditional alliance systems, or Leagues of Nations.

Nationalism was the disease, and the American Constitution the cure:

> A constitution that is already universal in its scope, that allows for the admission to its Union of any state on earth, that never even mentions territory or language, and that mentions race and color only to provide that freedom shall never on that account be denied to any man.[37]

Streit suggested a world state built around an Anglo-American nucleus, with fifteen North Atlantic democracies plus Australia, South Africa and New Zealand: "A government that bases itself on a continent or sea limits its possibilities of expansion, but a government that is based on an ocean is headed straight toward universality."[38]

Streit's Union would have power over foreign and defense policy, trade, money and communications. It would be ruled by a two-chamber parliament and a plural executive, along with a premier, a cabinet and a supreme court. Other nations could accede to the Union as they became politically adult. Meanwhile, the Union would control all remaining colonies.

Streit's Atlantic federalism had an important economic dimension. He praised the usual liberal virtues, but noted how impossible they were to sustain without power. For Streit free trade was not the antidote and alternative to power as it was for Cobden and Hull. On the contrary, Streit believed hegemonic power essential to a liberal world economy. The Gold standard, Streit argued, had worked in the nineteenth century only because of Britain's overwhelming hegemony in the industrial, commercial and financial world. After Britain's eclipse, control over money was divided among several roughly equivalent rivals. None could restore stable money "without first restoring its essential basis, namely, a single overwhelmingly powerful government that is responsible for it."[39]

Streit's sort of vision became increasingly popular in the

overwrought and apocalyptic atmosphere of wartime. In 1943, Roosevelt's Republican opponent of 1940, Wendell Willkie, published his popular *One World*. The book was a rag-bag of half-baked ideas—interesting because it reveals so many of the currents, eddies and winds circulating through semi-literate political opinion. Three strong themes were notable: the need for a single universal security system as opposed to inter-locking or regional accommodations, the beneficent influence and widespread popularity of American business throughout the world, and a strong hostility to European colonialism. All three themes were, in fact, fundamental elements in the official American design which Hull and his friends sought to impose on the postwar world.

In any event, Europe's respite from superpower hegemony was over. In World War II, the tragic drama had played itself over again. Britain, Germany and France could still reach no lasting accommodation. British policy toyed with appeasing Germany, but never decisively enough to forge a real alliance.

After the second catastrophe, America, impelled by the Cold-War threat, returned to play consciously her full role as the dominant superpower in the West. Mahan doubtless would have agreed that the moment had come. The Atlantic Alliance, celebrated prematurely by Adams, marked the hegemony of America over Europe. Henceforth an American general, answerable to the President, was to assume the primary responsibility for Europe's defense.

Most Europeans, as we have noted, were glad enough to have their American protectors. As long as the Cold War was raging, and Russia seemed menacing, there was relatively little difficulty in maintaining appearances in the Atlantic Community. If the American protectorate required the elaborate multilateral charade of NATO, Europeans were willing enough to play the game. Serious military integration was more or less limited to the Germans, who were fortunate to have any army at all.

Moreover, as we have seen, military hegemony carried its rich economic and political compensations. After the quarrels of the Hullian era, America finally brought the aid Europe so desperately needed. In addition, in the crucial question of the arrangements for economic reconstruction, Europeans were not seriously constrained either by Hull's liberal universalism or by NATO's Atlanticism. Instead, as we have seen, they were encouraged to form an economic bloc of their own, to discriminate against American dollars and American goods.[40] Later, the European Coal and Steel Community and then the Common Market, with its common external tariff, all received warm American support.

America's Ambivalence

It is not difficult to see a fundamental ambivalence in American policy toward Europe. The Eurocentric focus of the Marshall Plan, carried forward in our heavy support for the European Communities, violated the spirit not only of Hull's free-trade universalism, but also of Streit's geopolitical Atlanticism. As we have seen, Hull's liberalism and Acheson's Atlanticism were easy enough to fit together in Cold War partnership. The IMF and NATO had many features in common. Both reflected America's hegemony. But the European Payments Union and the European Economic Community were something else again. The EEC became the focus for a distinctive and permanent European bloc, a formation which was clearly a potential challenge not only to America's continuing leadership within an Atlantic bloc, but in the long run, a challenge to the very continuation of any Atlantic bloc at all.

Nevertheless, the American Europeanists assiduously promoted the official American view: the political gains of a European union would be well worth the economic costs. In its preoccupation with security, American official policy accepted the

Europeanist argument and embraced European union. If Western Europe could become a federation, it was said, the United States would have a true and equal partner in the Atlantic Community. Russian ambitions in Europe would be blocked permanently. But what about American ambitions in the Atlantic? What would happen to the dreams of Hull and Streit?

The issue was never faced in the American government. Instead, three strands of policy lived in uneasy co-existence. These may be described as the Europeanist, the Geopolitical Atlanticist and the Rump Hullian. Each had its own set of bureaucratic partisans and European clients.

The Europeanist influence tended to see the Atlantic system built around American hegemony as a transitional construction, born of exceptional European weakness, bound to be transformed if not discarded once that weakness had passed.[41] Implied was the view that Europe was too big to be dominated indefinitely. A united Europe would be strong enough to accept American partnership for common world purposes. But a divided and weak Europe would shrink from American domination and hence become protectionist in its economics, unstable in its politics and adventurous in its diplomacy. These views were seldom challenged directly until the 1960's.

The geopolitical Atlanticist influence, meanwhile, remained preoccupied with NATO, the Cold War and a continuing Soviet threat to security. For the future, it dreamed of a political *Atlantica* growing out of a rejuvenated NATO. Beyond, perhaps a grand Russian-American world condominium would resolve the problems of world peace.[42] Partisans of this geopolitical view had originally accepted the idea of a European economic bloc as a more efficient way to promote the economic recovery essential to military security. They were reluctant, however, to see the European bloc extended to military affairs, especially nuclear. In these matters, they followed a frankly hegemonic policy.[43]

The third group, the Rump Hullian influence, is the most interesting for our study. From its perspectives, it was not the Atlantic Community that was transitory, but the European. The conflict between this Hullian view and that of the Europeanist goes back to the origins of the Marshall Plan itself. The Treasury and its allies were less than enthusiastic at the Europeanist trend, and the whole period saw severe fighting within the American bureaucracy. Unable to stop the Europeanists, the Hullian Rump fought a long guerilla war to keep the new European bloc "outward-looking" and firmly embraced in Atlantic partnership. Trade discrimination, if unfortunately necessary for recovery and federation-building, was to be transitional only. Throughout the 1950's, United States representatives in the GATT and the IMF pressed constantly for the end of bilateral trade and financial restrictions.[44] By the late 1950's, the prospering Europeans were themselves inclined to a more liberal view. The GATT promoted a series of broad tariff cuts. The EPU was formally ended in 1958 and European currencies returned to convertibility. Thus the IMF and the GATT began to take something like the place for which they had been designed—if not on Hull's universal scale, at least within the Atlantic Community which had come to substitute for it. Transatlantic trade and investment, meanwhile, had begun to grow by leaps and bounds.

Thus, as the 1950's drew to a close and Europeans congratulated themselves on the formation of a European Economic Community, the Hullian Rump was beginning to celebrate an emerging world capitalist economy—extended from the integrating Atlantic outward to Japan and the white Commonwealth. Meanwhile, with détente in the air, the remaining group, the geopolitical Atlanticists, began to search for new ties to hold together their Alliance. Their quest led to a new fusion with the Hullians. The Atlantic economy became the substitute for the Cold War. For even as the security threat appeared to decline, Atlantic economic interdependence, it seemed, was growing more intense. What had begun as the Atlantic Alliance was becoming the Atlantic Economy as well. In the end, it would be the Atlantic Community. America's historic partnership with Europe would thus be sustained and legitimized and perhaps someday transform itself into the first genuinely modern world state.

The Gathering Conflict

The Hullian-Atlanticist alliance was, of course, quite in keeping with the general thrust of America's advance to Western hegemony and eminently compatible with America's geopolitical tradition. But American military hegemony, when joined with a free-trade empire, was quite unacceptable to Europe, as the early postwar experience had strongly suggested. Even in the late 1940's, an enfeebled Europe resisted adamantly the Hullian schemes for liberal economic interdependence. Nevertheless, the American government, its Atlanticist and Hullian views in phase together, sought relentlessly through the 1960's to reinforce the faltering military alliance with increasing economic "interdependence." The policy cannot easily be called a success. The Europeans, unwilling to accept economic hegemony when they were weak, were even less inclined to it when they were strong. Indeed, Europeans began to undermine the foundations of those institutional survivals of the Hullian era—the IMF and the GATT. By 1970, it was not so far-fetched to speak of transatlantic economic war. The Hullian policies of the mid-forties were repeating their failure. Only this time, there was no Stalin to save the situation.

By the beginning of the 1970's, there were visible outlines of a great impending tragedy. For, in its economic dimension, the Atlantic Community had, in truth, accomplished a great civilizing task, an important advance toward an orderly world economy. The sounder parts of Hull's dream were becoming increasingly real. But the inability to separate these accomplishments from an outdated American hegemony has threatened more and more the whole Atlantic structure. For this inability to separate hegemony from community, we should blame not only the lingering vision of Mahan, but unfortunate tendencies in the American federalist tradition itself.

CHAPTER FOUR

Federalism

Federalism in the United States and Europe

No one can understand the place in American postwar policy of either the Atlantic or the European ideal without considering the influence of a certain kind of "federalism" over the American political imagination. This particular form of political idealism illuminates the entire American view of the international scene and gives to much of our foreign policy a characteristic rhetoric and bias.[1]

Federalist ideas have also enjoyed great popularity in postwar Europe. The war gravely damaged the prestige of the traditional nation-states. Many expected that a supranational government built around the Common Market would ultimately absorb the historic states into a continental federation. But while impressive progress has been made in harmonizing economic and political policies among the governments of the Common Market, the nation-states have nevertheless proved surprisingly durable. However much the European Communities have become the arena within which European governments organize their mutual relations, the governments remain national. National states continue to be the political organisms which generate popular loyalty and participation and hence are the sources of legitimate political power. It is still the national states which organize democratic "consensus," that shared identity and civic spirit sufficient to rally the contentious elements of society to rational cooperation within an organized and accepted constitutional framework. Hence federalist institutions in Europe, for all their striking progress, remain intergovernmental or *confederal*. The popular political communities remain the nations and not the federation.

In the United States, such a distinction between nation and federation is meaningless. For a century, no American "state" has pretended to be national. All have been provinces of a larger national union. The national state is the federal union. The overriding impulse of the American federalist tradition has favored strengthening the central "federal" authority at the expense of the component states. Unlike Europeans, Americans are thus nationalists and federalists simultaneously. The American federation is a nation-state.[2] American federalism and American nationalism are thus interchangeable. In this respect, what is called federalism in America is not so different from what is called nationalism in Europe, except that the nation in America corresponds to a unit the size of all Europe. American federalism is nationalist in a pathological sense as well: American federalism has proved a remarkably suitable ideological base for American imperialism.

Federalism and American Imperialism

The guiding principles of American federalism are admirably set forth in the *Federalist Papers*, the most famous of which is Madison's *Federalist No. 10*. Writing in 1787, Madison presented the startling proposition that the more heterogeneous a community, the more likely it was to be stable. Democracies, Madison observed, tended always to break up into warring factions. The causes lay in the very nature of man. In a free society, no one could cure the causes of faction, but modern political science could deal successfully with its effects. One invention of political science, representative government, mitigated faction by refining popular passions through an assembly of notables. Another invention, federalism, defeated factionalism by deliberately proliferating factions. The orbit of the federal commonwealth was expanded to encompass so great a variety of separate factions that no one special interest could seize control.[3] The result was a political system characterized by perpetual maneuvering and compromise, where no stable majority could form to oppress the others.

It is remarkable how Madison's formula, taken as a general theory of government, ignores the particular features and overall character of the populace over which it is to be applied. Whereas a nationalist writer would stress the need for cultural consensus to hold together a free political community, Madison's formula thinks to replace consensus by a superior political technology of presumably universal application. In theory, the American formula could be applied anywhere. The large-scale union achieved in North America could be achieved by any community wise enough to employ the same advanced political machinery—as Seeley suggested in *The Expansion of England* and Streit took for granted in *Union Now*.

A more historical view might decide that the durability of the American Union depended less on the cleverness of its Constitution than upon the power of those devoted to its preservation. The American nation-state, like most others, was confirmed in blood. Indeed, while "nationalist" Europe was in the midst of nearly one hundred years of general peace, "federalist" America dissolved into the biggest war of the century. The Union was preserved not by Madison's clever checks and balances but by Lincoln's popular dictatorship.

Madison's *Federalist No. 10* was not the whole of the American federalist formula. Had it been, we would probably not now have a Union. The other half of the tradition, ably represented by Hamilton, called for a strong and energetic executive power at the center of the Union. Hence the strong monarchical presidency, the energetic mercantilist policy and the national elite which Hamilton and John Adams fostered in the early days of the Republic, and which those self-conscious neo-federalists—Henry and Brooks Adams, Lodge, and Theodore Roosevelt—hoped later to revive. For Hamilton, the presidency ought to gather power not merely as an arbiter among multitudinous conflicting interests, but as the embodiment of the national interest. The presidency was to be the institution which generated and mobilized a national consensus, a General Will as opposed to the particular sectoral and class wills expressed in Congress.

When the two elements of our federalist tradition are taken together and examined against the realities of American history, the American system appears, in essence, not so very different from that of any other modern constitutional nation-state. Above all, the American state, like any other, depends upon a national consensus to support its unity. Therefore, the claim that the federalist formula could be extended over an indefinite orbit, a claim implied by Madison and later advanced by writers like Seeley and Streit, is not substantiated by our own national history. The United States is a nation built around a republican monarchy with a national parliament and judiciary, institutions sustained by a cultural and political consensus—a union buttressed by flags, anthems, "Americanization," coercion, bribery and war. In short, we are a nation like any other. Our unity depends upon a consensus mobilized by institutions derived from our own particular history and situation. We managed to cover most of the North American continent not because we invented some unique machinery suited for world government, but because we were growing and the land was nearly empty. Where we found others strong enough to maintain their own nations, we stopped. Our institutions could absorb neither Mexico nor even Canada.

All the same, the Madisonian pretension to universality lives on, particularly in a characteristic American view of world politics. According to this view, amply illustrated by Streit, the American federal formula is ready for export. If extended over other advanced nations, it will succeed as in America. For generations, American experts on foreign affairs, enboldened by the Madisonian pretention, have been partial to elaborate organizational schemes for resolving the problems of "world peace" and "interdependence." Americans have become the world's political mechanics—everywhere tirelessly peddling, installing and servicing some advanced model of governmental machinery. Only establish federal institutions like our own, we are given to saying, and ballots will replace bullets, and conflict be avoided by superior organization.[4]

All in all, the rhetoric of federalism and the particular characteristics of the American federalist formula are highly serviceable to the needs of a hegemonic power, as the American use of international organizations in recent years makes apparent. The Hamiltonian formula of combining a heterogeneous and unfocused legislature with a homogeneous and powerful executive is easily adapted to international organizations meant to organize and legitimize hegemony. In such organizations, the American government, principally its presidential branch, assumes the executive role and the others the legislative. But whereas in the American system the presidential executive is the principal emanation of that popular consensus which constitutes the community itself, in the international sphere the American president is an alien, even if benevolent overlord. The President becomes the Emperor.

NATO is a prime example of such organizations. Its "orbit" encompasses fifteen separate governments who meet to discuss policy in a legislative council. Meanwhile, the executive military command, the SACEUR, is occupied by an American general who depends upon the President and the Pentagon for the weapons, orders and strategies to make deterrence credible. Nothing disturbs that hegemonic line of command. In practice, the heterogeneous council has no real control over SACEUR or his masters in Washington. Within the council, no contrary consensus is likely to emerge to challenge the governing will automatically provided by the United States. The majority on the council, the bulk of whom are dependent in one way or another, go along with the Americans. Passive resistance, of course, is developed to a fine art. But openly rebellious member governments are dismissed as "nationalist."

These institutions unquestionably represent a politer and probably more responsive form of hegemony than that practiced by most others in the past. But the gentle effectiveness of these hegemonic international organizations is both a strength and a danger. Multinational institutions used for these purposes may find it difficult to evolve into more genuine plural communities. The rigamarole of packed international organizations becomes a substitute for genuine negotiations among the principals. The forms of pluralism may become so corrupted by the practices of hegemony that they become difficult to rescue for more straightforward purposes. And Americans never learn to distinguish between the mere forms of pluralism and the genuine practice. They become addicted to the specious internationalism of "interdependence."

Europe's Union: the Shortcomings of Theory

The most successful of the postwar federalist institutions, the European Communities, does not have the United States as a member. Within the European grouping, there is no hegemonic power, even if the French have enjoyed a certain preeminence. The foundation of the EC rests upon a fundamental Franco-German reconciliation, in itself a revolutionary transformation of the European scene. But France and Germany, even when in concert, have not been able to dominate the Six, let alone the larger European Communities of the present.[5] This nonhegemonic European grouping, with its extensive administrative bureaucracy, complex political balances and elaborate confederal procedures, has evolved into a remarkable political organism. Indeed, federalist theory does not yet seem to have caught up with this new reality. The new Europe was supposed to have been *supranational*. As economic decision-making became more and more concentrated in Brussels, integration in one field was to spill over into others. National governments were gradually to lose initiative and authority and hence cease to be the principal receptacles of political legitimacy and power. In the usual theoretical model, the Commission was expected to evolve into a technocratic European executive, responsible to a popularly-elected European parliament.

So far at least, the reality is quite different. The nation-states, acting through the Council of Ministers, very much retain their political vitality. The Communities are, in effect, a sort of permanent diplomatic conference in which the various national political and bureaucratic structures are in constant formal and informal interchange with each other, their deliberations assisted by a skilled international staff, itself in considerable part seconded from the national structures. While the arrangements for making decisions seem cumbersome by most national European standards, they appear less so in comparison with the chaotic untidiness of the American system. In any event, federalist theory seems to have underestimated the possibilities of the confederal form. In many respects, as we shall argue in due course, the present structure of the Communities may be better adapted to the needs of modern societies than those tidier supranational models which have never yet achieved reality.

Europe's Union: American Expectations

Americans have been among the most distinguished students of European "integration" and most fertile theorists of its mechanism. American diplomats and scholars have provided some of the most avid enthusiasts for the EEC, and American policy steadily sought to promote its success. Why? The potential dangers of a European bloc to American political and economic predominance might well have been thought obvious.

American motives were varied, shifting and intangible. At least three broad hypotheses have grown up about these motives. Roughly speaking, the first hypothesis holds that we were naive, the second that we were clever, and the third that we were good.

The first hypothesis sees us so carried away by the prospect of Europe's imitating our own continental federation that we overlooked the dangers of fostering so formidable a potential rival to ourselves. It is certainly true that nearly all American enthusisasts for the Communities have also been fierce partisans of its supranational model. These Americans sometimes appear to find it more difficult than the Eurocrats themselves to be reconciled to the "failure" of the Communities to achieve this model. Many Americans, reflecting now on the inconvenience of so powerful an institution as the Communities, yield to the suspicion that we have been not only duped, but that many of us have also been active partners in our own deception. In this view, Europeanists in the American government, disarmed by their enthusiasm for the trappings of federalism, seriously miscalculated the consequences of a separate European bloc.

This Frankenstein hypothesis surely carries some truth. Anyone experienced in American diplomacy knows how doctrinaire and active the partisans of European federalism have been in the American diplomatic establishment. Personal connections have played a large role in this enthusiasm. So wide was Jean Monnet's circle of important American acquaintances, and so great his influence within it, that Americans took Monnet for one of their own and frequently intervened in European affairs to support his pet projects.[6] Few seriously entertained the notion that Monnet might be creating institutions that might turn against America, or that the institutions being created were not his work at all. In later years, the running ideological quarrels between the Gaullists and the Good Europeans deflected our attention from the intrinsic dangers of any Community, Gaullist or supranational. Even when the Brussels machinery had become a powerful instrument for European economic protection, we tended to blame de Gaulle rather than the Communities.

To be sure, Americans had some reasons for blaming their European problems on de Gaulle rather than the rest of Europe. The Gaullist quarrel with the Good Europeans did, in fact, revolve around America's future role. De Gaulle maintained that Monnet and Hallstein were workers for American imperialism, a charge which Hallstein, at least, hotly denied.[7] It was no secret why the Americans supported the Good Europeans, de Gaulle argued. Monnet's Europe would be an amiable, apolitical technocracy encumbered with an incoherent multinational parliament, a perfect structure for American purposes. Such a community would suppress whatever strong national policies there might be, but lack internal cohesion or popular support to develop strong new policies to replace them. Thus, a supranational Europe would allow easy access for American influence and be a thoroughly pliable partner for the Atlantic Alliance.[8] A European customs union, without any strong government, dominated by the liberal ideals of Germany and the Low Countries and bullied by the GATT, would provide a splendid opportunity for American exports and investments:

> It is true that in this "integrated" Europe, as they say, there would perhaps be no policy at all. This would simplify things a great deal. Indeed, once there would be no France and no Europe, once there would be no policy—since no one policy could be imposed on each of the six States—one would refrain from making any policies at all. But then, perhaps, this world would follow the lead of some outsider who did have a policy. There would perhaps be a federator, but the federator would not be European.[9]

In vetoing Britain's first application to join the Communities, de Gaulle concluded with the following observation:

> It is foreseeable that the cohesion of all its members, who would be very numerous and very diverse, would not hold for long and that in the end there would appear a colossal Atlantic Community under American dependence and leadership which would soon completely swallow up the European Community.
>
> This is an assumption that can be perfectly justified in the eyes of some, but it is not at all what France wanted to do and what France is doing, which is a strictly European construction.[10]

Whereas the Frankenstein theory makes the American Europeanists seem exceptionally naive, the Gaullist theory makes them appear diabolically clever. While the latter view may be more flattering, it is for the same reason less convincing. De Gaulle's hypothesis cannot be dismissed, however, merely by declaring that no responsible American official was ever consciously motivated by it. If a policy with predictable consequences is pursued tenaciously and if those consequences favor those who pursue the policy, their claims to disinterested motives are not only suspect, but irrelevant. For self-deception and rationalization are scarcely less developed among governments than among individuals. As any good Jansenist Frenchman might know, a proper examination of conscience in these matters requires a sturdy worm-like self-suspicion not common among official apologists for foreign policy. Moreover, Americans were neither wicked nor unreasonable to assume the permanent eclipse of the old European states, or of any European will to independent world power. At the time, they were accepting the judgment of innumerable distinguished Europeans. And why not gather the fragments of a broken Europe into a more convenient supranational container? What de Gaulle saw as imperialism Americans saw as charity. The nurse often seems a tyrant to the patient.

The full truth about American motives requires, however, the third strand of explanation, one which does more credit both to our intelligence and our good will. It should not seem inconceivable that some Americans, appalled by the ruin of a

Europe they loved, were more interested in restoring the old continent than in ruling it. Some in the American government accepted from the beginning the possible consequences of those policies that began with the Marshall Plan. They understood quite well that the great nations of Europe, once revived, would have minds of their own. Out of their abundance and self-confidence, Americans were simply generous. Imperialism is not the only American instinct. The extraordinary admiration for de Gaulle in America, more evident after his death to be sure, suggests a more than grudging respect for people with the courage to resist being pushed around, even by the United States. We ourselves are a people not without grandeur.

Perhaps these more generous attitudes to Europe owe something to another side of America's political tradition. That tradition, after all, has produced not only the *Federalist,* but the *Declaration of Independence.* Unlike Madison, Jefferson gave great significance to the nature of a "people"—to their social and political culture, and was less sanguine about the automatically beneficent effects of constitutional machinery. Indeed, Jefferson once counselled a revolution every twenty-five years just to shake up and refresh a country's political institutions.

From the Jeffersonian strain sprang a primordial American sympathy for the national independence of other peoples. The persistence of this Jeffersonian tradition has made it difficult to transform the country from isolationist nationalism to imperialism as abruptly as Lodge, Mahan or the Adamses would have liked. A certain characteristic circumlocution and nervous moralizing has been the inevitable result. Hence the Open Door Policy, which combined lust for economic penetration with moralistic opposition to Europe's overt colonialism. Hence, too, Woodrow Wilson's rather tortured rationale for intervention in World War I: American power—but to make the world safe for democracy.[11]

Perhaps something can also be said about the influence of what might be called an American humanist tradition—a relatively conservative view of the world, suspicious of both the national pretention to exceptional virtue and the national zeal for social and political engineering. One of the most perceptive and devastating contemporary critiques of Wilsonian idealism came from the humanist critic and scholar, Irving Babbitt. Babbitt's theme is not so different from that of Senator Fulbright's *Arrogance of Power*. The quiet current of national sanity which this tradition embodies, a force aroused in reaction to unmeasured ambitions and bloated pretensions, may well have operated, consciously and otherwise, to make sensible men draw back before the dream of a permanent American hegemony over Western Europe.

Europe's Rising Will to Power

Insofar as our postwar Europeanists did expect the new Europe to be a docile dependency, they have been increasingly disappointed. Instead of a politically pliable and economically open dependency, we now see a hostile mercantilist power bloc. Particularly outrageous to American officials, opposition to the United States now often seems, in itself, the principal incentive to European solidarity. But in truth, we have no claim to feel either surprised or aggrieved. The world neither began nor ended in 1945. History was unlikely to stand still for our convenience. Only a moderate effort at achieving the historian's detached vision makes Europe's postwar predicament and behavior quite understandable. Europe, gravely enfeebled by two self-destructive wars, found herself caught between two rival imperialisms. The Russian threat was crude and military; the American subtle and economic. One was Ivan the Terrible; the other Woodrow Wilson. While the Russian threat was infinitely worse, it also, in time, came to seem far less credible. In any event, neither Russian nor American hegemony is particularly appealing to a strong Europe. Quite naturally, Europeans grope for a way out of their predicament.

To a number of prominent Europeans, both the predicament and its solution were already obvious after World War I. If the European states wished to escape domination by their giant neighbors, they would have to stop fighting each other. Instead, they would have to build themselves into a coalition both to defend their collective integrity and to assert their interests in the outside world. No longer the unchallenged center of world power, Europe could no longer afford the luxury of internecine quarrels.

This simple but compelling observation lay behind Coudenhove-Kalergi's idea of *Paneuropa*, a European federalist movement which sprang up after World War I. In many respects, Coudenhove's ideas prefigure the evolution of Europe's response to America's hegemony after World War II.

Coudenhove, a former Hungarian diplomat, founded his movement and began to send forth an influential stream of ideas in the early 1920's, when he labored for Franco-German reconciliation and exercised considerable influence over Aristide Briand. Coudenhove's fundamental aim was a European economic and political coalition, *Paneuropa*, as a third force between Russia and America. Another European war, he argued, would leave Europe dominated either by Russian communism or American capitalism. Only by reconciling ancient differences and coming together into a strong coalition could European nations resist the superpowers and become their own masters. Only by uniting could Europeans play a constructive role in the world. Only *Paneuropa* could be an American ally without being an American protectorate. Only *Paneuropa* could draw Russia back to a normal relationship with the rest of the continent. Once consolidated, *Paneuropa* could be the center of a triple alliance to secure world order.

In many ways, Coudenhove's ideas anticipated those of General de Gaulle. Indeed, in his later years, when de Gaulle was in power, Coudenhove saw the General's European program as the true continuation of Briand's enlightened policy.

Like de Gaulle, Coudenhove envisioned not so much a single unitary European state, as a grand coalition of Europe's nation-states. Coudenhove also shared de Gaulle's suspicions of England's commitment to Europe—at least until the British more decisively abandoned their imperial and transatlantic perspectives. And he shared de Gaulle's wariness both toward the United States and, in particular, toward the dangers of a Russian-American condominium at Europe's expense.[12]

The contrast between Coudenhove's federalist vision and the American Atlanticist ideal was clear before the War, as can easily be seen by contrasting Coudenhove's plans with those of Clarence Streit. Coudenhove's federalism was to counter American power, not embrace it.

Jean Monnet's postwar schemes tried to combine Atlanticism and Europeanism. For a long time, he succeeded. As with America's relations with Britain, the Cold War solved—or postponed—many problems. The strong anti-communism of most of the Chirstian-Democratic Good Europeans helped obscure any tension between European union and Atlantic partnership. But when recovery was followed by détente, America began to experience not the Europe of Streit or even Monnet, but the Europe of Coudenhove, a Europe determined to be independent of the superpowers on its periphery.

General de Gaulle was, of course, the principal occasion for these confrontations. In effect, his policy challenged the whole notion of an American Atlantic bloc. As the United States pursued détente with the Russians, de Gaulle raised the specter of Yalta and launched an ambitious diplomatic campaign of his own with the East.[13] His search for a special relationship with Bonn began to cause trouble with our hitherto docile German allies. His dogged persistence with the *force de frappe* challenged the cherished NATO concept of a division of labor within a single Atlantic security community. His vehement opposition to America's intervention in Vietnam mocked the Atlanticist pretensions to a partnership for world peace-keeping.

Finally, just as a declining security threat seemed to make economics increasingly significant in maintaining Atlantic solidarity, de Gaulle used the Common Market to promote a European economic bloc with distressing "inward-looking" tendencies. In particular, the Common Agricultural Policy was bound to hurt American exports seriously. Moreover, as Franco-American tension increased, de Gaulle began to foster European resentment of American monetary hegemony which had evolved from Bretton Woods. In short, events began to shake the easy assumption that European unity and Atlantic partnership were complementary. As the European idea gained flesh, it began to challenge its Atlantic rival.

America's Inappropriate Reaction: the New Atlantica

Unfortunately, the reaction of the Kennedy Administration was not particularly enlightened. Perhaps the rhetorical quarrels among the Six over supranationalism, the rancorous anti-Gaullist propaganda of our old European clients, the disappointment of our own Europeanists, or the dramatic style of the General's diplomacy all led us to underestimate the broad significance of the Gaullist challenge. In any event, we treated it as a passing aberration. Instead of seeking to accommodate what was, in reality, a rising Europe, the Administration launched a powerful drive to isolate France and consolidate and extend America's Atlantic hegemony. European and American halves were to be bound ever more tightly in the Atlantic Community. The old federalist formulas inspired a new round of hegemonic policies and institutions.

In the military sphere, the Administration proposed the Multilateral Nuclear Force as well as a new counterforce strategy which stressed centralized command. In the political sphere, the United States promoted British membership in the EEC, tried to break up the Franco-German alliance, sought to gain European support for American "peace-keeping" and launched an elaborate exercise to coordinate "détente management" through NATO. Few of these initiatives enjoyed serious success. Instead, a Johnson administration saddled with the Vietnam war was soon on the defensive in the entire political and military sphere. De Gaulle's withdrawal from NATO in 1966 appeared to threaten the Alliance itself.[14]

In its Atlanticist strategy, the Kennedy Administration unfortunately relied heavily upon economic policy. The "Grand Design" to cement Atlantic interdependence was essentially economic. It was as if the ghost of Cordell Hull had returned to preside over American policy. A new round of tariff cuts was to inaugurate a new era of interdependence. To emphasize the importance of his new trade measures, Kennedy went himself to speak before Congress:

> As members of the Atlantic Community we have concerted our military objectives through the North Atlantic Treaty Organization. We are concerting our monetary and economic policies through the Organization for Economic Cooperation and Development. It is time now to write a new chapter in the evolution of the Atlantic Community. The success of our foreign policy depends in large measure on the success of our foreign trade, and our maintenance of Western political unity depends in equally large measure upon the degree of Western economic unity. An integrated Western Europe, joined in trading partnership with the United States, will further shift the world balance of power to the side of freedom.[15]

The same Atlanticist federalism informed the speeches of former Secretary of State Christian Herter, named to head the American team for the trade negotiations:

> Those, whether in Europe or America, who urge us to declare independence from one another are at best ignorant and at worst malevolent. . . . Our goal is a genuine Atlantic partnership, adequately organized to meet the political, military, and economic challenges of the era.[16]

End of the Liberal System?

In the economic sphere, as in the political and military, the American drive fell far short of its hopes. By the late 1960's, Americans were on the defensive in the economic sphere as well as the others. Our own dollar's increasing weakness menaced the whole liberal monetary system and our industry's declining competitiveness threatened our own liberal trade policy. European resentment of American investment foreshadowed serious trouble for America's "Atlantic" corporations.

To be sure, there were some American successes. The Kennedy Round was a considerable advance in trade liberalization even if we ourselves could not meet all our own commitments to it. A series of brilliant expedients staved off monetary disaster for a decade and perhaps helped prepare the way for a new system. American corporations, their access to American capital blocked, found in the Eurodollar market the way to continue their heavy European investing.

Even our successes, however, had a certain makeshift quality. De Gaulle's departure brought no lasting relief. Fundamental changes in the transatlantic relationship seemed inevitable, above all in economic relations. Still, American policy, bemused by the old Atlanticist federalist rhetoric, seemed paralyzed before the need to accommodate a risen Europe. As the dollar fell in 1971, Nixon's New Economic Policy suggested not so much accommodation as belligerant withdrawal from cooperation. America and Europe seemed to be pulling back into those hostile mercantilist blocs so feared by Cordell Hull.

With America's hegemony faltering can the liberal Atlantic Community survive at all? As the next three chapters discuss in detail, American policy has not been much help. Ironically, the most avid partisans of the "Atlantic" system are major obstacles to its survival. Their ideological vision of "Atlantica"—

an integrating multinational system, dominated by a super-power and gradually eroding the economic, political and social base of its other nation-states—greatly impedes the American-European accommodations that must soon be made.

These tendencies to confuse liberalism with antinationalism, federalism with hegemony, and interdependence with dependence are all part of that specious internationalism which history has woven into our Atlantic ideal. If we are to acquire a more realistic view of international economic and political relations, if the Atlantic Community is to be saved, we must somehow break the spell of those superannuated and rotting idols that still enchant the American mind.

Introduction

In the early 1970's, the Atlantic Community's liberal economic system drifted into a major crisis. The American payments deficit in 1970, calculated on the "official reserves transactions" basis, grew to a colossal $9.8 billion. By 1971, even the American trade surplus was gone and the Nixon Administration, confronted with massive speculation, declared the dollar no longer convertible into gold and imposed stiff protectionist measures against imports. The liberal order broke down, and negotiations to repair it promised to be complex, arduous and uncertain.

Although we were quick to blame others, the blame was essentially ours. American policy throughout the sixties ran counter to the fundamental rule of equity necessary for a stable international system. We had used a privileged position in the monetary system to sustain the exchange costs of our massive foreign military positions and our heavy program of capital investment overseas. After the dollar's debacle in 1971, the Nixon Administration changed tactics but America's abuse of the international system continued. The attempt to create through devaluation a trade surplus large enough to meet military and investment exchange costs was no less a violation of fundamental rules of the game than the old policy of meeting these exchange costs through a deficit. Both the earlier policy of relying on a monetary deficit and the later policy of relying on a trade surplus have constituted, in effect, taxation by America of the other Atlantic countries. As such, our policy has been an obvious and continuing abuse of the liberal system. If not changed, our policy will very likely break up that system and create those mercantilist blocs which the policy was initially designed to avoid.

The crisis of the seventies, however, encompasses more than the inequities of the monetary system and the imperialist vagaries of American policy. For not only is a supposedly liberal monetary system in question, but these very ideals of free trade and international investment which that monetary system was designed to assist. In the United States, and elsewhere, the "neo-isolationist" mood seems to be spreading into economics no less than politics. Protectionism and autarchy are in the air. For some, they indicate the wind of the future.

The next section examines first the monetary system—to show how American policy has worked to destroy the postwar liberal order, and then proceeds to a more general discussion of the place, within the evolving Atlantic economy, both of free trade and of the international corporation.

CHAPTER FIVE

The Monetary System

The Postwar Dollar System

Monetary Systems and Political Systems

In the postwar era, America's role in the monetary system and America's role in the military alliance have been two sides of the same imperial coin. Nuclear hegemony in NATO has matched dollar hegemony in the IMF. Dollars support troops, and troops support dollars. It is difficult to know, particularly in recent years, which leans more on the other. The relationship need surprise no one. The design of a monetary system, underneath its technical drapery, naturally reflects the basic political pattern governing the overall relations of the member states.[1]

Postwar history amply illustrates the correspondence. Hull's universalist Wilsonian program encompassed money as well as trade and security. As Morgenthau argued at the time, support for the UN meant support for the IMF. Security and monetary institutions were, he said, complementary as the blades in a pair of scissors.[2] Russia's refusal to join the IMF was one of the early signs of the Cold War which was to reduce Hull and Morgenthau's universalism to Acheson's Atlanticism. Similarly, the European Payments Union was a logical monetary parallel to the Marshall Plan and the OEEC. America's Europeanist policy encouraged a European regional bloc, an impulse eventuating in the formation of the European Communities. As Europe's economies recovered in the 1950's and American economic policy sought to nudge the nascent European bloc back to Pan-Atlanticism, the European Payments Union closed down. The general monetary convertibility envisaged at Bretton Woods finally came into being among the Atlantic powers. In monetary matters in the IMF as in military affairs in NATO the frame was America's *Atlantica*.

The Rise and Fall of the Dollar Exchange Standard

Convertibility, once established, was not, however, sustained in the fashion that Hull and Morgenthau had presumably imagined.[3] Instead of that rapid adjustment of balance-of-payments deficits and surpluses which the United States had initially favored, the actual system built itself around a chronic American deficit. Thanks first to the Marshall Plan and then to America's continuing heavy spending abroad for defense, aid, tourism and investment, the dollar gap became the dollar glut. In spite of a constantly favorable American balance of trade, we continued to spend overseas substantially more than we earned. As a result, the United States eventually passed from being the world's major short-term creditor to being its principal short-term debtor.

The dollar soon became the world's chief "reserve currency," meaning that foreign governments and individuals proved willing to hold dollars rather than cash them in for gold from our reserves. Hence our dollar deficits were unredeemed. Instead, expatriate dollars came to constitute a large part of the monetary reserves of most foreign countries and were the principal currency in world trade and the international short-term capital market. America's military protectorate, huge gold reserves, and giant productive capacity all made the devolpment seem only natural.[4]

The distinctions between these actual arrangements—a gold-dollar system, and the Bretton Woods formula—carried with them great economic and political consequences.[5] The gold-dollar system was still "liberal"—based on fixed exchange rates and easy convertibility. But at Bretton Woods, such a system was thought to require rather firm domestic discipline and occasional adjustments in parities. Neither proved as significant as had been imagined. Instead, with America's lavish and continuing deficits greatly increasing the world's supply of international money ("liquidity"), everyone else found it relatively easy to run a surplus. With their share of the surplus dollars, nearly all developed countries had ample monetary reserves. Hence, once popular recovery got underway, the developed Atlantic countries maintained convertibility without frequent devaluations, stern domestic discipline, protectionism, or tight exchange controls.[6] It was, in short, economic liberalism without tears.

The United States, its unredeemed deficits flowing into the reserves of other countries, became a sort of world central bank, constantly adding to the world's money supply and thus promoting expansion. This dollar system, allowing us to run deficits without restraint, constituted, to be sure, an American monetary hegemony with many special privileges. The system nevertheless had many advantages for everyone. In a climate of easy money and secure exchanges, world trade and investment grew by leaps and bounds.

There was, nevertheless, a fatal flaw in the system. It was based on the assumption that the liquidity-creating reserve currency, the dollar, was still convertible into gold. Yet a regularly increasing liquidity depended upon a continuing American payments deficit. In time, it was inevitable that America's net short-term debt would come to exceed her gold supply. The system would then break down—either because the United States brought its payments into balance, and liquidity-creation ceased, or because foreign dollar-holders, realizing that the dollar was no longer solidly backed with gold, would grow reluctant to hold it.[7]

The latter is what happened. Europeans, delighted to hold dollars when the United States had most of the world's gold, grew increasingly restive as the American short-term debt came to exceed American reserve assets several times over.[8]

In the face of growing European discontent in the 1960's, the American government turned to a series of inventive expedients to bolster the dollar.[9] These expedients, however successful *ad hoc,* appeared to presume, in time, some more fundamental solution for the continuous American deficits.[10] But as the 1960's wore on, the American performance gradually eroded confidence that a solution would be found.

Private holders of dollars became increasingly inclined to exchange them for gold or for stronger national currencies. By the late sixties, speculative monetary crises, stemming in large part from the dollar's weakness, became a regular feature of economic relations among the Atlantic powers.[11] Finally in August 1971, the American government, faced with the rapid loss of its remaining gold reserves, officially suspended the redemption of foreign-held dollars. By December of 1971, the United States agreed to an official devaluation. Dollar convertibility, however, seemed indefinitely postponed.[12] The Bretton Woods system, or rather the dollar standard, formally broke down.

American Apologia: "Benign Neglect"

By late 1971, the need to reconstitute the monetary system seemed obvious to everyone. But until the last moment, a great many American monetary experts had denied any need for major changes. All along, distinguished economists had readily supplied plausible arguments to support the status quo. The existing system was supposed to go on indefinitely. Foreign central banks, it was argued, were unlikely to precipitate a major crisis either by refusing to accept more dollars or by demanding gold for those dollars they already held. The postwar monetary arrangements, despite America's special privileges, gave too many advantages to everyone. American spending abroad not only protected the Free World, but energized its economy. An ever-growing dollar deficit created that ample liquidity which had, in turn, fueled the remarkable postwar growth of the world's economy. America's international corporations, with their heavy direct investment abroad, efficiently channeled that liquidity into productive investment throughout the world. It was not America's fault if foreigners preferred to hoard their dollars rather than spend them. If Europeans were worried about holding so many dollars, they could, after all, buy American goods or invest in American securities.[13] If a country in chronic surplus wanted neither to spend its dollars nor to hold them, it could always revalue its own currency upward.[14] In short, America's deficit was beneficent. Our attitude toward it should be "benign neglect."

European Objections

The theory of benign neglect only carried the postwar status quo to its natural conclusion. Europeans were asked to acknowledge openly what had been true all along. The dollar was not backed by gold. What did gold matter? Imaginative and logical, the theory nevertheless proved impractical. It not only under-estimated the growing inconvenience to Europe of so one-sided a monetary interdependence, but tacitly presumed Europe's continuing military and political dependence would justify overlooking that inconvenience. Technically, the system might well have worked. But politically it was no longer feasible. It was not the moment to ask Europeans to walk under the yoke. For in the political sphere at least, many believed American hegemony was coming to an end.

To be sure, few Europeans were in a hurry to precipitate major changes. Most, while not accepting benign neglect in theory, only grudgingly contemplated any fundamental alterations in the status quo. Few wanted to initiate the breakdown of that system of fixed exchange rates on which Europe's own internal integration had obviously depended. Gradually, however, revisionist forces have grown into a formidable coalition whose varied arguments reflect not only irritation and dismay with the increasingly chaotic functioning of the monetary system, but a growing sense of Europe's collective interest and power, and a growing impatience with America's singular privilege and weakness.

In the monetary sphere, as in so many others, de Gaulle was the first major leader to articulate Europe's discontent. Characteristically, he focused on the political implications of supposedly technical questions. De Gaulle regarded the use of national currencies for international reserves as the economic counterpart to political imperialism.[15] America's payments deficit was an involuntary tax imposed on other nations to finance America's imperial military and economic activities around the world. For de Gaulle, the system was not only politically unjust but economically unsound. American deficits fueled Europe's inflation. International reserves, he argued, should be held only in some objective medium, preferably gold, which was limited in quantity and could not be created by the fiat of a single nation and used for its own special purposes.[16]

The Vietnam war gave point to de Gaulle's attacks on America's world-wide military imperialism. The growing opposition to America's "take-over" of European industry reinforced another side of his argument.[17] Above all, the rash of currency troubles that afflicted all European countries in the late 1960's fed the uneasy sense that governments and banking systems were losing control of national economies. The immense waves of speculation throughout the later sixties lent credence to the old Gaullist charge that the United States had steadily exported an excess liquidity which, if unchecked, would unhinge European economies and frustrate plans for their rational development. In 1969, Europe's capital market in expatriate dollars, the Eurodollar market, had mushroomed to $40 billion of credit, seemingly beyond the effective regulation of any public authority. Moreover, the growing internationalization of business and banking, especially American, greatly increased the mobility of money and the consequent violence of speculative flows. Hence abrupt shifts in America's domestic monetary policy quickly produced disruptions in Europe's money markets. Europe was the can tied to America's tail.[18]

In addition, the waves of monetary instability profoundly upset the Common Market. In the late sixties the revaluation of the mark and devaluation of the franc severely strained the Common Agricultural Policy, thought by many to be Europe's biggest step toward genuine economic integration. The elaborate formulas balancing national interests were undone and could be restored only by complex negotiations.[19] No sooner had the agricultural structure been restored than the crisis of 1971, in which the mark and the guilder floated and the franc remained fixed and controlled, once more threw the system into confusion.

In the late sixties the swelling coalition of European forces dissatisfied with the monetary status quo began to turn to the idea of a European monetary union. The members of the European Community began by forming a caucus within the IMF. By the end of 1969, the Six committed themselves to a formal monetary bloc. The Commission promptly developed a plan for seeing a common currency achieved in ten years and three stages.[20]

No sooner had the Six launched the scheme than they were swamped by the renewed dollar crisis of 1971. That crisis revealed both how difficult it would be for Europeans to sustain a monetary bloc and how reluctant European governments were to accept its logical conclusions. While they grew increasingly united in their determination not to accept dollar hegemony—in other words, to reject an ever-increasing flow of inconvertible American deficits—they nevertheless found it difficult to agree on how to end or replace that hegemony.

An optimist could believe Europe's disarray only temporary. It was difficult to concert six and later nine governments on fundamental changes in policy. The monetary crisis had come before Europe was ready to cope with all the implications of America's retreating hegemony.

Failures of American Policy

Ambivalent Motives

Whatever the shortcomings of the Europeans, the history of American international monetary policy over the past decade makes a puzzling and depressing chronicle. While our government never officially embraced the theory of benign neglect, monetary policy throughout the period has nevertheless been bedeviled by a basic and disabling ambivalence: were we trying to end our deficits, or were we aiming for the dollar standard proposed by many of our leading economists? The choice carried broader implications: were we preparing to adjust our policies to a new plural system, in which we would be a country subject to the same rules as the others, or were we trying to make permanent the postwar Atlantic imperial system, in which we played the hegemonic role?

In monetary affairs, at least, our official policy was the former: we were to bring our payments into balance. Nevertheless, we invested our principal energy and prestige into a series of initiatives, often praiseworthy themselves, but with highly questionable prospects for improving our balance of payments. At the heart of our failure to end the deficit lay an obstinate refusal to do anything serious about its causes.

When a competent government pursues a course of action which appears contrary in many aspects to its declared policy, can that government be sincere in its declarations? Was the real American policy, in fact, to establish dollar hegemony permanently, as many economists had recommended? No one can easily answer such questions, even those intimately involved in the conduct of affairs. Governments are highly plural institutions, the American government in particular. Many policies, personalities and agencies struggle for pre-eminence. Bureaucratic compromises or simple lack of coordination often result in official actions contradicting policies. If a counter-policy has considerable support in the government, it can often hamstring the implementation of its official rival, even if it cannot unseat it. Moreover, even those who reject a policy can unconsciously be strongly influenced by it.

The theory of benign neglect, by suggesting that nothing at all needed to be done, helped sap any will to make hard decisions. An embattled politican, faced with the alternatives of promoting domestic recession or else restricting tourists, business or the military, was all too eager to hear distinguished experts counsel inaction. Even if he was unwilling to accept their position formally, he was comforted in his reluctance to do anything drastic. In any event, with the course we did follow, our failure to end the deficit should have surprised no one, as a look at the nature of the deficit and its causes quickly reveals.

Why an American Deficit?

The American balance of payments can be measured in several ways. One way is to count the net change in the quantity of dollars held by foreigners. This flow is what the government seeks to depict in its "reserves transactions" and "net liquidity" balances. The balances inevitably contain a large element of "short-term" capital, those volatile, speculative dollars which compose, for example, the Eurodollar Market. The number of dollars in the category of short-term capital held by nonresidents is now enormous, estimated at some $60 billion in 1970.[21] Today, the still-mounting accumulation of foreign-held short-term dollar capital hangs as a perpetual menace over the American balance of payments and makes it extremely difficult to restore convertibility. Our monetary reserves now cover less than one-fifth of these foreign dollar holdings.

The extreme volatility of this short-term capital pool has led the government to employ, along with the reserves transactions and liquidity balances, the concept of a "basic" balance, a measurement which disregards short-term capital flows and records only the net movement on current account and "long-term" capital.[22] The practice may somehow suggest that the basic balance is more real, measuring as it does the flows from current expenditures and serious investment as opposed to the flows sparked by currency speculation. An historical relation, however, links the relatively small basic deficits over two decades with the huge reserves transactions and liquidity deficits common since the late sixties. For the latter deficits, springing from massive movements of so-called short-term capital, clearly are more volatile because so large a pool of dollars is now held abroad. That pool is not the creation of any single flow at any one time, but the accumulated foreign savings which are the counterpart of our own accumulated foreign debt, a debt built in turn by the basic deficits which have continued for nearly every year since the Marshall Plan.[23]

A close look at the components of the basic deficit year after year reveals a good deal about its cause and the failure of our policies to end it. Throughout the 1960's, the United States ran a favorable balance, generally substantial, on merchandise trade and services. In addition, repatriated income on foreign investments brought a large and growing net inflow. But this positive inflow from trade, services and investment income was overwhelmed by the outflow for government expenditures, tourism and new foreign investments. The figures for 1970, a

year when we enjoyed a comfortable trade surplus, illustrate
the basic situation. (See Table 5–1).

TABLE 5–1

Elements of the U.S. Basic Balance of Payments, 1970

	seasonally adjusted, millions of dollars
Merchandise trade balance	$ 2,110
Exports	41,980
Imports	− 39,870
Other services, net	588
Travel and transportation, net	− 1,979
Investment income, net	6,242
U.S. direct investments abroad	7,906
Other U.S. investments abroad	3,503
Foreign investments in U.S.	− 5,167
Remittances, pensions and other transfers	− 1,410
Military transactions, net	− 3,371
U.S. Government grants (excluding military)	− 1,739
U.S. Government capital flows excluding nonscheduled repayments, net	− 1,837
Non-scheduled repayments, of U.S. Government assets	244
U.S. Government nonliquid liabilities to other than foreign official reserve agencies	− 436
Long-term private capital flows, net	− 1,453
U.S. direct investments abroad	− 4,445
Foreign direct investments in U.S.	969
Foreign securities	− 942
U.S. securities other than treasury issues	2,190
Other, reported by U.S. banks	199
Other, reported by U.S. nonbanking concerns	576
BALANCE ON CURRENT ACCOUNT AND LONG-TERM CAPITAL	− 3,038

Source: U.S. Department of Commerce, *Survey of Current Business*, June 1971, Table 1.

As Table 5–2 indicates, in 1970 the American government
added over $7 billion net to our exchange outflow, a sum more
than twice the entire year's basic deficit of $3 billion. Of that
government expenditure, $3.4 billion alone was the net out-

flow for current foreign military expenditures.[24] Military expenditures have, in short, played a key role in the basic Ameri-

TABLE 5–2

U.S. Government Transactions And Their Effects on the
Basic Balance of Payments, 1970

	seasonally adjusted, millions of dollars
Military transactions, net	$ − 3,371
U.S. Government grants (excluding military)	− 1,739
U.S. Government capital flows excluding nonscheduled repayments, net	− 1,837
Nonscheduled repayments of U.S. Government assets	244
U.S. Government nonliquid liabilities to other than foreign official reserve agencies	− 436
	$ − 7,139
BALANCE ON CURRENT ACCOUNT AND LONG-TERM CAPITAL (basic balance)	$ − 3,038

Source: U.S. Department of Commerce, *Survey of Current Business*, June 1971, Table 1.

TABLE 5–3

U.S. Basic Balance and Net Military Transactions Compared
1960-1970

	U.S. Basic Balance[1]	U.S. Net Military Transactions
1960	− 1,155	− 2,752
1961	20	− 2,596
1962	− 979	− 2,449
1963	− 1,262	− 2,304
1964	28	− 2,133
1965	− 1,814	− 2,122
1966	− 1,614	− 2,935
1967	− 3,196	− 3,138
1968	− 1,349	− 3,140
1969	− 2,879	− 3,341
1970	− 3,038	− 3,371

[1] Balance on current account and long-term capital.
Source: U.S. Department of Commerce, *Survey of Current Business*, June 1971, Table 1.

can payments deficit. In an unusually candid statement, in itself a sign of desperation, the American government, through its new Secretary of the Treasury, John B. Connally, finally admitted on May 28, 1971, the intimate relation between military expenditures and the basic American deficit:

> I find it an impressive fact, and a depressing fact, that the persistent underlying balance-of-payments deficit which causes such concern, is more than covered, year in and year out, by our net military expenditures abroad, over and above amounts received from foreign military purchases in the United States.[25]

The fact, of course, has been impressive for a decade, but no American government seems yet to have faced up to it, the Nixon Administration included.[26]

Figures like those cited above suggest that America's basic payments deficit, at least until 1971, has been essentially political rather than commercial. To be sure, it is not strictly accurate to trace our balance-of-payments deficit to any one outflow as opposed to another. Foreign exchange to pay for troops could theoretically come from reducing other forms of spending abroad. Americans might, for example, have given up foreign investing or travel. But travel restriction, seriously contemplated by the Johnson Administration, would abridge what seems a fundamental liberty in a supposedly open society, and make the metaphor of a garrison state uncomfortably apt. While the interest-equalization tax passed in 1963 did, in fact, discourage American portfolio investment abroad, curbs on direct investment, businessmen argue, threaten the market position of American companies abroad, a position which in 1970 yielded nearly $8 billion in repatriated earnings. Thus the government has only reluctantly curbed direct business investment abroad and declared its intention to remove the impediments as soon as possible.[27]

Thus, for one reason or another, no American government throughout the sixties and early seventies was able either to reduce its own political and military spending abroad or curb private investment and tourism—at least not significantly enough to bring America's foreign account into balance.

Other solutions, therefore, had to be sought. One series of policies has hoped to boost America's trade surplus high enough to cover the political and investment outflow, while another has tried to alter the monetary system to make it easier to finance our deficits without losing reserves.

Official Solution I: Trade Surplus Through Deflation

On the face of it, the possibility of ending the deficit through more trade would seem promising. If, for example, in 1968, 1969, or 1970, we had achieved the same favorable trade balance as in 1961, 1963 or 1964, our basic payments would have been in balance. In 1970, a favorable swing of only $3 billion—in a turnover of some $42 billion of exports and $39 billion of imports—would have achieved a basic balance. But although when put in such terms the task seemed small, it proved impossible. Instead, 1971 saw the first American trade deficit in the twentienth century. Why did our policy fail?

When a European country wants to boost its trade, it normally imposes a deflationary stabilization plan on its economy. Devaluation is a last resort. The Nixon Administration's deflationary policy of 1968 and 1969—devised in some part to help the balance of payments—did encourage, by 1970, a noticeable improvement in the trade balance.[28] But as unemployment mounted and the election drew nearer, reflation seemed a political necessity. The trade deficit of 1971 was among the results. It is not easy to fault the Nixon Administration for inconstancy. For reasons that seem obvious in an economy with only 9 per cent of its GNP in foreign trade, no American Administration is likely to sustain a deflationary policy long enough to cure a payments deficit. The cost to the domestic economy—in employment and growth forgone—seems excessive.[29]

Official Solution II: Trade Surplus Through Parity Changes

If restoring a trade surplus or our balance of payments generally were the only consideration, it would seem simpler for a country like the United States to devalue, much easier in fact than for most European countries. Why? For a country with a high proportion of its GNP in foreign trade, changes in the value of the currency have widely unsettling effects on the domestic economy; but for a relatively self-sufficient economy like the American, parity changes have proportionately little effect on general domestic price levels.

A number of other factors, however, have made the United States reluctant to devalue. Since the dollar was the "key currency," the only currency directly convertible into gold and hence the standard against which all other national currencies measured their relative values, it would be difficult, we argued, for the dollar to change its value. To change the dollar's gold content, moreover, would require Congressional legislation, always dilatory and unpredictable. And dollar devaluation might well carry unfortunate psychological connotations for our prestige and the cohesion of the Free World.

It was therefore better, we argued, that those particular countries which enjoyed a large surplus with the United States should themselves revalue their currencies upward, instead of expecting us to move the dollar downward. Hence, we have strongly pressured the Germans and Japanese to revalue and, in 1971, the rest of the developed countries as well. Revaluation was meant not only to offer at least a temporary respite against further speculative pressure on the dollar, but also to affect the flow of trade and hence our basic deficit. For precisely this reason, however, revaluation was strongly resisted by our trading partners.

Since the United States ran a general trade surplus throughout the 1960's, and a highly favorable balance with Europe as a whole,[30] it was difficult for a European government to convince its own exporters that the dollar was overvalued for trading purposes. Broadly speaking, until 1971 our exports were competitive and not overpriced. To our foreign competitors, lowering the dollar's relative value would have seemed an unjustified boost to American products, an unfair currency manipulation inviting retaliation. Even in a country like Germany, which enjoyed a trade surplus with the United States, exporters could note revaluation's negative effects on their trade with nonrevaluing neighbors, like France, whose trade with Germany was far larger than our own.

After the rapid deterioration of American trade in 1971, the American case for a dollar depreciation was obviously sounder, although we sought to depreciate enough not only to balance our newly acquired trade deficit, but also the entire long-standing basic deficit, including large sums to cover military exchange costs and several billions more to cover American foreign investments.[31] But to expect commercial transactions to shift in our favor sufficiently to bear the burden of non-commercial outflow was only to invite foreign retaliation. It seemed doubtful that European governments could permit our still highly favorable trade surplus with them to increase further until it covered our deficit for nontrade outflows. Shifts of such magnitude would almost inevitably mean serious losses for European producers. Again, because of the greater significance of foreign trade for Europe's economies, and their smaller size, such effects are felt more generally and severely in Europe than here. Economics, like politics, is the art of the possible. Of course, the commercial effects of currency changes are generally delayed for a year or two and even the most refined predictions can give only extremely rough and uncertain estimates of those effects.[32] All the same, if devaluation should succeed in its object, and trade were affected substantially, the political pressure for retaliation would very likely grow correspondingly.

Similar limitations apply to the academically fashionable

solution of an open currency market with "floating" rates. In such a scheme, the dollar is supposed to decline in response to market forces until the deficits disappear. To begin with, our huge overhang of volatile short-term capital poses a considerable danger of panic-selling in such an arrangement. Moreover, as the dollar depreciates, the foreign exchange costs of our military commitments increase as well. Thus, unless our government reduces its own outpourings, or severely restricts private outflows, a floating dollar might well sink downward until American export prices become so depressed that trading partners would almost certainly be forced into protectionist measures.

All this is not to say that depreciating the dollar, by devaluation or a selective revaluation by surplus countries, can never be an effective policy to restore trade equilibrium. Nevertheless, as the means for restoring an overall payments balance without any fundamental change in the size and composition of our nontrade outflow, a trade surplus induced by depreciating the dollar runs a high risk of generating protectionism abroad, protectionism which will defeat both the immediate and the broader aims of the depreciation. All societies, American and foreign, have a limited tolerance for shifts in trade that severely disrupt local producers. No country can be expected to bear willingly any more than its reasonable share of the social and political costs of free trade.

The old problem remains. The basic American deficit is not merely commercial but has a large political and investment component. Even after 1971, the basic deficit came less from an unfavorable balance of trade than from overseas government expenditures and direct business investments. In 1971, for example, with the dollar crashing around it, the Nixon Administration used every pressure to fight Congressional moves to reduce troops in Europe, a major drain contributing to the basic deficit. In so doing, it has the apparent support of those Western European governments, France included, who were at the same time refusing any longer to accept surplus dollars. Americans are not the only people unwilling to face the causes of America's basic payments deficit.

Official Solution III: Trade Surplus Through Liberalization

A great deal of American energy has gone into the various GATT negotiations to liberalize trade. While much of this dedication doubtless springs from the old Hullian view that trade promotes political interdependence, American officials have sometimes spoken as if trade liberalization would, in itself, improve our balance of payments. As we have seen, the payments deficit was presented as a major reason for supporting the Kennedy Round. In the negotiations over the dollar's depreciation at the end of 1971, the United States demanded trade liberalization, to remove "unfair" handicaps which presumably have harmed our trade over the years.

That further general trade liberalization would help American trade seems highly questionable, for reasons discussed in the next chapter. As it happened, the Kennedy Round did achieve substantial liberalizing of transatlantic trade barriers. That it worked to improve our own balance is not supported by the figures, which show a decline from a surplus of $6.8 billion in 1964 to a deficit of $2.7 billion in 1971—or a swing of nearly $10 billion in seven years. Improvements in our trade balance will more likely come from the numerous restrictive measures of the early seventies—the quotas and gentlemen's agreeements to stem imports in that increasing range of industrial products where our producers grow less competitive.[33]

The protectionist reaction in the United States in recent years only further illustrates a fundamental axiom of international trade relations. No democratic government can be expected to remain indifferent to the economic interests of its own producers. Hence the implausibility of curing America's basic deficit through a huge trade surplus.

Official Solution IV: The SDR

Alongside our efforts in trade, American policy has sought a cure to the monetary predicament through the "liquidity" approach, the principal fruit of which is the Special Drawing Right. Like our approach to trade, our approach to international liquidity is an uneasy combination of general ideology and particular self-interest. Also like trade liberalization, the liquidity approach is rather elliptical in its treatment of the real causes of the basic deficit. In advocating Special Drawing Rights, American experts went back to the old debate at Bretton Woods about liquidity versus adjustment. Keynes, they argued, had been right. The IMF system, as originally framed, did not provide adequate international liquidity. Hence the dollar had subsequently been forced to play the role of reserve currency, to be the principal new source for otherwise desperately short international liquidity. But if some new source of non-national liquidity could be devised, the dollar could retract form its overextended position.[34] The IMF was to be that source. Periodic credits, or Special Drawing Rights, issued to members could accumulate and become, in effect, part of the members' monetary reserves.[35]

While a new and nonnational form of liquidity was doubtless desirable for the reasons stated, the analysis presented by its advocates seemed to suggest that the United States had been running postwar deficits mainly out of an altruistic determination to make amends for the limited vision of Cordell Hull and Harry Dexter White. But, as we know, the American deficit sprang from our government's unwillingness to rein in its own spending abroad or curtail that of any of its citizens. If the dollar's role as a reserve currency was a cross, it was one we had embraced with alacrity and fought fiercely to retain. For it was the dollar's position as reserve currency that allowed the United States to run deficits. And it was these deficits that financed world "responsibilities" without forcing cutbacks in the private outflow. If the deficits also created much-needed liquidity for others as well as ourselves, so much the better. But making the dollar's incidental liquidity-creating role superfluous would not end the deficit, however sound an idea the SDR might be in itself.

Underneath the rhetoric about general world liquidity, many American officials saw the SDR primarily as an additional form of finance for a continuing American deficit. It was ironic for the Americans to dress up their special pleading for more credit with a concern for international liquidity. For it was the continuing American deficits which, by calling into question the value of the immense dollar reserves already extant, threatened to precipitate the possibly catastrophic decline in real world liquidity.

The SDR scheme, of course, was more than an elaborate American plea for additional credit. Both Europeans and Americans glimpsed its potential for replacing dollar hegemony with a truly multilateral system of liquidity creation. In accepting the scheme in 1967, the EEC countries insisted on a collective veto over SDR creation, thus trying both to stop any new form of unlimited credit for the United States and also to go ahead with machinery for an orderly multilateral creation of liquidity, should the United States finally get its deficit under control.[36]

The Settlement of 1971

Pushing through the SDR was the last major triumph of American monetary leadership within the collective Pan-Atlantic system. Since that time, American monetary policy has become increasingly unilateral, not so much from any diminished enthusiasm for managing a collective international system, as from inexorable deterioration of the dollar. When the Nixon Adiministration, *in extremis,* formally and unilaterally suspended convertibility in August 1971, it had little choice.

America's subsequent devaluation, and the revaluation of

Japan and several Western European countries, were at best only halfhearted attempts to restore the old system of fixed exchange rates. The United States did not restore convertibility; short-term capital which had migrated to Europe stayed there; and exchange markets remained uneasy. By the summer of 1972, the pound was floating and the dollar again precarious.

With a huge pool of expatriate dollars still available for speculation, trade prospects uncertain, and no letup in official spending and private investment overseas, more dollar crises seem not unlikely in the next few years. After the experiences of 1971, dollar holdings are likely to be even more volatile and European central banks even less likely to support the dollar in a major crisis.[37] The dollar is not only tottering, it will continue to be pushed. The resulting situation, if prolonged, will represent not only the collapse of the dollar exchange standard, but the breakdown of the whole postwar system of easy international convertibility. The nationalist fragmentation during the dollar crisis of 1971—the "dirty floats," two-tier markets and various other interventions and controls—suggested not so much a new system as the beginning of anarchy.[38] Nations cannot tolerate perpetual uncertainty and frequent disruption in monetary affairs. Inevitably, to protect domestic stability they will impose exchange controls and tariffs.

Is all this inevitable? Must the dollar standard collapse and pull down the liberal monetary order with it?

If the answer to the second question is still uncertain, the answer to the first is very probably yes. Beyond the economic and technical reasons for the dollar's weakness lies a fundamental political evolution. The foundation of the dollar standard has been the hegemony of the United States. In this era of postwar reconstruction, Western Europe and Japan have depended on the United States politically, militarily and economically. Now, in every sphere, all are going back, often haltingly and reluctantly, to a more normal, that is to say a more plural world.

In such a world, it is no longer appropriate for the United States to control the creation of international money. Perhaps some one state, if it were a kind of monetary Vatican City, might be ceded the function of creating new world credit and distributing it equitably. But the United States is still the world's biggest economy and its biggest military power, also its principal borrower and principal foreign investor. These years when the United States has acted as the world's central bank have reflected an institutionalized and imperial economic system, a system never likely to survive the restoration and consolidation of Western Europe.

Prospects for a Liberal Restoration

Plural Liberalism?

The fading of American hegemony presumably need not be the demise of a liberal world monetary system, any more than it need be the end of all transatlantic military cooperation. It can be argued, of course, that no closely integrated monetary system can survive without a hegemonic power to hold it together. According to such reasoning, the decline of American hegemony means the end of an integrated monetary system. Unquestionably, a plural political system poses difficult conditions for a closely integrated monetary system. With no hegemonic power to overawe them, independent national states cannot easily be compelled to subject themselves to the discipline of any integrated system, if that system appears not to work in their interest. At the very least, independent states are likely to require two conditions for their participation.

First, the workings of the monetary system must not interfere excessively with the internal equilibrium of the national states, nor prevent orderly private and public economic planning. Second, the system must not be imperial, must not appear to give special advantages to any one state or group of states within it at the expense of the others.

The present system fails on both counts; hence the present shambles.

Clearing Away the Debris

To reconstruct a liberal system requires liquidating the destabilizing remnants of America's dollar hegemony and creating new stabilizing institutions to replace that hegemony.

The first task requires a resolute end to America's balance-of-payments deficit as the principal source of international liquidity and a resolute phasing out of the dollar's role as the principal vehicle for the liquidity. This means bringing America's basic balance out of its deficit. Regaining stability will also very likely require funding a great part of the enormous dollar balances now held by foreign governments and private persons. Otherwise, these huge balances, remaining volatile, will continue to menace monetary stability. Once the dollar balances are funded, central banks should limit their dollar holdings to relatively small "working balances" needed to stabilize exchange markets. As a technical matter, it seems unlikely that the dollar can or should retain its role as the "key currency" used to intervene to support other currencies in daily exchange operations. In a new plural system, some more neutral or collective unit would seem more appropriate and convenient.[39]

No one should underestimate the difficulties of clearing away these remnants of the old system. The Atlantic world will be fortunate to avoid serious dislocations.

Old Problems: Liquidity and Adjustment

Even if the dollar standard can be dismantled without catastrophe, the familiar problems of "liquidity" and "adjustment" will remain to be solved by a new system. If deficits end and dollar balances are funded, some new system of liquidity-creation will be needed, preferably some system which does not recreate the instability of the dollar standard by giving some other national currency the advantages and burdens of the reserve role.

Actually, experts are in considerable agreement on these matters. Many propose a larger and more active role for the IMF.[40] In a plural system, an international organization with considerable autonomy can, like the Commission in the European Communities, play a useful managerial role, guard the rules of the game and often act as a catalyst crystallizing consensus around the common interest. The IMF thus would seem the logical agency for converting the huge floating dollar debt into some form of internationally backed asset, like the SDR.[41] The SDR already provides the means for systematic increases in world liquidity without relying on dollar deficits. But while it is easy enough to imagine the techniques whereby an international organization could perform the functions of liquidity-creation, establishing a multilateral agency for creating liquidity will not, in itself, solve the problems of the current system. The problem today is not liquidity but adjustment. The SDR, plus American deficits, have in fact provided more than ample liquidity in recent years. While an ample supply of international credit can ease, it cannot eliminate altogether the necessity for adjustments. Thus, despite the leeway of increasing credit provided by the SDR, the United States has not been able to stop its payments deficit, nor to avoid depreciating the dollar. Therefore, some "adjustment mechanism" whereby a deficit currency can return to equilibrium is the critical element in any new system. Even more fundamental than the machinery is the question of whether rates between currencies should be fixed firmly or change with ease.

Fixed Rates versus Changing Parities

Traditionally, a nation with a payments deficit has had to

choose between a domestic deflation or currency devaluation. The postwar system has been strongly biased in favor of fixed exchange rates, in other words, against devaluation and in favor of deflation. But, as we note above, throughout the postwar period the special features of the dollar system have given the world the benefits of fixed exchange rates without many of the usual costs. Now that this comfortable system is breaking down, the domestic costs and benefits of fixed exchange rates are assessed with a more realistic eye.

The abstract advantages of fixed exchange rates are obvious, particularly for those heavily engaged in international transactions. The relative costs depend, in great part, upon the nature of the domestic economy. For small or medium-sized economies with a relatively high participation in foreign trade, frequently shifting exchange rates, especially with major trading partners, seriously disrupt domestic markets and planning. Moreover, when the inflationary rate of such an economy differs markedly from that of neighboring economies, the consequences are usually soon apparent. Thus among a group of such states who trade heavily with each other, the nation's most pressing domestic interest strongly encourages stabilization policies to sustain currency parities and avoid frequent disruptions, even if these stabilization policies are occasionally painful to particular domestic interests. As long as the economically interdependent countries are politically stable, have adequate monetary reserves and are roughly similar in the evolution of factor costs and business cycles, the effort to sustain parities is not only desirable, but usually feasible as well.

For large and self-sufficient countries, on the other hand, a change in the exchange rates has relatively little effect on domestic prices and unemployment. Therefore, the domestic incentive to maintain the currency's parity is far less. Moreover, for the reasons discussed earlier, a policy of deflation severe enough to balance the trade accounts would be politically difficult to justify. Devaluation, with its minor effects on the overall price level, would seem far superior.

This general view suggests a basic difference between the European and American national interests in fixed parities. Europe's economies fit the first category, America's the second. Among the Six, for example, exports and imports added together equal 40 percent of the national GNPs. The comparable figure for the United States is 9 percent. (Table 5–4.) Thus parity changes are far more likely to disrupt European economies than our own. Moreover, not only are the European nations heavily engaged in trade, but much of their trade is with each other. Roughly half the trade of the Six is with other members of the EEC.[42] Thus, frequent shifts in exchange rates are particularly disruptive when they occur among the Six themselves. Hence the interest in sustaining fixed exchange parities is especially compelling among these close neighbors, who absorb a large share of each other's production. Maintaining fixed rates, moreover, is likely to be easier among European neighbors, precisely because of this proximity, similarity and heavy interdependence. France and Germany, each the other's best customer, are more likely to be in economic phase together than either is with the United States. Thus both France and Germany have a strong incentive and a relatively easy time maintaining close similarities in factor costs, rates of inflation and general business cycles.

By contrast, with exports and imports equal to only 9 percent of the American GNP, the domestic constraints necessary to maintain our economy in phase with Europe's are simply not worth the trouble. The cost of defending the dollar is much greater to us than the cost of devaluing it.

This line of reasoning clearly points toward a certain regional differentiation of the adjustment mechanism within Pan-Atlantic monetary relations. The United States has a strong incentive to encourage more flexible exchange rates. The European states have a strong incentive toward maintaining fixed exchange rates among themselves. A European monetary union, with fixed rates among its members and a common rate toward outsiders, seems the logical solution.

TABLE 5–4

GNP, Exports and Imports as Percent of GNP

EEC AND THE UNITED STATES, 1970
(billions of U.S. dollars)

	GNP	Exports (f.o.b.)	Imports (c.i.f)	Exports & Imports as % of GNP
United States	927.6	43.2	40.0	9
EEC	452.8	88.7	88.6	
Belgium–Luxembourg	25.0	11.6	11.4	40
France	138.0	17.9	19.1	(includes
Germany	172.7	34.2	29.8	intra-EC
Italy	87.3	13.2	14.9	trade)
Netherlands	29.8	11.8	13.4	

Sources: U.S. Agency for International Development, Gross National Product: Growth Rates and Fund Data, by Region and Country (May 15, 1971); OECD, Statistics of Foreign Trade, Series A. Reprinted in: Committee for Economic Development—*The United States and the European Community: Policies for a Changing World Economy*, Washington, Nov. 1971, Table 6, p. 74.

European Monetary Union I: Advantages

By fixing rates among themselves, the nations of the Communities would avoid those especially severe disruptions that occur from intra-European currency shifts. Occasional transatlantic devaluations would disrupt far less with only one rate change between the United States and a European bloc, as opposed to constantly shifting rates between the dollar and each European currency. While the Communities are collectively still less self-sufficient than the United States, enlargement and association will probably make them more so. As long as internal rates remain fixed, they should be able to contemplate external currency adjustments with something like the same indifference as the United States.[43]

European Monetary Union II: Problems and Solutions

If a monetary union seems the logical way for Europeans to preserve the Common Market, reassert control over their collective economic environment, and adjust their monetary relations with the United States, still, such a union will be most difficult to consummate. Numerous economic and political reasons dampen enthusiasm among Europeans themselves. A currency union requires close coordination of national monetary and fiscal policies and possibly an unacceptable degree of supranational integration. Economists also note that a monetary union can easily bring disaster to its backward countries and regions.[44] Such areas, unable because of their backwardness to compete at the general price level, and unable because of the union to restrict trade and capital movements or to change their exchange rates, see their capital float away and their economy sink into permanent depression.[45]

For these and other reasons, many expect a monetary union will either precipitate genuine supranational integration or else founder on the resistance to that integration. But in the future as in the past, the Communities may develop rather differently from the theories which seek to anticipate them. The confederal pattern characteristic of the Communities in general may serve in the monetary field as well. Indeed it may be preferable to a supranational system. Any monetary union of separate states will have to be relatively loose and flexible and allow a variety of separate regional policies.[46] In a confederal system, general monetary policy would flow through national sluice gates, each channeling liquidity according to the varying conditions of the different European economies. To be sure, regional equalization would have to be a major task for the system's common reserve fund. But the principle that backward regions must receive special aid is thoroughly familiar to the mercantilist thinking implicit in the ideas of the European Communities. And the precedent for transferring resources already exists in the Common Agricultural Policy and its development fund.

A monetary union will have to contend not only with the intrinsic difficulties and oppositions among Europeans themselves, but also with America's increasingly ambivalent attitude toward further European integration, and monetary integration in particular. While we have always urged European union, in this era when Soviet-American relations seem relatively stabilized, a strong, coherent and self-sustaining European bloc seems less necessary, and a rich, open and pliable Atlantic Europe more beguiling. While we are unlikely to pursue wholeheartedly a policy designed to break up the Communities, our positions in various questions can do much to make intra-European cooperation unworkable. Our leverage in Europe remains great. In particular, the German government's commitment to an *Ostpolitik* based on Atlantic defense makes it highly sensitive to American displeasure, above all to threats of troop withdrawal.[47]

Still, in monetary affairs as in others, Europe is likely to continue its progress toward closer union. Neither we nor the Europeans are likely to tolerate willingly the uncertainty and disorder that has characterized the monetary system in recent years. No modern government can long forgo control of its internal economic environment. If the Europeans do not seek economic self-determination in some confederal union, they are likely to find it in nationalist isolation. Such a fragmented Europe is less likely to be a docile group of satellites than a troublesome group of volatile and adventurous middle powers. For them, and for us, the Communities are a better framework. For these reasons, Europe is likely to continue its consolidation. A monetary union seems both a desirable and likely prospect.

Two Blocs in a Common System?

A European monetary union will not, in itself, guarantee a stable and liberal transatlantic monetary relationship. While dollar and European blocs, once constituted, could remain within some common monetary system organized around the IMF, they could also grow increasingly isolated from one another, their relations characterized not only by frequently changing or even floating parities, but also by close trade and currency controls.

While all the steps outlined above—funding dollar debts, shifted liquidity creation to the IMF, as well as forming a European currency union—will make transatlantic interdependence more manageable, none will necessarily provide any satisfactory solution for the essential problem which has so racked the present system, namely America's basic payments deficit. Even with a European monetary bloc floating against a dollar bloc, as long as we insist on our current level of official and private nontrade outflow, any dollar depreciation that might finally generate a trade surplus large enough to balance our payments would also sharply increase Europe's large trade deficit with the United States. Protectionist retaliation would be hard for European governments to resist, and in turn would reinforce the already strong protectionist sentiment in this country. Europeans would maintain, as they have already, that Americans and not Europeans should bear the burden of America's adjustment. America's deficit, as they say, comes not from trade but from excessive government and private "investment."[48] In short, the more the dollar depreciates, the more the two monetary blocs will grow isolated from each other and the common Atlantic system disintegrate.

In a plural world, a liberal international economic system must base itself on mutually advantageous rules of fair play. If the system constantly disrupts the members, or gives one of them egregious advantages, the system will break down. The monetary system imagined at Bretton Woods, for all its shortcomings, was based upon the ideals of sound money and common rules. The United States, with its perpetual basic deficit, altered that system into an instrument of imperial taxation.

Now that our hegemony is fading, and with it the justification for our special position, we must reform the system or be prepared to see it fall down. If the United States returns to balance by reducing its foreign expenditures to where they are covered by a moderate trade surplus, the type of open transatlantic system imagined at Bretton Woods will very likely survive. But no stable transatlantic monetary system seems likely so long as it is expected to absorb the combined costs of America's official overseas spending and heavy private investment.

To be sure, the burden of adjustment does not lie entirely on our side. Europe's unwillingness to pay the costs of its own defense, for example, remains a principal cause for our continuing basic deficit. But the end of hegemony in one sphere inexorably implies its end in others as well. The Europeans must accept the costs of independence or else pay tribute to their protector. As de Gaulle knew well enough, liberty is seldom cheap.

Author's note: This chapter was written mainly in the summer of 1971 and completed in early 1972. The second devaluation of the dollar and the formation of a European monetary bloc would seem to make the authors reasonably good prophets. But for several years the situation is likely to remain highly volatile, and Europe's union uncertain. In short, while every low in the dollar's troubles is regularly hailed as the beginning of a stable new order, the issues and alternatives posed by the deteriorating system remain much the same. Indeed, they have changed remarkably little since their discussion in Calleo's *Britain's Future*, published in 1968. They will doubtless be with us for many more years to come.

—D.T.C. and B.M.R.

CHAPTER SIX

Atlantic Community Trade

Trade and American Postwar Policy

In Hull's grand vision, as we have seen, free trade was expected to engage nations in peaceful and prosperous interdependence. Hull linked nearly everything else to his trade policy. The Axis powers were to be defeated because their economic policies meant a closed world of blocs. Our Allies were to be supported only if they renounced their preferential systems. Monetary systems were devised to facilitate trade; security systems to protect it. However lightly he was taken by Roosevelt and his contemporaries,[1] Hull emerged as the figure who expressed most clearly the ideas that would dominate a good part of America's postwar policy.

In postwar America's Atlanticist vision, trade has in fact taken a central significance. Trade has been linked to the full complement of economic issues—including inflation, price stability, full employment and growth. Trade and growth are said to set up a "virtuous circle," the one stimulating the other.[2] And, following Hull's prescription, trade has also been linked to a closely-knit Atlantic political system. Interdependence in trade is said to mean interdependence in foriegn policy.

These two dimensions to trade policy, the economic and the political, have been mutually reinforcing. Assertions that trade policy injures domestic employment and production must contend with counter-assertions about trade's vital role in preserv-

ing international good will and "interdependence." Throughout
the past decade, moreover, trade has grown more rather than
less significant in American policy. On the one hand, as the
immediate and obvious threats to Atlantic security have appeared to recede, and the American balance-of-payments difficulties grown more acute, economics increasingly has become
the focus of international relations and the stuff of diplomacy.
On the other, as security links have grown looser, promoters of
Atlantic political unity have been inclined to rely all the more
on transatlantic trade and economic connections in general.
Thus for many in the Kennedy and Johnson Administrations, the
Kennedy Round seemed no less important to the future of the
Atlantic Community than NATO itself.

Disillusion with Trade Liberalization

After a quarter of a century during which trade liberalization has commanded an almost religious deference from Western statesmen and economists alike, many signs now suggest
a major shift, in the United States particularly. No new trading
initiatives of significance have followed the Kennedy Round,
completed in 1967, and indeed, Congress has only partly and
conditionally accepted the fruits of those negotiations. In the
early seventies, the American protectionist mood in general
and the popularity of Nixon's trade measures in particular revealed a surprising fragility in the whole liberal trade policy—
a fragility which suggests a certain erosion of its foundations
and a growing disenchantment with its fundamental assumptions.

Several theories vie to explain why trade liberalization is now
embattled. The most cheerful explanation sees the Kennedy
Round so successful that nothing further remains to be done
with tariffs. Trade liberalization now means the reduction of
nontariff barriers, a complex task awaiting the development of
new negotiating machinery.[3]

The current militancy of protectionism in this country, however, threatens to undo more than the Kennedy Round and belies such facile optimism for the future. But nearly forty years after Hull's first trade legislation why should Americans be renouncing the Calico Goddess?

As the British experience suggests, free trade appeals most to those confident of their ability to compete in an open market. American goods, however, are growing less and less competitive; hence Americans are becoming more and more protectionist. Since 1971, the American balance of trade has officially fallen into deficit.[4] While our exports have continued to grow, our imports have jumped at a substantially greater rate. Trade with Canada and Japan has shown the greatest and most rapidly increasing imbalance;[5] but even the traditional surplus with the Common Market, while persisting through 1971, has shrunk (see Table 6–1).*

Explanations for the decline in America's trade balance and prescriptions for correcting it are both many and complex. Special factors like the Canadian-American Automobile Agreement may have sharply affected trade with particular countries.[6] Special negotiations, it is hoped, will ultimately eliminate the deleterious effects of these special situations. More generally, the decline in our trade balance can be blamed on the peculiar American economic situation in recent years. The Vietnam war has placed extraordinary stress on the national economy, increasing imports, rendering exports less competitive, and setting off a spiralling inflation.[7] Analysts hope that as an aberrant policy can be said to have caused the decline, a sane policy can reverse it. Phasing out the war, combined with internal correctives like wage and price controls, should end America's rapid inflation, restore price competitiveness to her products and hence rejuvenate the usual liberal trade constituency. Many

*Tables for Chapter Six follow the Chapter—See pages 144–162.

analysts also expect much from the dollar's devaluation.[8] As the key currency, the dollar had not been devalued since before World War II, whereas most of our major trading partners have devalued several times. An overvalued dollar has gradually sapped competitiveness, which, it is hoped, can now be restored.

Another set of explanations, however, sees America's trade balance declining less from short-term than from secular historical factors.[9] Many Americans in the seventies, like many British in the sixties, perceive a general decline in their society, or at least in those virtues most conductive to economic efficiency. Others see the gap between American and foreign wages not closing rapidly enough to compensate for a general loss of America's traditional advantages in management, technology and marketing. The loss of these advantages is often blamed on the overseas migration of so many American companies. To many with such views, restrictions on imports and foreign investments seem the obvious remedies.[10]

Certain liberal analysts take a more hopeful view of the declining trade balance. The American economy is seen entering its mature phase. Hence manufacturing is a diminishing—and services are an increasing—constituent of GNP.[11] In this view, all but the most advanced technological industries tend to move abroad. Regulations against pollution will hasten the migration. While the United States will thus earn less and less abroad from selling goods, more and more earnings will come from the sale of services and royalties. Above all, the steady stream of American investing overseas will yield a return to compensate for our trade deficit. Like Britain before World War I, the United States will be a rentier economy. Protectionism, therefore, is unwarranted and harmful to our own consumers.

This latter view, however cheerful and tidy it may seem to economists, appeals less to workers and those who represent them. Many of the arguments, moreover, are highly problematical. While manufacturing abroad may enhance a company's earnings, repatriated profits are scarcely as remunerative to

American labor as domestic production. The assumption that new jobs can be created in "advanced" industries and services to compensate for a general decline in almost all the major manufacturing sectors seems highly questionable, even with "adjustment" assistance on a far more lavish scale than has ever been provided.[12] Selling American services to foreigners on a scale to compensate for the dwindling exports of goods seems an equally uncertain prospect.

Under the circumstances, no one need wonder at the growing militancy of American protectionist forces and the uncertainty and disaffection among many who formerly supported trade liberalization.[13] The whole policy, in fact, demands a fundamental re-evaluation, an inquiry conscious of the domestic costs as well as the benefits of trade liberalization.

An equally skeptical view seems imperative toward the political benefits which have been thought to accompany international trade liberalization. Even assuming that a more closely integrated pan-Atlantic economic and political community is a proper aim for American policy, and acceptable to Europe, is trade likely to promote that integration? Neither the trade figures themselves nor the recent experience of the Kennedy Round can confirm that trade promotes Atlantic integration.

To begin, it would be useful to consider the actual trading patterns of recent years. No one can deny that postwar transatlantic trade has grown significantly, or that the Atlantic countries as a whole have been trading more with each other than with third countries.[14] From 1948 to 1970, this "Atlantic Trading Community" increased its share of total free-world exports from 62.5 percent to 70.6 percent, and its share of free-world imports from 62.2 percent to 70.9 percent (See Tables 6–2 and 6–3).[15] Between 1958 and 1970, the percentage of its members' exports to each other has increased from 61.5 percent to 72.8 percent of their total exports (See Table 6–4).[16] In other words, the Atlantic Community's share of world trade has been rising, and turning inward.

But these shifts can give only ambiguous support to partisans of transatlantic interdependence, for within these broad trends, trade has shifted significantly within the Atlantic Community itself—a shift which reflects a more self-sufficient Europe, relatively less involved in trade with America. The shift, of course, is only relative, and easy enough to lose sight of in the continuous growth of world trade. Nevertheless, the trends are significant and suggest that for both Europe and the United States, trade is centering itself increasingly within mutually exclusive regional blocs.

If, for example, the flow of trade were really the determining indicator of an economic community, then it would be more proper to see the United States in an American hemispheric bloc rather than in an Atlantic Community (See Tables 6–5 and 6–6). Since 1963 our exports to Europe have grown significantly less than our exports to Canada, the Western hemisphere as a whole (despite the sluggish performance of our trade with Latin America), or Japan. In fact, only once between 1948 and 1971—in 1963—have we exported less to Latin America and Canada together than to Europe (See Table 6–7). In 1971, Canada alone absorbed exports from the United States nearly three-quarters the size of our exports to Western Europe. Moreover, for trade, the American bloc increasingly looks to the Far East rather than to Europe: Japan is now another major market for American goods—roughly one-third the size of EEC and EFTA combined and growing at a more rapid rate (See Table 6–5).

The European countries are, of course, increasing their trade more rapidly among themselves than with America. In 1958, 29.6 percent of all imports of the six EEC members came from each other; in 1970, 48.4 percent. During the same period, their exports to each other increased from 30.1 percent to 48.9 percent of their total (See Table 6–8). The comparable figures for EFTA are less striking, but indicate a similar tendency (See Table 6–9).

Furthermore, most of the EEC's trade with the outside takes place with their European, African and Middle Eastern neighbors and former colonies—a pattern which has been sustained through association and preferential trade agreements as well as a growing number of arrangements for increased East-West trade. In 1958, 59.8 percent of all EEC imports from nonmembers originated in countries in Eastern and Western Europe, Africa and the Middle East, and in 1970, 61.1 percent. Similarly, in 1958, 64.8 percent of the EEC's external exports went to countries and territories within this geographic area, and in 1970 66.5 percent (See Table 6–8).

In short, if a transatlantic economic community binds together the world's advanced capitalist nations, trade figures do not give it a conclusive demonstration. On the contrary, trade statistics would seem to reflect not so much a growing Atlantic interdependence, as a growing mutually exclusive regionalism on either side of the Atlantic. Nevertheless trade has continued to play its central role in Atlanticist ideology and American foreign policy, as the expectations attached to the Kennedy Round so clearly illustrated. But quite apart from whether it remains in America's interest to preserve an Atlantic political and economic bloc, the experience of recent years suggests that trade liberalization is a poor policy to accomplish that end. Although the Kennedy Round negotiated a significant reduction in tariff levels, by an arithmetic average of 30 percent, it has not been easy to see a corresponding improvement in Atlantic relations. On the contrary, since the late sixties quarrels over trade and money have increasingly dominated the transatlantic scene. Ironically, the Atlantic idea was never stronger than in the middle fifties, when Europe was encased in a cocoon of restrictive and discriminatory practices.

The whole experience of the Kennedy Round demonstrates significantly the limitations of trade as a political instrument and policy. The Grand Design relied upon the trade negotiation to achieve an impressive variety of objectives. The Kennedy Round was meant to hasten British entry into the Common Market—certainly no less a political than an economic aim.[17] It was meant to improve the American trade balance and stop the flow of American capital to Europe.[18] It was meant to demonstrate capitalist harmony and disprove Marxist predictions of inevitable trade war.

For a start, it is doubtful that the American initiative did much to help Britain's candidacy for the Common Market. Quite the contrary, America's eagerness only fed French suspicions. If the European Community was to succeed, de Gaulle pointedly observed, members must look to each other before looking to outsiders. Others, he noted had different notions. Some dreamed of a colossal Atlantic Free Trade Zone in which Europe, as a distinct entity, would be absorbed into a larger whole dominated by America. But France had other ideas for Europe.[19] The General was, he might have explained, an admirer of Coudenhove-Kalergi and not of Clarence Streit.

De Gaulle's veto upset not only our political strategy for an "outward-looking" Common Market, but also our negotiating strategy for the trade talks themselves. With Britain excluded, the United States was unable to apply the "dominant supplier" clause of the Trade Expansion Act—and hence, was prevented from negotiating the great cuts otherwise expected.[20] With the United States thus hobbled in its negotiating stance, the exercise is said to have deteriorated from grand strategy for Atlantic interdependence to "low-key commercial policy."[21]

In retrospect, however, it is doubtful that tariffs could have been cut much more than they were. On the contrary, the subsequent behavior of Congress suggests that the American negotiators went rather too far as it was.[22] There are limits to the tolerance of domestic economic interests for seriously damaging competition from abroad. In any democratic political system, those interests will very likely impress themselves upon the government. Some observers, not implausibly, see the wave of protectionism which has hit both Congress and the Administration in the late sixties and early seventies as a predictable backlash from the Kennedy Round.[23] Moreover, any assumption that broad tariff cuts would improve the American balance of trade seems questionable. In manufactures the overall consequences were at least as likely to be the contrary. In agriculture, of course, we might, in theory, have greatly increased our exports to Europe. But was it ever realistic to expect the Europeans to agree?

Studying the agricultural aspect of the Kennedy Round offers considerable insight into the complexities and limitations of trade liberalization. For the United States, agriculture seemed a highly appropriate field for tariff cuts. America enjoyed an undisputed comparative advantage in many basic agricultural products. Moreover, farm interests formed an essential element in the fragile domestic American coalition which favored free trade. Therefore, it was important that those interests be encouraged. As Kennedy explained to Congress:

> The American farmer has a tremendous stake in expanded trade. One out of every seven farm workers produces for export. The average farmer depends on foreign markets to sell the crops grown on one out of every six acres he plants. Sixty percent of our rice, 49 percent of our cotton, 45 percent of our wheat and 42 percent of our soybean production are exported. Agriculture is one of our best sources of foreign exchange.
>
> Our farmers are particularly dependent upon the markets of Western Europe. Our agriculture trade with that area is four to one in our favor.[24]

In addition, as European industrial goods grew increasingly competitive, we came to rely more and more on agricultural products to maintain our favorable balance with Europe (See Table 6–10). With these considerations in view, American negotiators arriving at the Kennedy Round insisted that agricultural issues be clarified before any serious progress might be made on industrial products.[25]

But, as it happened, agriculture seemed no less critical to the Europeans. Continental Europe, like the United States, had a long history of government support for agriculture. In the Common Market countries, farmers and agricultural workers constituted a much greater part of the total labor force and general population than in the United States, and agriculture contributed a substantially higher proportion to the Gross Domestic Product (See Table 6–11).

A Community-wide agricultural policy, moreover, had been an essential element in the Franco-German deal to create the Common Market in the first place. If there was to be a Common Market in industrial goods, which was expected to help German industry, there would also have to be a Common Market in agriculture, with provisions most likely to benefit French farmers. Anything which threatened that fundamental arrangement between France and Germany threatened the EEC itself. Nevertheless, for a variety of reasons, including American pressure in the Kennedy Round, it proved extremely difficult to complete arrangements for the Common Agricultural Policy. In June 1965, de Gaulle actually ordered his negotiators to leave Brussels. After his re-election in December, the Six agreed on the essential elements of the CAP.[26]

The resolution of the agricultural question was a considerable triumph for de Gaulle. American and British attempts to keep Europe's agricultural market open to outsiders were decisively defeated. French wheat farmers could look forward to an assured European market and to subsidies for exporting to the rest of the world. De Gaulle also foiled the Commission's attempt to parlay France's eagerness for a Common Agricultural Policy into a major increase in supranational control. In the Gaullist view, Europe had become more "European" without having to accept the supranational system of control favored by European federalists and their American allies, a system de Gaulle believed would increase European subservience toward the United States.

De Gaulle won his victory by tying the achievement of the Common Agricultural Policy to the very existence of a European Community. Once faced with the choice between European integration and Atlantic liberalization, the Six chose Europe. De Gaulle thus managed both to safeguard a vital French domestic interest and to unite Europe against the Americans. No doubt he did as he wished. Nevertheless, it is not easy to see what other course any strong French government might have taken, at least on the trade issue. Few democratic countries can afford to ignore the interests of a substantial part of their population in the interests of free trade. This is not necessarily because politicians are venal or stupid, but because states have vital social, human or strategic concerns which they are unwilling to sacrifice for wider or theoretically more efficient trade.

From time immemorial, agriculture has been regarded as the social, economic, and even cultural backbone of France. Moreover, in many parts of the country,, farming remains highly lucrative. The government's attempts to modernize agriculture —to eliminate uneconomic farms and provide a good income for those that remained—resulted both in increasing production from rich farmers and increasing dissatisfaction from poor. Agricultural population was already dropping at a rapid rate. In a country whose social structure was already severely strained by the rapid pace of modernization, no government was likely to ignore so vital and explosive a sector. To drive even more French agricultural workers from the land so that Europeans could buy the cheaper products of America's industrialized agriculture was a policy bound to be fiercely resisted by any French government. In the end, any neighbors serious about building an economic and political union with France would have to defer to that interest.

The perspective of classical economics offers, unfortunately, very little insight into the realities of such a situation. There is, in fact, something fundamentally defective and simple-minded about the classical economist's view of the world as expressed in the principle of comparative advantage. The principle is not "wrong" in its own terms; it is simply an insufficient guide to understanding the modern world. All governments today play a highly active role in shaping the economic environment of their citizenry. Governments are the agents by which people seek to impose their cultural ideas upon their environment. In this respect, we live in a mercantilist and not a liberal world. Undoubtedly economic intercourse among nations brings advantages all around. But when that interdependence begins to threaten the social and political values of society, or impinge seriously upon a government's ability to control its economic environment, then that government is bound to resist if it can. Thus, to push interdependence too far is to run the risk of violent and self-defeating reactions.

From the perspective of politics, such ideas seem self-evident; but less so from the perspectives of economics. As we discuss in Part I, throughout this modern era the political ideal of community has had to contend with the economic ideal of growth. The uneasy relationship, of course, continues to the present day and is clearly reflected in many of the issues raised by trade.

Economic Man versus the General Will

In a hungry world, as Ricardo saw it, the alternative to economic efficiency was mass starvation. The more the state interfered with the market to promote uneconomic ends, the more the society would suffer deprivation. And as we have seen, for Ricardo free trade was the essential element in achieving economic efficiency. Modern trade theory, for all its many refinements, has not moved far from Ricardo's fundamental view. Liberal trade is still believed vital to economic prosperity. While modern trade theories are often impressive intellectual constructions, in their essential points the arguments for international trade liberalization are not complicated, and are roughly analogous to the theory of domestic trade or even village exchange.

Trade began, economists will tell us, with the recognition that any particular person or tool was not equally well suited to perform every task. Specialization was therefore logical, and with specialization came the incentive for the exchange of goods. Trade let men share the benefits of specialization—within the village and region, or even across seas, deserts and mountains.

As specialization put men, machines and materials to work where they were relatively most useful and efficient, productivity increased. The larger the market and the fewer the obstacles between its parts, the greater the possibilities for specialization. Specialization moved an economy closer to its ideal state of *economic efficiency*—defined as that point of specialization where the return to no single factor of production can be increased by putting it to work in any other way.

The concept of ideal economic efficiency was and is, of course, highly theoretical. Realizing it requires a "perfect market" with "perfect competition," itself the product of several utopian conditions. In a perfect market, the unimpeded laws of supply and demand determine costs and prices. Neither suppliers nor buyers of a productive factor can fix its price and no producer or consumer can arbitrarily depress or raise the price of goods produced and consumed. Perfect competition, of course, assumes also that every buyer and seller of a factor or a product possesses perfect knowledge of market supply and demand, and that all factors of production are perfectly mobile and can be combined according to the principles of economic efficiency as dictated by the market. Finally, to achieve economic efficiency requires not only all these ideal objective conditions, but also the subjective will to use them as the ideal dictates, in other words, a determination by the actors in this perfect market to guide their behavior by strictly economic criteria of efficiency.

In the actual world, these conditions are elusive.[27] Various distortions, like monopolies and governments, inevitably influence the workings of the market, and hence prevent it from approximating the model. Nevertheless, the model market and its informing principle of economic efficiency stand as ideal constants against which, economists believe, reality should be tested. In a fallen world, if policy must deviate from the optimum of economic efficiency, economists should at least ensure that governments know the costs, and suffer from bad consciences.

The principle use of the model is to show how an economy ought to allocate its factors and determine what they should produce—in other words, how an economy should decide on its inputs and outputs. The object is to employ fully all the factors at a given state of technology and to maximize total production. Normally, there are a variety of product mixes which will employ all the factors. The market may decide to produce more of product A and less of product B. To use a simple diagram, the *production possibility curve* indicates both the maximum amount of either good an economy can produce with its given technological knowledge and with all its available productive factors fully employed, as well as every possible maximum combination of the two goods. The curve, thus, represents the production "frontier" of the economy, a frontier which in the real world, of course, may be altered, for example, by change in technology or labor conditions.[28]

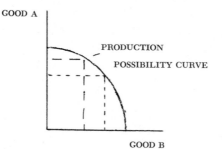

GOOD A

PRODUCTION
POSSIBILITY CURVE

GOOD B

To allocate more factors to the production of good A necessarily means to produce less of good B. Yet as long as the actual
point of production is located somewhere on the production
possibility curve, society as a whole is using its available factors
of production with maximum efficiency. To achieve economic
efficiency no one combination of goods is superior to another,
provided that the combination uses the existing factors to the
full.

How, then, does a society decide what to produce? In a free
market model, the consumer decides. Consumers may decide
to buy more of good A and less of good B—in response to price
or taste changes, for example. It is assumed, however, that as a
consumer acquires more and more of A, he becomes increasingly loath to accept any more of it in place of B. Indeed, it
is assumed that—beyond a certain point—one good can no
longer be substituted for another. Thus, no matter how much
lower A's price may fall the consumer will not buy any more
of it in substitution for B. This principle of the limited substitutability of goods can be expressed diagrammatically as a
consumption indifference curve, a curve which must necessarily be convex, as shown in the diagram.[29] The consumption
indifference curve, then, shows what increase in the quantity
of one good is necessary to induce the consumer to forgo some
amount of the other. For the sake of convenience, economists
postulate a *community consumption indifference curve* which
is, in theory, an average derived from the sum of all personal
consumption indifference curves.[30]

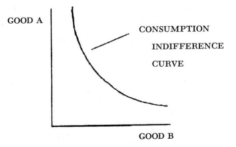

GOOD A

CONSUMPTION
INDIFFERENCE
CURVE

GOOD B

To sum up the market model in diagrams: the point of tangency between the production possibility curve and the highest possible consumption indifference curve marks the point at which the economy should actually produce. Consumer demand is satisfied and all available factors of production are employed in the most economically efficient fashion. The economy is then said to be in a state of *output consumption equilibrium.*[31]

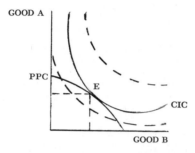

So far, we have been speaking, in effect, about a closed economy which contains its own production factors and consumers within itself. What happens when this economy enters into trade with another which is also in an optimum state of economic efficiency? In effect, trade simply creates a larger market. If either production possibility curves or consumption indifference curves are not identical, trade will satisfy consumer demand at a higher level in both economies. In other words, either a difference in consumer preferences or a difference in factor endowments (or in available technology) permits mutually profitable trade between two economies.

In short, trade creates a bigger market; a bigger market allows more specialization; specialization means more production at less cost—in other words: greater economic "efficiency." But for the efficiency to be realized, perfect market conditions must prevail. Ideally, nothing should interfere with the free expression of consumer preferences or with the free movement of productive factors in response to those preferences. Thus, the case for free trade is an extension to an international market of the case for laissez-faire in the domestic market.[32]

The case for freer trade is also, in its essentials, a case for achieving a maximum of consumption. The object of the ideal market mechanism is to organize economic activity so that the consumer gets all that he wants at the lowest possible price. The consumer is sovereign. While the consumer allegedly benefits all the time, a particular producer—an entrepreneur, or a laborer—benefits only so long as he remains competitive. Freer trade, in fact, increases the risk and vulnerability of any particular producer even as it enhances the benefits of consumers in general.

Herein lies a great flaw in classical free-trade theory, a flaw which is both practical and moral. Practically speaking, in Western societies, most consumers are also producers. Most people have to work to consume; the great bulk of consumption is by people who also work. From the perspective of the producer or the producer/consumer, a system which focuses on the welfare of consumers and expects producers to shift for themselves has its priorities backward. From this perspective, a more rational system would orient itself toward production, toward achieving the full and satisfying employment of its labor and capital. Consumption would then take care of itself. If there is thereby some loss in theoretical economic efficiency, if prices are somewhat higher, the corresponding benefits to society as a whole will more than compensate. So it is likely to seem to the producer.

In fact, in modern capitalist countries since the war, producers have more or less had their way. Full employment is at least the stated goal of economic policy for most governments. Neither modern business, labor, nor even capital will in fact submit willingly to the discipline of absolute economic efficiency. Labor's efforts to protect itself against risk are manifest, as are those of farmers and businessmen. For the successful company, limited risk is counterbalanced by general prudence.

Thus the corporation attempts to control its environment by manipulating the "sovereign" consumer through advertising or by spreading its risk through diversification.[33] Some liberal theorists still complain about how corporations pass the costs of risk-avoiding along to the consumer. Thus, it is said, the few exploit the many.[34] No doubt, some corporations, either from bad judgement or venality, greatly abuse the consumer. Certainly, the particular interests of unions and corporations lead them to a highly partial view of the general welfare. Nevertheless, the notion that lower prices for the consumer should be the principal value guiding economic policy reflects a view no less partial and simple-minded.

Governments, of course, introduce another set of perspectives about the general welfare and another set of "distortions" into the market. A government charged with the general welfare does not blindly submit the nation's security or independence to the dictates of the consumer's market. Like business corporations, states draw back from the logic of economic efficiency. Free trade is supposed to encourage national economies to specialize for a world market. In practice, rather than grow dependent on alien sources, governments in major industrialized nations prefer to conserve a full range of industries within their national boundries. The American government furnishes a particularly good example, as the growing number of our restrictive bilateral trade agreements suggests.[35] Even within the Common Market, where integration through trade liberalization might be expected to have proceeded farthest, the great bulk of trade across borders still occurs within groups of products which are produced in nearly all countries, as opposed to between groups produced in only one or two countries. A German, for example, may buy a French car, but both Germany and France make a full range of automobiles.[36]

It is, incidentally, a striking feature of contemporary trade that it grows fastest among countries with similar economies,[37] a phenomenon which suggests doubts about the marginal advantage of a good deal of international trade, even for the consumer. How heavy a price in the disruption of domestic industry and labor should be paid to get that putative consumer advantage?[38]

Deciding among the competing perspectives of various interests, and hence measuring and balancing social costs and gains, is in the end more a problem for philosophy than for economics. And in these matters, classical economics presents a primitive and even dangerous view. In the model world of the classical economist, the consumer is sovereign and that economy is best which is most fluid in response to the consumer's demands. That, after all, is what the economists' optimum state of *free factor mobility* means. But no economy is separable from the society it serves, and economic fluidity thus imperils societal stability. No association or institution is sacred. All must be prepared to be uprooted according to the dictates of the market place.

The moral poverty of such an economic model is apparent. Its basic assumption of consumer sovereignty is not only questionable practically, but morally as well. Most political philosophers would find it difficult to isolate the public welfare either within the "production function" or within the "consumption function." It lies in both and in neither. Nor can the public welfare be found automatically in some simple majority—organized either as consumers or producers. Rousseau, wrestling with this problem, assigns moral sovereignty neither to the will of a governing elite, nor to the "will of all," but to a "general will"—the general welfare as it ought ideally to be conceived.[39]

Rousseau's suggestions for the institutional structure to define the general will doubtless leave much to be desired. In any event, for the reason to which Burke gives classical expression, no simple, let alone universal, constitutional formula can ever be satisfactory. Finding the general will while engaging the citizenry in its formulation and expression will always be the fundamental and continuing business of any democratic political economy. And particular definitions of an ideal good tend naturally to be partial and incomplete in accordance with the particular perspectives of the definer. But in this era, we can really do better at locating the general welfare than equating it with the maximization of consumption. No political community has ever done so, for we continue to live in a fallen world where politics "distorts" economics. And why not? Why, for example, should consumer values necessarily be taken as superior to producer values? In an age of technological abundance, why shouldn't an economic system be set the primary task of providing the individual with a steady and interesting job, as opposed to providing the consumer with the cheapest price? Why isn't unemployment, insecurity or the dehumanization of labor a cost worse than lessened consumption? But neither production nor consumption is, in itself, an adequate standard for economic policy.

The individual, after all, is not only a producer/consumer, but a man and a citizen. Such a role calls for a broader set of values than even the most enlightened economics is likely to provide. To paraphrase Burke, a nation is not a commercial affair, to be taken up and dissolved according to the dictates of the market, but a fundamental human partnership—stretching across the generations—to build a good society.[40] It is this membership in the general community which, according to Rousseau, joins the individual will to the general will. In the ideal society, the general will of the citizen incorporates his particular will as consumer and producer into some broader ideal of a good life, and of a good society for achieving it. Economic prosperity is obviously an essential element in the general welfare, but scarcely the only one. No doubt the market remains one of the basic instruments for expressing and refining the general will, but only after the mechanism has been corrected by what the classical economist would call "distortions" and the rest of us might call equity and morality— in short, civilization.

Obviously, capitalist societies have long ago ceased using the market place as the measure of all things. Indeed, the progress of capitalist civilization over the past hundred years might be described as movement away from laissez-faire toward the "mixed economy" and the welfare state. The welfare state may or may not be economically "efficient." The money spent on social security for the aged would perhaps produce more if spent by IBM or General Motors. But economic efficiency is not the only goal of any modern state. Each seeks, in theory at least, to develop a broadly humanitarian society, not merely an efficient one. The achievement of a high degree of economic efficiency is highly desirable, but by no means a sufficent or exclusive objective for a good society.

In summary, quite apart from its manifest irrelevance because of the innumerable "distortions" which prevent its operation in the real world, economic efficiency is of questionable use, even as an ideal. Two of its basic principles, consumer sovereignty and free factor mobility, would—if they prevailed—mean the collapse of modern civilization.

Similarly, the discipline of economics in today's world derives its public utility not as a special source of prescriptive moral wisdom, but as a highly elaborate form of systems analysis whose concepts provide a means for predicting certain of the consequences of choice among economic options.

Whatever moral pretensions may linger around the ideal of economic efficiency and the free market should be banished to the museum of history. By the same token, free trade should be ejected from the pantheon of unquestioned precepts for the governance of foreign economic policy. The costs and benefits of trade, like those of any other economic activity, must be judged according to the broad criteria which define the general welfare.

Seen in this light, our postwar international economic policies have presented a curious anachronism. While we have been able to imagine, and have made great efforts to create, a humanitarian welfare system domestically, our vision and policy for the international economic environment has been very much dominated by the ideals of laissez-faire. This contrast between domestic and international ideals has become more than an anomaly; it has become a fundamental danger. The international dimension of our economy has been growing to a point where it threatens to encroach upon the achievements of the humanitarian state itself, both in America and abroad. Many of the arguments heard today which contrast the wisdom of liberalism with the perils of protectionism sound curiously like the conventional defense of laissez-faire in the bad old days of undirected nineteenth-century capitalism. Enthusiasts for free trade, perhaps regretting the demise of laissez-faire on the national scale, apparently hope to bring it back on a world scale.

Trade and Growth

To say that trade liberalization should no longer be seen as a prescriptive political principle, independent of broader criteria for the general welfare, is not to say that freer trade is an improper object of policy. Highly plausible empirical arguments, for example, assign trade liberalization a major role in the great postwar boom among the Atlantic countries. In periods of general economic growth, freeing trade, it is said, prolongs and stimulates that growth. Liberal access to imports can break the inevitable bottlenecks in a rapidly expanding economy and keep growth from stalling. A large and open export market reduces fears of overproduction and hence encourages efficient companies to produce to capacity and to expand.[41] Thus, as Andrew Shonfield has argued, trade and growth can come together to form a sort of "virtuous circle," where the growth of national product tends to call forth an even higher growth of trade.[42]

But even if it does prolong growth, there is no reason to

exempt international trade from the same conscious rational control which is applied increasingly to the rest of the economy. In the past two decades, after the terrible ravages of war and the dismal hardship of depression, governments have pursued economic growth with single-minded determination. No doubt, the virtuous circle has aided and abetted that growth. But as affluence has become the common state of Western society, many signs indicate a period of economic and social consolidation. After the rapid growth of the last two decades, there is a new awareness of the broader social and environmental costs of increased production. Blind enthusiasm for growth is slowly falling out of fashion, and with it, therefore, a principal justification for greater levels of trade.

In today's time of relative economic sobriety, many question whether growth, and incidentally the trade which is meant to sustain it, are proper goals for American policy at all. An environmental crisis of unparalleled proportions now threatens imminent danger. America, some feel, might not survive many more decades like the sixties.

In summary, free trade should be demoted from its central position in American international economic policy. Trade is not the panacea for all international economic and political problems. Carried blindly beyond a certain point, it becomes a cause of intolerable domestic disruption and increasing international friction. Trade, like all other economic elements, needs to be regulated according to some more general view of the national welfare. Modern nation-states have long ago abandoned laissez-faire for welfare mercantilism. There is no reason why trade alone should be exempted from the general progress of modern civilization.

Trade in a Mercantilist World

If the classical arguments are no longer determining, should the United States abandon trade liberalization as an

international policy? Not necessarily. Quite apart from particular economic benefits, a good case can be made for the liberal
trading system built up since the war precisely because we do
live in a mercantilist and not a liberal world order. The great
danger of mercantilism is its tendency to engage the power
and prestige of states in economic competition for world markets. Domestic difficulties resulting from over-production, insufficient consumption or other misallocations of resources are
simply exported to the world at large. Carried to its logical
conclusion, world trade, prompted by domestic inadequacies,
can easily degenerate into a form of warfare among states. For
all of Hull's naiveté, it is difficult to deny that he was concerned with a fundamental problem.

Within a mercantilist world, the liberal trading principles
serve an essentially political purpose. They form a code of conduct which seeks to refine and civilize the inevitable conflict
among nations. States inevitably base their policies upon considerations of domestic welfare. Close and harmonious coordination of domestic policies is difficult among more than a
handful of closely related states. Yet states must constantly be
reminded of the external consequences of their policies, and
schooled—in their mutual interest—to resist the temptation to
pass on the cost of domestic welfare to the world at large.
Countries, of course, will continue to grow and decay, form
new institutions and exert new pressures. A civilized code of
international economic behavior forms a framework within
which strong new forces can be allowed their fair measure of
international expression, and weak ones the dignity of a decline
according to the rules of the game. This is a goal considerably
more modest than the "interdependent" Atlantic Community
sought by the Kennedy Round of GATT negotiations. But the
GATT's true and great achievement has not been building some
version of Hull's liberal world order, but evolving a civilized
common law to govern the relationships among mercantilist
states. The negotiated body of concepts, regulations and

procedures is a code of mutual accommodation and restraint to remind states that trying to solve their domestic problems by ruining their neighbors is a policy which ends in disaster.

To recognize the great achievement of the GATT system, however, is also to recognize its limitations. In a mercantilist world, the liberal code is threatened when it begins to impinge on the ability of states to shape their own economic environment—be it because one powerful state is using liberalism as the instrument and ideology of domination or because unruly private interests use it to escape from political control altogether. Those concerned with preserving the achievements of the GATT should take care that its principles are not used to mask political imperialism or private greed.

As the preceding chapter suggests, the United States, in its rather literal-minded devotion to liberal trading and monetary policies—a devotion to "interdependence" which has only thinly masked the pursuit of hegemony—has in fact violated the cardinal principles of any genuinely liberal world system. Thus, for example, our insistence on a trade surplus large enough to cover our outflow for troops and investments risks inducing that very mercantilist seizing up of the world which our liberalism was presumably designed to avoid. Such worries seem less abstract since the summer of 1971. As our trade position has rapidly deteriorated, the American government has grown less bashful about asserting national interests without their liberal smokescreen. The will to power remains; the idealism has vanished. Our policy has not so much changed as become more honest. Nor is the basic change to be regretted. Quite the contrary. It may, we can hope, be the beginning of a long overdue adjustment of institutions, rules and responsibilities. But in abandoning that literal-minded liberalism which is no longer convenient to our interests, we should not ourselves become the wreckers of that system of mutual restraint whose absence we might rapidly come to regret.

Tables 6–1 to 6–11, referred to in the foregoing, Chapter Six, Atlantic Community Trade, appear in the following pages (144–161).

TABLE 6–1

U.S. Merchandise Trade Balance with Major Trading Partners, 1967-1971
(millions of U.S. dollars)

		1967	1968	1969	1970	1971
Canada	Exp.	7,165	8,072	9,137	9,079	10,366
	Imp.	7,107	9,005	10,384	11,092	12,762
	Bal.	+ 58	− 933	− 1,247	− 2,013	− 2,396
Mexico	Exp.	1,222	1,378	1,450	1,704	1,622
	Imp.	749	910	1,029	1,219	1,263
	Bal.	+ 473	+ 468	+ 421	+ 485	+ 359
Venezuela	Exp.	587	655	708	759	787
	Imp.	980	950	940	1,082	1,216
	Bal.	− 392	− 295	− 232	− 323	− 429
Australia	Exp.	893	872	855	986	1,004
	Imp.	406	488	588	611	620
	Bal.	+ 487	+ 384	+ 267	+ 375	+ 384
Japan	Exp.	2,695	2,954	3,490	4,652	4,055
	Imp.	2,999	4,054	4,888	5,875	7,261
	Bal.	− 304	− 1,100	− 1,398	− 1,223	− 3,206
EFTA[1]	Exp.	3,277	3,890	4,040	4,515	4,261
	Imp.	2,881	3,572	3,683	3,851	4,292
	Bal.	+ 396	+ 318	+ 357	+ 664	− 31
United Kingdom	Exp.	1,960	2,289	2,335	2,536	2,374
	Imp.	1,710	2,058	2,120	2,194	2,459
	Bal.	+ 250	+ 231	+ 215	+ 342	− 85

TABLE 6–1, Cont.

EEC	Exp.	5,643	6,127	7,005	8,423	8,389
	Imp.	4,453	5,885	5,798	6,609	7,524
	Bal.	+ 1,190	+ 242	+ 1,207	+ 1,814	+ 865
Belgium/Luxemb.	Exp.	704	823	960	1,195	1,078
	Imp.	584	767	683	696	845
	Bal.	+ 120	+ 56	+ 277	+ 499	+ 233
France	Exp.	1,025	1,095	1,195	1,483	1,380
	Imp.	690	842	842	942	1,088
	Bal.	+ 334	+ 253	+ 353	+ 541	+ 292
Germany (West)	Exp.	1,706	1,709	2,142	2,741	2,832
	Imp.	1,955	2,721	2,603	3,127	3,651
	Bal.	− 250	− 1,012	− 461	− 386	− 819
Italy	Exp.	973	1,121	1,262	1,353	1,314
	Imp.	856	1,102	1,204	1,316	1,406
	Bal.	+ 117	+ 19	+ 58	+ 37	− 92
Netherlands	Exp.	1,235	1,380	1,447	1,651	1,785
	Imp.	368	453	466	528	534
	Bal.	+ 867	+ 927	+ 981	+ 1,123	+ 1,251

Data refer to U.S. imports f.o.b. and U.S. exports f.o.b.

+ denotes American trade surplus, − denotes American trade deficit.

Exports are total exports of domestic and foreign merchandise, including special categories, military shipments, etc. Imports are general imports for consumption.

1. EFTA figures include Iceland and Finland.

Sources: U.S. Bureau of the Census, *Highlights of the U.S. Export and Import Trade*, Report FT 990, December 1971 (released January 1972), pp. 44–46, 86–88; U.S. Bureau of the Census, *Statistical Abstract of the United States 1971* (Washington, 1971), pp. 768–771; and *Statistical Abstract of the United States 1969* (Washington, 1969), pp. 808–811.

TABLE 6–2.A

World Exports (f.o.b.), by Major Regions, Countries and Country Groups
(millions of U.S. dollars)

	1938	1948	1953	1959	1963	1970
A. Developed market economies	15,200	36,700	53,700	75,700	103,900	223,900
"Atlantic Trading Community"	13,170	33,610	48,680	68,040	93,220	196,300
USA	3,064	12,545	15,661	17,472	23,104	42,593
Canada	865	3,109	4,220	5,365	6,466	16,187
Western Europe	9,240	17,960	28,800	45,200	63,650	137,510
EEC	4,360	6,680	14,680	25,470	37,550	88,520
EFTA	4,150	9,560	12,000	16,940	22,130	40,240
Other	730	1,720	2,130	2,800	3,960	8,760
Japan	1,109	258	1,275	3,457	5,452	19,318
South Africa	163	557	830	1,214	1,400	2,148
Australia	518	1,650	1,979	2,002	2,786	4,620
New Zealand	225	496	659	821	923	1,225
B. Developing market economics	5,900	17,100	21,100	25,800	31,500	54,200
Europe	10	20	20	20	30	60
Latin America	1,710	6,520	7,620	8,270	9,710	14,380
Other America	300	940	1,130	1,360	1,580	2,270
Africa	860	3,030	3,960	4,820	6,230	12,540
Asia	2,980	6,490	8,230	11,160	13,750	24,570
Asian Middle East	330	1,290	2,180	3,960	5,290	10,380
Oceania	30	80	110	150	200	430
C. "Free World" total (A + B)	21,100	53,800	74,800	101,500	135,400	278,100

Note: Exports of USSR and centrally planned economies in Europe and Asia are excluded.

Sources: United Nations: *Yearbook of International Trade Statistics 1969* (New York, 1971), pp. 12–19,
Table A. United Nations: *Monthly Bulletin of Statistics—June 1971*, pp. xii–xv, Special Table B.
United Nations: *Monthly Bulletin of Statistics—January 1972*, pp. 110–115, Table 52.

TABLE 6–2.B

Exports and Percent of "Free World" Total

	1938	1948	1953	1959	1963	1970
A. Developed market economies	72.0	68.2	71.8	74.6	76.7	80.5
"Atlantic Trading Community"	62.4	62.5	65.1	67.0	68.8	70.6
USA	14.5	23.3	20.9	17.2	17.1	15.3
Canada	4.1	5.8	5.6	5.3	4.8	5.8
Western Europe	43.8	33.4	38.5	44.5	47.0	49.4
EEC	20.7	12.4	19.6	25.1	27.7	31.8
EFTA	19.7	17.8	16.0	16.7	16.3	14.5
Other	3.5	3.2	2.8	2.8	2.9	3.1
Japan	5.3	0.5	1.7	3.4	4.0	6.9
South Africa	0.8	1.0	1.1	1.2	1.0	0.8
Australia	2.5	3.1	2.6	2.0	2.1	1.6
New Zealand	1.1	0.9	0.9	0.8	0.7	0.4
B. Developing market economies	28.0	31.8	28.2	25.4	23.3	19.5
Europe	...	...	...	...	...	...
Latin America	8.1	12.1	10.2	8.1	7.2	5.2
Other America	1.4	1.7	1.5	1.3	1.2	0.8
Africa	4.1	5.6	5.3	4.7	4.6	4.5
Asia	14.1	12.1	11.0	11.0	10.2	8.8
Asian Middle East	1.6	2.4	2.9	3.9	3.9	3.7
Oceania	0.1	0.1	0.1	0.1	0.1	0.2
C. "Free World" total	100.0	100.0	100.0	100.0	100.0	100.0

Source: See Table 6–2.A

TABLE 6–3.A

World Imports (c.i.f.) by Major Regions, Countries and Country Groups
(millions of U.S. dollars)

	1938	1948	1953	1959	1963	1970
A. Developed market economies	17,900	41,200	55,100	79,300	110,700	236,100
"Atlantic Trading Community"	15,550	37,180	49,540	71,580	98,670	207,510
USA[1]	2,180	7,183	10,915	15,478	17,072	39,768
Canada[1]	691	2,618	4,317	5,746	6,085	13,349
Western Europe	12,320	26,190	33,000	48,540	73,560	150,850
EEC	5,120	10,650	15,510	24,550	49,430	88,290
EFTA	6,290	12,880	14,570	19,960	26,450	47,800
Other	810	2,660	2,920	4,030	6,680	14,760
Japan	1,070	684	2,410	3,600	6,736	18,881
South Africa[1]	464	1,424	1,194	1,368	1,698	3,556
Australia[1]	517	1,227	1,293	1,851	2,478	4,479
New Zealand	225	450	538	648	905	1,245
B. Developing market economies	5,800	18,600	21,400	27,440	32,800	56,700
Europe	30	90	80	110	140	200
Latin America	1,540	6,180	6,530	7,910	8,700	15,430
Other America	400	1,270	1,420	1,870	2,090	3,570
Africa	1,060	3,600	4,610	5,890	6,730	10,730
Asia	2,690	7,390	8,720	11,400	14,870	25,900
Asian Middle East	330	1,370	1,710	3,000	3,620	7,070
Oceania	30	80	120	180	260	840
C. "Free World" total (A + B)	23,700	59,800	76,500	106,700	143,500	292,800

Notes: Imports of USSR and centrally planned economies in Europe and Asia are excluded.
1. Imports f.o.b.—The regional and overall totals are adjusted to c.i.f.

Sources: United Nations: *Yearbook of International Trade Statistics 1969* (New York, 1971), pp. 12–19, Table A. United Nations: *Monthly Bulletin of Statistics—January 1972*, pp. 110–115, Table 52.

TABLE 6–3.B

Imports as Percent of "Free World" Total

	1938	1948	1953	1959	1963	1970
A. Developed market economies	75.5	68.9	72.0	74.3	77.1	80.6
"Atlantic Trading Community"	65.6	62.2	64.6	67.1	68.8	70.9
USA	9.2	12.0	14.3	14.5	11.9	13.6
Canada	2.9	4.4	5.6	5.4	4.2	4.6
Western Europe	52.0	43.8	43.1	45.5	51.3	51.5
EEC	21.6	17.8	20.3	23.0	28.2	30.2
EFTA	26.5	21.5	19.0	18.7	18.4	16.3
Other	3.4	4.4	3.8	3.8	4.7	5.0
Japan	4.5	1.1	3.2	3.4	4.7	6.4
South Africa	2.0	2.4	1.6	1.3	1.2	1.2
Australia	2.2	2.1	1.7	1.7	1.7	1.5
New Zealand	0.9	0.8	0.7	0.6	0.6	0.4
B. Developing market economies	24.5	31.1	28.0	25.7	22.9	19.4
Europe	0.1	0.2	0.1	0.1	0.1	0.1
Latin America	6.5	10.3	8.5	7.4	6.1	5.3
Other America	1.7	2.1	1.9	1.8	1.5	1.2
Africa	4.5	6.0	6.0	5.5	4.7	3.7
Asia	11.4	12.4	11.4	10.7	10.4	8.8
Asian Middle East	1.4	2.3	2.2	2.8	2.5	2.4
Oceania	0.1	0.1	0.2	0.2	0.2	0.3
C. "Free World" total	100.0	100.0	100.0	100.0	100.0	100.0

Source: See Table 6–3.A

TABLE 6–4.A

Trade within the "Atlantic Trading Community," 1958
(exports f.o.b., in millions of U.S. dollars)

From	Total	To USA	To Canada	To Western Europe	To EEC	To EFTA	To "ATC"	To Japan	To "ATC 2"
USA	17,760	....	3,460	5,390	2,840	1,560	8,850	980	9,830
Canada	5,050	3,000	....	1,380	435	920	4,380	110	4,490
W. Europe	42,020	3,260	840	22,520	11,860	8,550	26,620	240	26,860
EEC	23,440	1,660	235	13,580	7,530	4,950	15,475	140	15,615
EFTA	15,980	1,370	600	7,370	3,650	2,800	9,340	90	9,430
"ATC"	64,830	6,260	4,300	29,290	15,135	11,030	39,850	1,330	....
Japan	2,880	690	80	320	120	170	1,090	....	1,090
"ATC 2"	67,710	6,950	4,380	29,610	15,255	11,200	....	1,330	42,270

Source: United Nations: Yearbook of International Trade Statistics 1969 (New York, 1971), pp 20–31, Table B.

TABLE 6–4.B

Trade within the "Atlantic Trading Community," 1970
(exports f.o.b., in millions of U.S. dollars)

From	Total	To USA	To Canada	To Western Europe	To EEC	To EFTA	To "ATC"	To Japan	To "ATC 2"
USA	42,590	....	8,810	14,270	8,330	4,300	23,080	4,610	27,690
Canada	16,710	10,920	....	3,150	1,190	1,790	14,070	790	14,860
W. Europe	138,060	11,150	1,760	92,810	56,690	27,440	105,720	1,710	107,430
EEC	88,500	6,630	730	63,060	43,300	14,840	70,420	990	71,410
EFTA	40,820	3,730	960	24,310	10,770	10,050	29,000	650	29,650
"ATC"	196,300	22,070	10,570	110,230	66,210	33,530	142,870	7,110	159,480
Japan	19,320	6,020	560	2,920	1,300	1,060	9,500	....	9,500
"ATC 2"	215,620	28,090	11,130	113,150	67,510	34,590	....	7,110	159,480

Source: United Nations: *Monthly Bulletin of Statistics—June 1971*, pp. xll–xv, Special Table B.

TABLE 6–4.C

Intra-"ATC" Trade as Percent of Total "ATC" Trade, 1958 & 1970

	1958	1970
"Atlantic Trading Community"	61.5	72.8
"ATC 2" (incl. Japan)	62.4	74.0

Sources: Tables 6-4.A and 6-4.B

TABLE 6–5.A

U.S. Merchandise Exports, by Area
(in millions of U.S. dollars)

	1949	1955	1960	1963	1965	1969	1970	1971
Total	11,560	13,838	20,586	23,387	27,521	38,006	43,224	44,137
Western Hemisphere	4,748	6,638	8,076	7,953	9,923	14,713	15,611	16,850
Canada	1,928	3,235	3,810	4,261	5,657	9,137	9,079	10,366
Other	2,820	3,403	4,266	3,692	4,266	5,576	6,532	6,484
Western Europe	3,980	4,187	7,211	8,198	9,258	12,392	14,463	14,190
EEC			3,991	4,921	5,256	7,773	8,423	8,398
Eastern Europe	65	11	195	167	140	249	354	384
Asia	1,997	2,121	4,187	5,448	6,015	8,261	10,028	9,850
Japan			1,452	1,848	2,084	3,490	4,652	4,055
Africa	594	612	793	1,053	1,229	1,392	1,579	1,694
Australia & Oceania	176	270	515	565	956	998	1,189	1,169
Developed countries			13,259	15,124	18,366	26,479	29,877	30,347
Developing countries			7,132	8,056	9,015	11,277	12,993	13,405

Sources: *Economic Report of the President* 1961, 1967, 1970, 1971, 1972; and "New Realities and New Directions in United States Foreign Economic Policy," Report by the Subcommittee on Foreign Economic Policy of the Committee on Foreign Affairs, U.S. House of Representatives (Washington, 28 February 1972), p. 29.

TABLE 6–5.B

U.S. Merchandise Imports, by Area
(in millions of U.S. dollars)

	1949	1955	1960	1963	1965	1969	1970	1971
Total	6,622	11,384	15,019	17,207	21,427	36,043	39,952	45,602
Western Hemisphere	3,995	6,262	7,117	7,887	9,256	15,547	16,928	18,801
Canada	1,512	2,653	3,153	3,851	4,858	10,384	11,092	12,762
Other	2,483	3,609	3,964	4,036	4,398	5,163	5,836	6,039
Western Europe	909	2,391	4,188	4,731	6,154	10,138	11,169	12,623
EEC			3,194	3,751	4,432	6,837	6,612	7,523
Eastern Europe	72	62	81	81	137	195	226	223
Asia	1,184	1,876	2,721	3,192	4,529	8,275	9,621	11,783
Japan			1,149	1,498	2,414	4,888	5,875	7,261
Africa	338	619	627	778	883	1,046	1,113	1,237
Australia & Oceania	125	174	266	504	455	828	871	895
Developed countries			8,951	10,832	14,101	26,460	29,259	33,781
Developing countries			5,984	6,283	7,173	9,373	10,442	11,552

Source: See Table 6–5.A.

TABLE 6-6.A

Indices of U.S. Merchandise Exports to Major Areas
(1963 = 100)

	1949	1955	1960	1963	1964	1965	1966	1967	1968	1969	1970	1971
Total	49	59	88	100	114	118	130	135	148	163	185	189
Western Hemisphere	60	83	102	100	116	125	144	150	169	185	196	212
Canada	45	76	89	100	115	133	157	168	189	214	213	243
Other	76	92	116	100	116	116	129	128	145	151	177	176
Western Europe	49	51	88	100	112	113	121	124	136	151	176	173
EEC	:	:	81	100	108	107	112	115	125	158	171	171
Eastern Europe	39	7	117	100	204	84	119	117	129	149	212	230
Asia	37	39	77	100	107	110	124	131	139	152	184	181
Japan	:	:	79	100	109	113	128	146	160	189	252	219
Africa	56	58	75	100	120	117	128	112	121	132	150	161
Australia & Oceania	31	48	91	100	142	169	142	180	182	177	210	207
Developed countries	:	:	88	100	114	121	133	142	156	175	198	201
Developing countries	:	:	89	100	111	112	126	124	134	140	161	166

Sources: See Table 6–5.A.

TABLE 6–6.ʙ

Indices of U.S. Merchandise Imports by Areas

(1963 = 100)

	1949	1955	1960	1963	1964	1965	1966	1967	1968	1969	1970	1971
Total	38	66	87	100	109	125	149	156	193	209	232	265
Western Hemisphere	51	79	90	100	107	117	138	150	179	197	215	238
Canada	39	69	82	100	111	126	160	185	234	270	288	331
Other	62	89	98	100	104	109	117	116	127	128	145	150
Western Europe	19	51	89	100	110	130	162	170	214	214	236	267
EEC	: :	: :	85	100	109	118	139	145	157	182	176	201
Eastern Europe	89	77	100	100	122	169	221	219	244	241	279	275
Asia	37	59	85	100	113	142	165	168	217	259	301	369
Japan	: :	: :	77	100	118	161	198	200	271	326	392	485
Africa	43	80	81	100	118	113	128	118	144	134	143	159
Australia & Oceania	25	35	53	100	88	90	118	116	138	164	173	178
Developed countries	: :	: :	83	100	110	130	163	175	223	244	270	312
Developing countries	: :	: :	95	100	107	114	124	123	141	149	166	184

Sources: See Table 6–5.A.

TABLE 6–7

U.S. Merchandise Exports to Western Europe
and Western Hemisphere, 1948–1971
(in millions of U.S. dollars)

Year	Western Europe	Western Hemisphere
1948	4,279[1]	5,307
1949	4,118[1]	4,861
1950	3,280	4,902
1951	5,118	6,607
1952	5,088	6,682
1953	5,709	6,514
1954	5,112	6,520
1955	5,119	6,903
1956	6,423	8,243
1957	6,751	9,001
1958	5,452	7,999
1959	5,464	7,692
1960	7,204	7,684
1961	7,237	7,673
1962	7,633	7,724
1963	8,171	7,944
1964	9,096	9,207
1965	9,224	9,917
1966	9,805	11,429
1967	10,187	11,890
1968	11,132	13,411
1969	12,392	14,713
1970	14,465	15,618
1971	14,190	16,850

1. All Europe, including USSR.

Sources: 1948–49; U.S. Department of Commerce, *Business Statistics,* *1969* (Washington, 1969), p. 111; 1950-66: U.S. Bureau of the Census, *Highlights of the U.S. Export and Import Trade,* Report FT 990, August 1967 (released October 1967), pp. 96–97; 1967–70: U.S. Department of Commerce, *Overseas Business Reports,* February 1971, Report OBR 71–009, p. 18; 1971: *Economic Report of the President 1972* (Washington, 1972), p. 299).

TABLE 6–8

Foreign Trade of the EFTA, 1959 and 1969
(by major regions and countries, in millions of U.S. dollars and as % of total)

| | EXPORTS F.O.B. | | | | IMPORTS C.I.F. | | | |
| | 1959 | | 1969 | | 1959 | | 1969 | |
	$	%	$	%	$	%	$	%
1. Total	18,099	100.0	38,254	100.0	21,099	100.0	44,017	100.0
2. EFTA	3,526	19.5	10,122	26.5	3,664	17.4	10,647	24.2
3. EEC	4,301	23.8	9,840	25.7	5,871	27.8	13,602	30.9
4. Other Western Europe	826	4.6	2,383	6.2	722	3.4	1,633	3.7
5. *Subtotal 2–4*	8,653	47.8	22,345	58.4	10,257	48.6	25,881	58.8
6. LDCs in Africa	1,169	6.4	1,777	4.6	1,258	6.0	2,336	5.3
7. *Subtotal 2–4, 6*	9,822	54.3	24,122	63.1	11,516	54.6	28,218	64.1
8. United States	1,858	10.3	3,687	9.6	1,887	8.9	4,428	10.1
9. Canada	676	3.7	995	2.6	1,010	4.8	1,464	3.3
10. Latin America	1,187	6.6	1,749	4.6	1,687	8.0	1,988	4.5
11. *Subtotal 8–10*	3,720	20.6	6,431	16.8	4,584	21.7	7,879	17.9
12. Japan	137	0.7	572	1.5	203	1.0	665	1.5
13. South Africa, Australia & New Zealand	1,518	8.4	2,139	5.6	1,618	7.7	2,039	4.6
14. LDCs in Asia	2,108	11.6	3,099	8.1	2,210	10.4	3,170	7.2
15. Eastern Europe	772	4.3	1,837	4.8	940	4.5	2,001	4.5
16. Other	23	0.1	55	0.1	29	0.1	45	0.1
17. *Subtotal for all LDCs*	4,487	24.8	6,679	17.5	5,185	24.6	7,539	17.1
18. *Subtotal for all developed market econ.*	12,841	70.9	29,738	77.7	14,975	71.0	34,477	78.3

Note: EFTA totals include trade of the original seven members plus Finland.

Source: Secretariat of the European Free Trade Association: *EFTA Trade 1969* (Geneva, December 1970), Statistical Appendix, Tables 8, 9, 12 & 13.

TABLE 6–9

Foreign Trade of the EEC, 1958 and 1970

(by major regions and countries, in millions of U.S. dollars and as % of total)

	EXPORTS F.O.B.				IMPORTS C.I.F.			
	1958		1970		1958		1970	
	$	%	$	%	$	%	$	%
1. Total¹	22,775	100.0	88,499	100.0	22,946	100.0	88,422	100.0
2. Intra-EEC	6,864	30.1	43,301	48.9	6,790	29.6	42,800	48.4
3. Extra-EEC	15,911	69.9	45,198	51.1	16,156	70.4	45,622	51.6
4. EEC	6,864	30.1	43,301	48.9	6,790	29.6	42,800	48.4
5. EFTA²	4,970	21.8	14,884	16.8	3,608	15.7	10,715	12.1
6. Other Western Europe	1,143	5.0	4,954	5.6	834	3.6	2,887	3.3
7. Subtotal 4–6	12,977	57.0	63,139	71.3	11,232	48.9	56,402	63.8
8. Soviet bloc Europe¹	626	2.7	3,040	3.4	678	3.0	2,776	3.1
9. Associated African States & Malagasy Rep.	712	3.1	1,265	1.4	914	4.0	1,862	2.1
10. Overseas departments of EEC-members	100	0.4	321	0.4	117	0.5	134	0.2
11. Associated overseas terr. of EEC-members	37	0.2	339	0.4	42	0.2	191	0.2
12. Algeria	1,012	4.4	812	0.9	473	2.1	859	1.0
13. Morocco & Tunisia	381	1.7	517	0.6	446	1.9	471	0.5
14. Other LDCs in Africa	364	1.6	1,597	1.8	524	2.3	3,510	4.0
15. South Africa	268	1.2	1,006	1.1	228	1.0	559	0.6
16. Western Asia (= Middle East)	693	3.0	1,831	2.1	1,803	7.9	3,899	4.4

TABLE 6–9, Cont.

17. *Subtotal 4–6, 8–16*	17,170	75.4	73,366	82.9	16,457	71.7	70,663	79.9
18. United States	1,664	7.3	6,633	7.5	2,808	12.2	9,038	10.2
19. Canada	237	1.0	728	0.8	430	1.9	1,260	1.4
20. Central and South America	1,640	7.0	2,845	3.2	1,647	7.2	3,591	4.1
21. *Subtotal 18–20*	3,505	15.4	10,296	11.6	4,885	21.3	13,889	15.7
22. Japan	139	0.6	986	1.1	117	0.5	1,232	1.4
23. Australia	171	0.8	553	0.6	382	1.7	567	0.6
24. New Zealand	45	0.2	90	0.1	118	0.5	153	0.2
25. *Subtotal 22–24*	355	1.6	1,629	1.8	617	2.7	1,952	2.2
26. Other LDCs in Asia and Oceania	1,027	4.5	1,921	2.2	779	3.4	1,588	1.8
27. *Subtotal for all LDCs*	6,125	26.9	11,546	13.0	6,824	29.7	16,105	18.2
28. *Subtotal for all developed market economics*	15,502	68.1	72,636	82.1	15,316	66.7	69,211	78.3
29. Soviet bloc Asia	354	1.6	364	0.4	111	0.5	273	0.3
30. Other, not included elsewhere	169	0.7	412	0.5	18	0.1	55	0.1
31. Intra-German trade[3]	191	(0.8)	656	(0.7)	204	(0.9)	546	(0.6)

1. Excluding trade between Federal Republic of Germany and German Democratic Republic (see Note 3).
2. Including Iceland after 1 January 1970.
3. Not included in subtotals or totals above.

Source: Statistical Office of the European Communities: *Foreign Trade—Monthly Statistics 1971—No. 10* (Luxemburg, 1971), Tables 2 & 5.

TABLE 6-10

Trade between the U.S. and the EEC—Agricultural and Non-agricultural Goods
(in millions of U.S. dollars)

	TOTAL TRADE			AGRICULTURAL TRADE			NON-AGRICULTURAL TRADE		
	EEC→US	US→EEC	Balance	EEC→US	US→EEC	Balance	EEC→US	US→EEC	Balance
1958	1,664	2,808	1,144	205	889	683	1,459	1,919	460
1959	2,371	2,651	280	225	900	675	2,146	1,751	−395
1960	2,242	3,830	1,588	235	1,198	963	2,007	2,632	625
1961	2,232	4,054	1,822	242	1,284	1,042	1,990	2,770	780
1962	2,447	4,458	2,011	250	1,299	1,049	2,197	3,159	962
1963	2,563	5,051	2,488	261	1,358	1,097	2,302	3,693	1,391
1964	2,849	5,438	2,589	271	1,627	1,357	2,578	3,811	1,233
1965	3,425	5,693	2,268	291	1,722	1,431	3,134	3,971	837
1966	4,098	6,022	1,924	326	1,887	1,561	3,772	4,135	363
1967	4,424	5,898	1,474	347	1,624	1,277	4,077	4,274	197
1968	5,769	6,393	624	381	1,634	1,253	5,388	4,759	−629
1969	5,958	7,335	1,377	381	1,599	1,218	5,577	5,736	159
1970	6,633	9,038	2,405	437	1,982	1,545	6,196	7,056	860

Note: − denotes U.S. trade deficit with the EEC.

Sources: Statistical Office of the European Communities:
Foreign Trade—Monthly Statistics, 1972—No. 1; 1971—No. 8–9 & No. 12; 1970—No. 6; 1969—No. 5;
1968—No. 3 & No. 8–9; 1967—No. 10; 1966—No. 8–9; 1964—No. 5.

TABLE 6—11

Employment in Agriculture as Percent of Total Employment,
and Percentage of Gross Domestic Product
at Factor Cost Originating in Agriculture
(in current prices)

	1960		1965		1969	
	% of GDP	% of Empl.	% of GDP	% of Empl.	% of GDP	% of Empl.
United States	4.0	8.0	3.4	5.9	3.0	4.4
Belgium	7.2	8.6	6.1	6.3	5.3	5.1
France	9.5	20.6	7.4	16.6	6.0	13.9
Germany (West)	5.7	13.7	4.3	10.9	3.6	9.5
Italy	14.8	31.8	13.3	25.2	11.3	20.5
Luxemburg	7.6	16.4	6.3	13.5	4.9	11.6
Netherlands	10.5	11.1	8.3	8.6	7.0	7.4

Notes: The agricultural sector includes fishing and forestry.
Total employment includes armed forces.

Sources: GDP data from OECD, *National Accounts of OECD Countries, 1953–1969* (Paris, 1970), pp. 377–390; and from Statistical Office of the European Communities, *National Accounts, 1960–1970* (Luxemburg, 1971), p. 197; Employment data from U.S. Bureau of the Census, *Statistical Abstract of the United States 1971* Washington, D.C., 1971), p. 210; and from Statistical Office of the European Communities, *National Accounts, 1960–1970*, Country Tables No. 7.

CHAPTER SEVEN

International Corporations

American Business Goes International

Despite the extraordinary emphasis given to trade both in our economic theory and in our public policy, America's growing international investment has been far more significant in the postwar era than America's trade. American firms now manufacture three times as much abroad as they export from the United States, and their repatriated earnings more than match the country's trade deficit.

Liberal economic theory has often seemed not quite at ease with the phenomenon of international investment, especially in its corporate form, and hence perhaps slow to grasp its significance. In Ricardo's vision of the international market, for example, only goods were to move from country to country, not the factories themselves, or even the capital to create them. A rational international economy required only that each country make the best use of its endowment of factors. But the factors—land, labor and capital—Ricardo thought relatively immobile:

> Experience shows that the fancied or real insecurity of capital when not under the immediate control of its owner, together with the natural disinclination which every man has to quit the country of his birth and connections, and entrust himself, with all his habits fixed, to a strange government and new laws, check the emigration of capital. These feelings,

which I should be sorry to see weakened, induce most men of property to be satisfied with a low rate of profits in their own country, rather than to seek a more advantageous employment of their wealth in foreign nations.[1]

Ricardo's advice notwithstanding, British factors moved abroad increasingly throughout the nineteenth century. Emigrating British capital built foreign mines, railroads, and even factories. British entrepreneurs sometimes went along to manage these enterprises. And millions of British workers emigrated to America and the Empire. Well before the First World War, Britain had come to depend on the repatriated earnings from these foreign activities to offset a large trade deficit.[2]

The United States, especially since the Second World War, seems to be evolving along somewhat similar lines.[3] American business corporations, their perspectives widening from national to international enterprise, have been the prime movers in this evolution. Almost all big American companies have greatly increased their foreign operations in recent years. Even if wide allowances are left for distortion, the usual figures are startling. Taken altogether, American firms in 1970 controlled $78 billion out of the estimated $120 billion of foreign direct investment in the non-communist world.[4] One expert recently estimated the overseas production of United States-based multinational firms at $220 billion.[5]

Such figures, inevitably imprecise, nevertheless indicate roughly the relative scale of America's foreign operations. Investment patterns suggest no sharp diminution in the continuing growth of these foreign operations. Since the mid-sixties, investment in plants and equipment for foreign affiliates of United States manufacturers has been roughly one-fifth the comparable domestic United States investment. In 1965, new investment abroad accounted for 33.9 percent of the overall new American investments in rubber manufacturing, 25.4 percent in the manufacture of transportation equipment, 25.0

percent in chemicals, 22.1 percent in non-electrical machinery and 21.4 percent in electrical machinery. In 1970, new investments in manufacturing, petroleum, mining and smelting abroad amounted to almost 35 percent of domestic investments in the same sectors (See Table 7–1).

Aggregate figures, moreover, do not always reveal the particularly heavy involvement abroad of certain of our major industries and many of our biggest corporations.[6]

Multinational firms, of course, are hardly an exclusively American phenomenon. European firms, even if set back by the war, still occupy an important, and indeed growing, role in multinational enterprise. Some recent estimates claim that foreign firms, mostly European, already produce together more goods and services outside their national borders than do the Americans.[7]

Not surprisingly, certain features of the remarkable postwar expansion of foreign investments, and of American foreign investments in particular, have caught the imagination of several economic and political analysts. For many, not only the size, but also the nature and location of American investment abroad have seemed to prefigure a new era of international economic integration.

Traditionally, foreign direct investments went mostly to the petroleum and other extractive industries for exploiting raw material sources to feed home factories. The balance of postwar American investment, however, has gradually been shifting into manufacturing. In 1950, American direct investment abroad was about equally divided between petroleum, manufacturing and other industries. By the end of 1970, out of a total book value of $78 billion of direct foreign investments in all industries, $32 billion was manufacturing, $22 billion in petroleum, and only $6 billion in mining and smelting.[8] Over the preceding five years, nearly half of all new investments abroad has gone into manufacturing.[9]

This shift in the nature of investments has been accompanied by a pronounced shift in their geographical location. As Table 7–1 shows, in 1950 our largest direct investment was in Latin America, with Canada second and Europe far behind. At the end of 1970, the order was strikingly reversed. Europe led, with Canada close and Latin America far behind. While sizable investments had also grown up in white Commonwealth countries other than Canada, and in parts of the developing world other than Latin America, Europe's relative share had doubled in two decades—from roughly one-sixth to roughly one-third the total.

It is this "Americanization" of European manufacturing which has particularly exercised economic and political analysts. To many, the wave of American investment in Europe clearly suggests an increasingly integrated Atlantic economy. According to this view, not only will the world's developed countries trade more and more with each other, but their giant corporations will plant factories throughout North America and Europe with as little attention as possible to national boundaries. The developed Atlantic capitalist countries are thus fated not only to the interdependence of national markets preached by free-traders, but also to that amalgamation of national economies dreamed of by federalists. That integration, even if still far from achieved, nevertheless is said already to characterize the most advanced industries and forms of corporate organization.

This kind of analysis reverberates widely among the informed public and carries implications for the future of the capitalist world. A good deal is thus inferred from the postwar investment surge of American business abroad, particularly its investment in Europe. Why has this investment been so enormous, particularly in this postwar period when tariffs and transport costs have fallen to historic lows and trade increased to an historic high? Any serious answer to such questions must go beyond the usual statistics and explanations to the very nature of the modern business corporation—its world-wide views and its relations with the political economies within which it seeks to flourish.

Why American Corporations Invest in Europe

For a start, it would seem useful to assess the various immediate and conscious considerations that are said to attract American corporations to Europe.

An economist attempting to explain why producers invest directly in a promising foreign market, rather than export to it from home, searches for comparative advantages in factor costs, high transport costs, or "politically inspired" interferences with trade, like high tariffs or currency restrictions.[10] In addition, any analysis of the attractions of postwar Europe has to take particular account of the Common Market, for the past fifteen years the most obvious special feature of Europe's economic environment. The great surge in American investment, in fact, began with the establishment of the Common Market.[11] What is its special attraction?

Economic theory proposes straightforward explanations. Tariff reductions promote trade, while tariff differentials promote investment. As it happens, in Europe both a reduction in tariffs and an increase in differentials have been occurring simultaneously. As the liberal GATT gradually cut transatlantic tariffs, the mercantilist Common Market created a differential between members and non-members. Thanks to the EEC, members of the Six gained an advantage over outsiders in each other's markets. Americans, by contrast, still faced a tariff which, however low, was a significant disability against rival producers with no comparable obstacle.[12] Hence American corporations sought to establish themselves beyond the barriers, directly within the new markets.[13]

Economists closer to business operations often offer a somewhat different explanation for American direct investment in Europe. Businessmen, they argue, do not necessarily

TABLE 7–1

U.S. Direct Investments Abroad: Book Value at Yearend,
by Geographic Area and Sector of Activity
(in millions of U.S. dollars)

	Year	Total	Mining & Smelting	Petroleum	Manufacturing
World total	1950	11,788	1,129	3,390	3,831
	1957	25,394	2,634	8,991	7,898
	1960	31,865	2,997	10,810	11,051
	1965	49,474	3,931	15,298	19,339
	1970[1]	78,090	6,137	21,790	32,231
Canada	1950	3,579	334	418	1,897
	1957	8,769	996	2,154	3,512
	1960	11,179	1,325	2,664	4,827
	1965	15,318	1,851	3,356	6,872
	1970	22,801	3,014	4,809	10,050
Other Western Hemisphere	1950[2]	4,576	628	1,416	781
	1957	8,052	1,238	3,060	1,675
	1960	8,365	1,319	3,122	1,521
	1965	10,886	1,474	3,546	2,945
	1970	14,683	2,037	3,929	4,604

TABLE 7–1, Cont.

Europe	1950	1,733	21	424	933
	1957	4,151	50	1,184	2,077
	1960	6,691	49	1,763	3,804
	1965	13,985	54	3,427	7,606
	1970	24,471	71	5,487	13,704
United Kingdom	1950	847	3	123	542
	1965	5,123	2	1,093	3,306
	1970	8,015	1	1,852	4,988
EEC	1950	637	+	210	313
	1965	6,304	16	1,624	3,725
	1970	11,695	15	2,525	7,126
Japan	1950	19	··	+	+
	1960	254	··	125	91
	1965	675	··	321	275
	1970	1,491	··	540	753
Australia, New Zealand, South Africa	1950	366	+	+	+
	1960	1,195	79	373	602
	1970	4,348	572	909	2,241

1. Preliminary data.
2. Excluding European dependencies.
+Included in totals, but not itemized.
Source: *Survey of Current Business*, October 1971, August 1964, Sept. 1960, Aug. 1957, Jan. 1951.

reason like economists. As a practical rule of thumb, big corporations measure their success in terms of their overall share of the world market. With a rapidly expanding regional market in Western Europe, a great many American corporations were determined to establish themselves within that market, lest they lose out to their European rivals. To operate effectively in a big foreign market, they reasoned, it is useful to be established in it on a substantial scale. If the market is growing, profits will take care of themselves. Once a large investment is made, moreover, businessmen believe it essential to go on investing. To cut back on investing risks losing market position to a more enterprising rival, a loss not only of marginal new earnings, but of the whole market position and the bulk of the earnings that depend on it.[14] In short, once in a market, the dynamics of competition force continued investment. For similar reasons, once a major American firm has gone to a promising foreign market, all its American rivals feel constrained to follow. If one firm is left to dominate a new and growing market, it will gain over its competitors in overall share of the world's production and threaten to alter the terms of competition in *all* markets, new and old.[15]

Such arguments tempt some economists to see American investment in Europe as the result more of fashion than calculation. Indeed, when asked by a Department of Commerce study in 1964, many corporate executives could give no very precise economic rationale for deciding to manufacture abroad rather than export. Once convinced of a growing market, many American firms simply expanded to Europe, factories and all.[16]

No doubt an academic economist in the government might recommend more refined calculations, but for many firms with a wide variety of products, the move was rational enough. Throughout the fifties and sixties there was no shortage of capital or foreign exchange. Local conditions made it feasible to manufacture in Europe with success. On balance, many plausible reasons suggested direct investment rather than exporting: lower factor costs in Europe, greater market knowledge from actually being there, the growing ease of communications, the risk of a later hike in restrictions and tariffs for balance-of-payments reasons, the urge to diversify.

Once in Europe, many American companies, moreover, appeared to enjoy a number of advantages over the local competition. Profits for American subsidiaries, on average, were higher than for their European counterparts.[17] Success naturally encouraged further migration.

Many reasons are given for the American advantage. Management in America is said to be studied and practiced more scientifically. United States companies not only invest more in research, but are much quicker to develop new products.[18] Marketing is considered another American strong point. Being multinational also helps in negotiating concessions from governments, avoiding heavy taxes and finding credit.

Why Corporations Go International

The Liberal View

While these particular explanations for America's corporate invasion of Europe are plausible enough in themselves, they tacitly assume a traditional liberal model for economic behavior, the model, springing from Smith and Ricardo, which tends to emphasize profit margins in a competitive market. In this view, competition among rivals spurs a ceaseless search for more attractive products and greater productive efficiency. While Ricardo, sensitive to diminishing returns, feared ultimate stagnation, the updated liberal view, confident in boundless spiralling technology, foresees interminable expansion. From this liberal view, the multinational corporation is the catalyst of an ever more integrated, and hence more perfect, international market. World-wide specialization will promote ever greater efficiency. The highly developed economies will concentrate on the new products spawned from their advanced capital-intensive technology and spin off to the less-developed economies those familiar products of an earlier and labor-intensive stage of development.[19]

The Marxist View

The liberal vision, and the role it assigns the international corporation, is challenged from many sides, but most unequivocally by the Marxists. According to the general Marxist view, the free market is a fraud and capitalism tends inevitably toward monopoly. Multinational corporations are simply a more advanced stage of monopoly. Giant firms, in collusion, control supply and demand within captive markets. Through its domination of these firms, a small exploiting class continues to control the fruits of enterprise and prevent that revolution in income distribution which the abundance of modern technology would otherwise promote.[20] But without such a revolution in income distribution, overproduction and stagnation dog the system. Evolving capitalist economies are thus driven to dispose of their overproduction and surplus capital in foreign markets.[21] Since the dominant capitalist class controls the nationalist state as well as the giant firm, the advanced stage of capitalist competition becomes an imperial struggle among capitalist states for control of foreign markets.[22] More recent Marxist writers, of course, also stress the essential economic role of the militarism that accompanies imperialism. Defense expenditures absorb domestic surplus and prevent stagnation, while still leaving the dominant class in control and avoiding any revolutionary income distribution.[23]

From this Marxist view, the spread of American corporations to Europe, as to the Third World, merely reflects the imperial dominance of American over European capitalism in their mutual and desperate competition for markets.

Both the liberal and even much of the Marxist world views were well formed before the huge business corporation became the dominant type of economic organization. As a result, although each ideology gives profound insights into the workings of modern capitalism, both constrain the corporation to fit within an elaborate model which took its essential form in a different era.

A "Corporatist" View

A sounder view of the corporation and the system which it forms is likely to come from later analysts who begin with a study of the institutions as they are. In recent decades, an American school—building on the foundations of modern sociology as well as traditional liberal and Marxist theory—has contributed greatly to the understanding of the corporation itself and of its economic and political role. Observation discloses that today's typical giant corporation is run neither by its stockholders nor by the heroic boss-figure of an earlier age, but by a class of professional managers. Today's big firm is thus rather like a medieval religious order—a corporate body whose members share in and are measured by a common intellectual outlook and discipline. With the growing influence of business schools, this vocation is seen increasingly in professional, that is to say, academic and bureaucratic terms.

These commercial monks, the business technocrats, have been widely analyzed—in for example, the celebrated writings of John Kenneth Galbraith.[24] Galbraith notes that certain technical skills, especially in the organization and communication of information, are increasingly indispensable to advanced economies. Those who possess these skills in one form or another are today's governing elite. They form the technocracy. They inhabit the bureaucracy, public and private, and especially the great corporations—the "technostructures" which they run.

Galbraith finds self-perpetuation the governing drive of these managerial technostructures—self-perpetuation with minimal interference and disruption from the outside. To achieve this ideal state, a technostructure must produce steady profits. Otherwise the holders of capital grow restive and rival managers move in.

It has, moreover, become a fundamental axiom of the American system that profits depend ultimately upon continuing growth. When a company ceases to grow, profits eventually do likewise. Stock prices, based on future expectations, drop. Decay, disruption and doom follow in due course.

To avoid such extremities, every corporate technostructure tries to plan an orderly, assured growth of its markets and production. Planning is thus the critical skill. But planning requires a predictable external environment. Corporations naturally seek as great a measure of control as possible over the environment in which they must operate. Thus, in every capitalist country, industries have concentrated themselves into vertical and horizontal monopolies, whose power over markets very often invites abuse and leads to state regulation and policing. But the state does not limit itself to policing the corporations. States carry out an enormous welfare function not only for their citizens but also for their industries. All states seek to shape the national economic environment—to regulate economic life so as to avoid those recurrent convulsions characteristic of earlier capitalism. In particular, contempory states have sought to maintain that assured general demand which is essential to rational industrial planning for growth and full-employment. As a result of this all-embracing role for the state, the modern economy is not Ricardo's free market, but rather a Keynesian version of mercantilism, an economic system which reflects the close interpenetration of government and business and their common interest in a predictable and favorable economic environment.

To be sure, the relationship between corporations and government is not always easy. Anti-trust policies may seriously increase business risk and otherwise interfere with what business might regard as the ideal management of production and marketing. Government regulation is not always benign, nor efficient. Large firms seek further insurance from risk and also further means of leverage and independence against unfavorable political interference.

This search for security leads corporations not only to seek monopoly in making and marketing one product but also to diversify into several types of production. Profits which fall in one product can be made up in another. Carried to its logical extreme, the drive toward diversification leads large firms to international operations.[25]

This general view of corporations, we believe, also provides the most convincing general explanation for their tendency to invest abroad. A giant firm with many products in many markets and producing in many different places feels itself less vulnerable to any particular set of unfavorable circumstances. Operations in an environment which becomes unfavorable can more easily be shifted to another.

In effect, these giant firms reject the classical doctrine of comparative advantage and embrace their own form of mercantilism. In place of specialization for higher returns, they substitute diversity for greater security. The modern mercantilist corporation seeks, in its own sphere, to imitate the modern mercantilist state.

This broad explanation for the spread of international business does not, of course, supplant the particular cost-benefit analysis of liberal economists. It merely places the calculations in broader perspective. Moreover, our kind of explanation does not refute the Marxist charges about the capitalist system's essential exploitation and instability. In effect, we reject the Marxist view in that we do not assume the inevitable captivity of political power by a selfish economic elite. Our view acknowledges the pluralism and conciliatory nature of modern society and stresses the independent mediating and creative role which the state can play in shaping that society.

Such a corporate view perhaps reflects a certain bland pluralist optimism which may seem unwarranted to those convinced of the inevitable exploitation and instability of modern capitalism. But by emphasizing the shaping and creative role of politics in economic matters, our view at least provides an intellectual foundation for conscious and humane reform short of bloody revolution.

Consequences of Foreign Investment for the United States

Economic Profits and Political Frictions

Whatever the causes, the spreading of American corporations around the world, and especially to Western Europe, obviously has important immediate and long-range consequences for economics and politics in both the United States and Europe.

At least one immediate consequence appears highly beneficial to the American economy—or at least for its balance of payments. In 1971, American business repatriated $9.3 billion of income from its direct investments abroad.[26] To be sure, there is a price for this income. There is, first of all, the trouble it brings the American government and secondly, perhaps, a long-range cost to the American domestic economy.

The more American business becomes international, the more the American government is likely to find itself embroiled in the domestic decisions of foreign states. Oil companies in the Middle East or mining companies in Latin America are classic examples. Difficulties in Europe are generally more subtle. The relationship between an American parent and its foreign offspring creates innumerable legal and tax problems. When the American government constrains the parent to impose financial or political policies on subsidiaries, foreign governments are understandably upset.[27] Antitrust regulation is an especially thorny aspect. American courts have claimed

jurisdiction over the mergers and agreements of foreign subsidiaries, or even over foreign corporations that sell in the
American market. Foreign resentment is understandable, yet
foreign arrangements can very well have serious effects upon
competition in the American market.[28] In other words, the
international corporation complicates for all governments their
fundamental task of regulating and shaping their own national
economic environment. In this respect, more internationalization of production will mean more friction among governments.[29]

Foreign Investment and Domestic Growth: Two Views

It can also be argued that the constant export of entrepreneurial energy and skill, capital and technology saps the
American domestic economy of resources needed to meet foreign competition. According to this view, America's huge
direct investments hasten the rapid dissemination of technology and hence the erosion of America's competitive edge in
the advanced industries.[30] Without this edge, we cannot meet
competition from countries with lower wage costs. These considerations raise a fundamental question: are the interests of
the American corporation and the interests of the American
economy similar? While foreign investment may loom large
in a corporation's plans for future prosperity, does the capital
invested abroad contribute to the economic well-being not only
of the corporation, but of America's domestic economy?[31]

The general argument over an alleged tension between
domestic production and foreign investment is as old as modern capitalism. Historical analysts seem divided between those
who see the propensity for capital to go abroad as the mark of
an economy's exuberant strength and those who see it as a
sign of advancing decay.[32] The first view now sees the United
States as an economy more and more specialized in advanced
technologies and spinning off lesser manufacturing to the

periphery.[33] The second sees the American economy less and less competitive in its factor costs and spinning off investment capital to a more productive world outside. The former view has long been popular among businessmen and economists, but the latter has been gaining ground.

There is considerable evidence that the technological lead once characteristic of domestic American industry is diminishing. Common sense suggests that the corporate migration abroad has at least hastened the process. For the migrants have spread not only the more old-fashioned technologies, like automobiles, but also the newest and most advanced parts of the computer and electronics industries. But would not the dissemination have occurred in any event? Technological information spreads with increasing rapidity among developed countries. Throughout much of the nineteenth and twentieth centuries, our technological lead, combined with a huge and growing market and abundant natural resources, was enough to sustain our competitive position in spite of high labor costs. Today, increasingly, those rarified sectors of advanced technology in which we are still unexcelled are too small and commercially insignificant to compensate for the disadvantages of our wage differential.[34] Hence the view that America's economy, like Britain's at the end of the last century, is entering a great secular decline. American savings, like British, are hastening abroad. In an age of corporations rather than capitalists, the technostructure itself migrates, rather than capital alone. It takes with it the accumulated fruits of a fading superiority.

Foreign Investment and Domestic Priorities

Such analysis suggests radical domestic reform. Galbraith's celebrated description of the American economic system as private affluence and public squalor seems today more pointedly relevant to the American system than a decade ago.[35] United States Government expenditure as a percentage

TABLE 7–2

Public Income and Expenditure (Central Government,
Local Authorities and Social Security) in Western Europe's Economies

	TOTAL RECEIPTS AS % OF GNP, 1969	CURRENT EXPENDITURE[1] AS % OF GNP		INVESTMENT[2] AS %	
		1959	1969	OF GNP 1969	OF NATIONAL INVEST. 1969
Sweden	49	28	37	6.5	29
Norway	43	22	37	7.0	28
Netherlands	42	27	37	6.0	28
U.K.	39	29	33	5.0	24
France	38	31	33	5.0	20
W. Germany	38	30	32	4.5	20
Austria	38	27	31	4.5	19
Denmark	37	22	32	4.5	18
Finland	36	23	28	4.0	18
Belgium	34	28	33	4.0	16
Italy	33	27	33	3.0	13
Ireland	31	23	26	2.0	11
Switzerland	28	20	23	2.5	10
Greece	27	18	24	..	..
Spain	22	13	18	..	..
U.S.	32	25	29	3.0	17

1. Current expenditure equals total expenditure minus investment and capital transfers.
2. Gross fixed asset formation.

Source: *Vision*, February 1972, p. 39.

of GNP, even including our massive defense expenditures, ranks only twelfth among those of the industrialized nations of the West (Table 7–2). The spiralling difficulties of urban governments, the manifest inadequacies in public transport, housing, city planning, health, welfare, education, and general control of the environment all suggest a fundamental imbalance in the American political economy.

The imposing institutional role of the giant business techno-structure in that economy suggests at least a reason for the imbalance. The corporate giants are the principal engines of private saving and investment in the American economy.[36] Their investments are dictated by their own need to make increasing sales and profits. Hence with corporations controlling savings, the nation has continually overinvested its resources into manufacturing for private consumption. With the American market for private consumer goods supersaturated, even with frantic advertising, American corporations have had to go abroad to grow. In recent years, American foreign direct investment has equalled about a sixth of overall American domestic corporate investment and a substantially higher fraction in particular industries. (Table 7–3) The apparent availability of capital for investment abroad contrasts sharply with its scarcity for public purposes at home. Corporations are not so much wicked, as themselves caught within a system in fundamental societal and cultural disequilibrium. Corporate emigration is itself a symptom of America's economic and social malaise.

TABLE 7-3   Annual Expenditure for New Plant and Equipment by U.S. Business and by Foreign Affiliates of U.S. Corporations (in billions of U.S. dollars)

YEAR	TOTAL		MINING & SMELTING		PETROLEUM		MANUFACTURING, TOTAL	
	For.	Dom.	For.	Dom.	For.	Dom.	For.	Dom.
1965	7.53	51.96	0.68	3.91	2.27	3.82	3.89	16.02
1966	8.64		0.79		2.53		4.58	
1967	9.27		0.92		3.00		4.53	
1968	9.39		1.04		3.31		4.19	
1969	10.79	75.56	1.13	5.09	3.64	5.63	4.98	22.82
1970	13.05	79.71	1.39	5.13	3.81	5.62	6.50	23.09
1971[1]	14.20	81.21	1.68	4.94	4.69	5.85	6.42	21.36
1972[2]	15.24	89.77	1.71	5.11	5.09	5.82	6.86	23.88

YEAR	MANUFACTURING, CHEMICALS		MANUFACTURING, MACHINERY		MANUFACTURING, TRANSP. EQUIPM.		OTHER INDUSTRIES	
	For.	Dom.	For.	Dom.	For.	Dom.	For.	Dom.
1965	0.86	2.59	0.86	3.06	0.73	2.56	0.69	28.21
1966	1.04		1.05		0.97		0.74	
1967	1.21		1.09		0.80		0.82	
1968	1.21		1.02		0.62		0.85	
1969	1.12	3.10	1.34	5.47	0.80	2.76	1.04	42.02
1970	1.28	3.44	1.92	5.74	1.06	2.43	1.36	45.87
1971[1]	1.33	3.44	1.86	4.94	0.90	2.13	1.41	49.06
1972[2]	1.34	3.43	2.03	5.39	0.91	2.49	1.59	54.96

1. Data for foreign investment are estimates.   2. Data for foreign and domestic investments are estimates.

Sources: *Survey of Current Business,* March 1966, Sept. 1966, June 1971 & March 1972.

Consequences of American Foreign Investment for Europe

Balancing Costs and Gains

The growth of international business obviously raises acute and far-reaching problems for Europe as well as for the United States. These difficulties of the "American challenge" have provoked numerous studies and controversies and become a major consideration for European national governments, the Common Market, and European business itself.

Europeans, like Americans, can point to many gains. Investments, especially from the outside, have a multiplier effect on the general economy. Heavy American investment has helped to fuel Europe's remarkable growth over the last two decades.[37] Direct investment has spread to Europe much of America's postwar technological advantage. Europeans can purchase advanced American goods produced by European workers and bought with European currency.

Complaints accompany the benefits. American corporations, it is said, upset labor conditions with extra blandishments in hiring and brutal abruptness in laying off. Aggressive American marketing is said to disrupt long-standing arrangements and force unwelcome changes in the structure and style of European business. According to a "manifesto" from UNICE, the Union of Industrial Employers in the EEC:

> It has become clear that certain American firms have been badly informed about the price mechanisms used in the European market—mechanisms which the various continental rivals respect. A joint study of the production costs has allowed us to set up rules which, while safeguarding competition, have proved beneficial to all. We must not allow the American firms, from lack of knowledge of our own methods, to provoke a price war that would cause serious difficulties in the market.[38]

European governments cannot easily stop these practices, moreover, because within a customs union American firms can easily play off one government against another. As the mobile international firm moves to a more conciliatory neighbor, the offending nation loses the investment, while its producers still face the competition.

While businessmen naturally complain if shaken by new competition, something more fundamental is involved. Even if American practices should bring more efficient production and distribution, the displacement of native elites and values by foreigners may itself be a heavy cost. The social, cultural and psychic structure of a nation is sometimes extraordinarily fragile. If rapid social and cultural dislocations can bring forth new talent and new material progress, they can also unleash demons. Thus what might seem enlightened economic internationalism, can from another perspective be seen as the insolent commercialism of profit-seeking nomads.

The Decline of Planning

Many Europeans are particularly disturbed by a growing sense that their native political and economic system is losing control over the national economic environment. Recent years, for example, have witnessed the increasing irrelevance of the French Plan, once considered an intellectual and administrative model for national economic coordination.[39]

In theory, the Plan was primarily cooperative and indicative rather than coercive. Business and government collaborated in predicting demand for the five-year period and deciding on a rational allocation of resources for production. Through its pervasive control of credit, government influenced business toward the choices indicated. The Plan has had notable success in encouraging French big business to combine to meet foreign competition. But the wider pretension to shape a more rational and humane society, whatever its prospects otherwise, has become increasingly irrelevant as the economy itself has grown subject to outside factors beyond control or even prediction. These exogenous factors result primarily from internationalization of the French economy. International corporations are an important, although certainly not an exclusive cause of this internationalization. Huge international companies, with large credit resources and the ability to shift investments from one country to another, can easily defy a national plan. These corporations, moreover, have fostered the growth of the Eurodollar market, which among its other effects has tended to break government control over investment credit.

While American corporations are a highly visible and convenient target, and do indeed contribute importantly to the decline of European economic planning, the Common Market itself is a far more important disruptive factor. On the one hand, the EC introduces most of the exogenous factors that now defeat the French Plan and, on the other, prevents the stronger European governments, like the French, from taking a firmer hand with the Americans. In time, no doubt, many of these problems can be settled within the Communities by more concerted national policies and the likely growth of the EC's own political and administrative infrastructure.

Much will depend, however, on the pattern which European business itself adopts—whether Europe's big companies remain national or become "European" like the Americans.

The Future of Corporate Organization in Europe

While some European national corporations have extensive holdings beyond Europe, few, so far, have either merged with corporations in other Common Market countries or expanded production directly into those countries. European governments, moreover, have sometimes actively discouraged such an evolution.[40] Hence the common view that only American corporations have taken advantage of the EC, while European businesses have not yet risen to the opportunities of the new multinational market.

Such a view is perhaps somewhat over-simple. European big business has been consolidating to a remarkable extent. In industry after industry, mergers and consolidations have sharply decreased the number of firms. In several countries, all that remain are one or two giants, which have absorbed scores of small and medium firms. Mergers, however, have taken place largely within individual nations.[41] The Common Market's pattern of industrial organization, like the pattern of political organization, has thus remained confederal. Hence while the new market is transnational, production for it remains national.

This confederal economic pattern, like its political parallel, is often seen merely as flawed federalism—a transitional stage before firms escape national boundaries to become "European." Certain advantages, however, suggest a more durable future for this industrial confederalism. In nearly every European country, the state plays a major role in shaping the economy and, in one way or another, guides closely the conduct of the big corporations. States and industry are in close partnership and sometimes, state-owned industries form a major portion of the national economy.[42] Under the circumstances, transnational mergers would pose numerous problems. European corporations would easily escape the governmental embrace which now both regulates and sustains them. By contrast, with a regional system that combines national production—guided by a single state—with a transnational market managed by a committee of governments, Europeans may get the best of both liberal and mercantilist worlds. The big market's beneficial effects can be enjoyed without national governments abdicating their traditional controlling functions over economic activity generally. To be sure, the system tests the ingenuity of the governments. When competition cannot be shut out by protectionism, national planning and control will become increasingly difficult unless governments can coordinate policies. But so far, the record in the Communities is sufficiently impressive to suggest that the national states can continue to exercise their mercantilist functions in the foreseeable future.

It is important to realize the full significance of this question, and not to underestimate its implications for the future of capitalism in Europe. It is especially important not to take American big business as a universal model. For the continent-sized American firm grew up in an era when governmental authority—both state and national—was in many respects at its nadir, even by our own historical standards. The age of trusts in American history was a time of brutal and chaotic competition with little effective public regulation. Even many of those who hoped to reform the system sought to enhance laissez-faire rather than suppress it.[43]

Europe's evolution has been rather different. For many reasons, by no means all economic, European companies have come to prefer orderly growth and accommodation rather than fierce and unremitting competition. These views go back to the last century. On the continent, especially, the deeply rooted mercantilist traditions of a corporate society strongly resisted allowing a free market to dictate the social and political order.[44] Traditional mercantilism left government the authority and responsibility to shape the society's general character. A surprisingly wide range of political men and movements—from Bismarck on the continental Right to the Fabians of the British Left—assumed that public authority should intervene to shape the economy toward the general welfare. Hence the European state took a modern role much sooner than the American. When America was at the height of laissez-faire capitalism, Europeans had already laid the bases of economic planning and the welfare state.

It is frequently said that, as a consequence, European business is unenterprising, that it is not as interested in thrusting expansion as is American, that European governments impose a heavy hand on the initiative of European corporations. In Europe, it is said, the state is too strong and business too weak.

But it might also be said that in America, the institutions of the general community are underdeveloped and the private economic organizations too strong. In any event, the European pattern is not easily to be displaced, nor indeed is it right that it should be. On the contrary, Americans interested in reforming their own society might study Europe with some considerable profit.

Business Internationalism and the Nation State

However much thoughtful businessmen might themselves subscribe to the conclusion of the preceding section, it clashes directly with the seductive internationalist ideology common in American business and academic circles. This ideology harks back to Hull's old vision of free trade strongly spiced with world federalism, and has an especially close affinity with the ideal of the Atlantic Community. Indeed, this business internationalism now eclipses security as Atlanticism's primary sustaining force. As a creed, it has two main tenets: nation-states are out of tune with the essential economic evolution of modern times, while multinational corporations are the harbingers of a new cosmopolitan age. According to this view, nation-states are the principal obstacles to a sane world order. "The nation-state is just about through as an economic unit," according to the distinguished economist, Charles Kindleberger, one of the more active creators of the new vision.[45]

Big international business corporations, by contrast, seem the catalytic agents of the new era. The multinational corporation is the new form of social organization which conforms to the world-girdling potential latent in modern technology.[46] According to General Lauris Norstad, an advanced Atlanticist with distinguished credentials:

> Already the bonds developed through normal business relations are more in tune with the realities of this age than are differences at the political level. It is proper, therefore, that as

businessmen and citizens, corporate executives undertake to discourage restrictive nationalism, with all its dire international and domestic consequences. They must take as their position the positive potential of multinational economic growth.[47]

Gene Bradley, a prominent publicist, takes an even sterner view of businessmen's responsibilities to history:

> In charting a more dynamic business community, capable of meeting the world's growing (and often desperate) human needs, it is the private sector which must take the lead—with, of course, indispensable cooperation from the several governments. Such progress cannot come through governmental edict; it must flow from literally thousands of decentralized decisions by corporate executives.[48]

Like Marxism, business internationalism has a strong Hegelian streak. Just as economic progress dictated that medieval city-states give way to nation-states, so now the internationalization of business is supposed to doom nations.[49] Corporations are the world-historical figures which reveal the new reality.

It is interesting how much it now seems taken for granted that free trade and the nation-state are fundamentally opposed. Ricardo, Bentham and Adam Smith were all firm believers in national self-determination. But, of course, Ricardo never imagined an international free market for factors of production as well as goods.

For a contemporary business theorist like Judd Polk, international economics is still clouded by Ricardo's failure to establish a theoretically adequate rationale for the international movement of factors of production. Moving factors, Polk observes, are far more significant than moving goods. The world's national political system obstructs this movement of factors and their remuneration and hence precludes the rational use of a hungry world's scarce resources. In making economic decisions, national perspectives are too "foreshortened":

In the present phase of rapid United States investment build-up abroad, important problems of a basic political nature arise. Investment viewed as a process inevitably modifying the deployment of resources is a disturbing factor in any economy. When the investment comes from outside the country this disturbing aspect is likely to appear in foreshortened perspective; the aspect nearest the viewer looms large and distorted, and the favorable impact of the investment on the production structure looks correspondingly small and remote. Thus United States investment is now almost everywhere viewed with some degree of anxiety even in countries seeking this investment as a crucial supplement to their own savings and technology.[50]

Among these writers, antipathy toward national states is generally more evident than plans for a federalist replacement. As with Hegel and Marx, Utopia is cloudy. World government, to be sure, seems a visionary goal for people who earn their livings as hardheaded analysts of the international scene. A structured Atlantic Community of the developed countries is somewhat more plausible, but the form it might take not much clearer. As General Norstad sees it:

The Atlantic Community will come. The forces that tend to divide us, strong as they may seem at times, are as nothing compared with the forces bringing us together, impelling us inevitably toward great unity. It will not be a new superstate, but it will be a magnetic nucleus—the heart and core of an eventual world order of peace, freedom and opportunity. [51]

It is difficult to avoid the suspicion that antinationalist federalism is, in reality, an updated version of laissez-faire. As national states have gained greater control over national economies, business goals have been subjected to political goals. While the corporation has not done badly in its partnership with the state, and would certainly be loath to do without its government's support, the corporation going international reaches toward a new era of freedom. Its protean international character will give it powerful leverage against all governments, its own included.

Philosophically, it is probably inaccurate to describe this new corporate ideology as liberal. Whatever the metaphorical imagery of its economists, big business today is very far from supporting the free markets imagined by Smith, Ricardo or Cobden. Essentially, the big corporation practices a private form of mercantilism. It seeks to create a secure environment for itself, just as a state does for a national society. The two forms of mercantilism inevitably clash.

While no one can sensibly deny the indispensable role of big business corporations in the modern world, in the contest between states and business no one should seriously want business to dominate. In an age when congestion, pollution and alienation test human organizational capacities to the full, a program which calls for enfeebling the structures of national control carries more than a touch of frivolity. In an era when political authority faces unprecedented challenges to the viability and cohesion of human society, it is no time to pull old established states up by the roots. A viable political community, with a firmly institutionalized respect for human rights, is a somewhat more extended, precarious and noble accomplishment of human genius than an efficient international business corporation. Democracy, finally, is not simply a problem of marketing or engineering. The network of habits, loyalties and general perspectives that permits constitutional governments is a complex and fragile achievement, not easily dismantled and recreated at will. To say this is not to denigrate the importance of business enterprise. To deny it, on the other hand, argues a certain moral imbecility.

Federalist overtones give a certain respectability to ideas that would otherwise be dismissed out of hand. For the federalist, it may seem that the peoples of lost nations make the best citizens of a new world. But it is psychologically unsound to assume that demoralized nations and cultures are the proper foundations for an open world system. A sound international order cannot be built on the wreckage of nation-states. There are, to be sure, many parts of the world where national political communities scarcely exist, where nation-states are artificial creations with no past and little future—where the long and often bloody test of nation-building lies ahead. Europe, however, hardly fits this category.

What of the belief that Europe's national economies are too small to sustain the level of economic abundance demanded by advanced modern society? Is there an irreconcilable tension in Europe between the demands of domestic political cohesion and economic growth? Do the alternatives thus lie between impotent national states and an impotent supranational federation?

To this fundamental question, the experiment of the European Communities gives considerable hope for successful resolution. The confederal organism seeks to knit yet preserve the strong states. Nation-based firms form a parallel confederal economic pattern. Because it preserves strong democratic states, the system seems more promising than a supranational Europe of giant multinational companies matched with incoherent and feeble political institutions. Insofar as the American corporation threatens that emerging European pattern, it is not an agent of progress but a sower of discord. For the business corporation cannot replace the state. The ends of the corporation are not the ends of society. Industrial growth is not an end in itself.[52] The world cannot much longer sacrifice its human, social and physical endowment to mindless expansion. If there is to be rational, measured control of human affairs, it will come from the political community.

Perhaps such views are hopelessly quixotic. Perhaps it is no longer possible to impose restraints on growth. But anyone who argues this way can hardly describe his position as pragmatic in any ultimate sense. For it is difficult to see how the modern world can long avoid the catastrophes foreseen for the environment without a firm control over industrial growth. And this control implies a much stronger, more confident and more legitimate public authority than the American system has ever yet provided, or than a supranational state in Europe would be likely to provide. The nation-state may all too seldom speak with the voice of reason. But it remains the only serious alternative to chaos.

PART IV
THE ATLANTIC COMMUNITY AND
THE WORLD OUTSIDE

Introduction

Whereas the first group of chapters discussed the birth of the Atlantic Community, particularly as it took form in the American political imagination, the second group has stressed that Community's gradual disintegration. As American political will and power has flagged, and as the old Cold War threat has lost its terrors, Europe and America have increasingly been inclined to go their own ways. The attempt to sustain the Cold War's community through old-fashioned liberal economic interdependence has only exacerbated the transatlantic frictions that would, in any event, have inevitably accompanied postwar Europe's revival. Transatlantic economic relations, we have argued, do not require, or indeed tolerate, a close measure of political integration—let alone the demise of the traditional political functions and structures of the nation-state. Paradoxically, the attempt to retain imperial political ties through economic integration is, in itself, breaking down the existing cooperative international monetary and trading institutions and practices—structures which should be adapted to promote liberal cooperation in a non-hegemonic system. Thus transformed, these structures would remain as the proud achievements of America's enlightened and self-liquidating trusteeship over Europe, rather than the vestiges of a decaying but stubborn hegemony. It is perhaps all too easy to call attention to the tendency in recent American statecraft to destroy things in order to save them. But the parallel has a certain disturbing force.

Our analysis, of course, depends upon the assumption that no common external threat will drive the transatlantic countries back to their postwar intimacy. In the present era, no such development seems likely from the communist world. And even if some such collective and overriding menace should appear in a decade or two, a cohesive European bloc would presumably be a very different "partner" from the shattered and demoralized European states of the postwar era.

Aside from their relations with the communist countries, Europe and the United States do share at least two other major problems in the extra-Atlantic world. Both problems are political in the broadest sense, but with a major and immediate economic focus. The first problem is Japan. How are its dynamic energies to be contained and satisfied within an orderly international system? The other is the general problem of Third-World development. How are the Third World's aspirations for political self-determination and industrial abundance to be dealt with? What are the proper responsibilities and capabilities of the Atlantic countries?

And finally, do these two problems, in themselves, constitute a sufficient common danger to justify that transatlantic economic and political integration which cannot be sustained for purely internal reasons alone? Are Japan and the Third World really so great a threat and can they be dealt with successfully only by a closely concerted Western policy, and within a single Hullian world economy?

Distinguished analysts can be found, of course, who would answer yes to all or most of these questions. And in the past decade and before, American policy toward Japan and the Third World has often reflected such assumptions. Only a closely integrated Pan-Atlantic Community, it has been said, can absorb Japan successfully and mobilize the resources needed to transform the Third World.

In neither case do we find the arguments convincing. While international cooperation is obviously helpful in these as in most other matters, in relation to Japan and the Third World, America's doctrinaire Hullian and Atlanticist solutions often seem irrelevant, and occasionally pernicious. The next two chapters take up these questions.

CHAPTER EIGHT

Japan and the Atlantic Community

The Japanese Challenge and the American Response

Of all the various postwar economic miracles, the Japanese is the most spectacular. Japan, nearly prostrate at the War's end, has become, in less than a quarter century, the free world's second-ranking industrial power.[1] Since 1950 Japan's GNP has grown an average of 10 percent per year.[2] From 1960 to 1969, it rose at an annual average of 11.4 percent per year. In 1960, the Japanese planned to double their GNP in a decade. Instead, they reached their goal by 1966.[3] Some scholars imagine the Japanese GNP catching up with the American by 1985 or 1990. The year 2000, it has been said, will begin the "Japanese century."[4]

Many in the Western world have been inclined to see Japan's surging industrial power as a major threat in both foreign and domestic markets. Japan would not only squeeze the West out of the vast potential markets of Asia, but undersell Western producers in Western markets themselves. None of these feelings is new. Ever since the Japanese began to show signs of their formidable technological and industrial prowess, they have presented a disquieting challenge to the Atlantic capitalist powers. Japan is notoriously the first of the great Asian civilizations to challenge the West on its own technological ground. In some respects, even more than Russia, Japan has managed to achieve a modern economy without becoming a

Western society. Ironically, Japan's non-Western society appears to be a determining asset in beating the West at its own industrial game. Japan thus fulfills at least part of Mahan's classic apprehension—of the power of the West combined with the culture of the East. The Second World War, it might be said, represented Mahan's way of dealing with the challenge—forward outposts and aggressive seapower to keep the enemy from consolidating his position.

Historians know well, of course, the connection between the economic and military dimensions of the American-Japanese conflict. Before World War II, trade relations between the United States and Japan deteriorated steadily.[5] Japan, frozen out of the West, sought to conquer her own exclusive economic sphere in Asia—a goal which conflicted directly with American plans for trade expansion into the East.[6]

To avoid a similar collision, and prevent Japan's being absorbed into Russian and Chinese communist spheres, the United States has resolutely sought since World War II to include Japan within our own "Atlantic" liberal trading community. But our European trading partners have never accepted this aim, nor cooperated in achieving it. As a result, Japanese exports, discouraged by European barriers, have fallen ever more heavily on the American market. American protectionist resistance has grown increasingly powerful, and Japanese-American trade relations increasingly tense. The good will accumulated from a quarter century of mutual accommodation and profit has dissipated itself with disturbing swiftness. With disconcertingly intemperate candor, more and more American officials have talked openly of the menace of Japan.[7] By the early seventies, with the collapse of the dollar, America's whole postwar policy toward Japan, like America's policy toward Europe, seemed at an impasse which compelled fundamental re-evaluation.

While we cannot do more here than sketch the complex issues in the Japanese-American-European relationship, our general assessment of American policy toward Europe must at least consider the Japanese dimension. Moreover, the difficulties in America's policy toward Japan, in particular the difficulties of bringing Japan into an Atlantic bloc, help throw into relief the fundamental weakness of the whole of our postwar economic policy, above all the impracticality of our schemes for closely integrated transoceanic economic "communities." Our policy toward Japan reveals not so much enlightened generosity as a characteristic blindness to the unique national heritage of others. It also reveals with particular clarity our continuing penchant for cloaking American geopolitical aims in the rhetoric of liberal free trade, a habit which, of course, makes it all the more difficult now to salvage a liberal economic system from the collapse of American political hegemony.

Early Occupation Policy

Since World War II, Japan, like Germany, has been an American protectorate. For a brief spell, our policy hoped to crush and reform the Japanese, according to the best Wilsonian formula, so that they would never again be able to dominate the Far East and menace American access to the Pacific. An early American report on reparations policy illustrates our initial strategy:

> The overall aim should be to raise and to even up the level of industrialization [in East Asia]. This aim can be served by considered allocation, to different countries, of industrial equipment exacted from Japan for reparations. Reconstruction is an urgent need of all the countries against which Japan committed aggression. Reconstruction is also needed in Japan. In the overall comparison of needs, Japan should have last priority.[8]

The official view of these early days tended to hold Japan's prewar mercantilist system responsible for the war. That system—with its concentrated economic power, regional exclusiveness and intimate government-industry cooperation—not only empowered Japan to wage war but fed her desire to do so. Extensive political, economic and social restructuring was necessary before Japan could take her place in the community of peaceful nations. Moral rehabilitation would precede economic rehabilitation. In one of his semi-annual lectures to the Japanese, MacArthur declared that Allied economic policy required breaking up "that system which in the past has permitted the major part of the commerce and industry and natural resources of your country to be owned and controlled by a minority of feudal families and exploited for their exclusive benefit. The world has probably never seen a counterpart to so abnormal an economic system. It permitted exploitation of the many for the sole benefit of the few. The integration of these few with the government was complete and their influence upon government policies inordinate, and set the course which ultimately led to war and destruction."[9]

Economic and political reform, even if it slowed economic recovery, was nevertheless deemed essential. The highly unpopular purging of key industry and government officials elicited the following explanation:

> Even if . . . this cleansing of the economy of Japan of undesirable influences is destined seriously to handicap industrial revival for lack of essential leadership—or even if such revival is wholly impossible without the guidance of those several thousands of persons involved who directly contributed to leading the world into a war taking the toll of millions of human lives and effecting the destruction of hundreds of billions in material resources—then, in that event, the interests of those hundreds of millions of peoples who want and seek peace leave no alternative than that Japan must bear and sustain the consequences, even at the expense of a new economy geared down to the capabilities remaining.[10]

Whatever its other shortcomings, our early postwar policy toward Japan created few problems with our European allies. A strong Anglo-American consensus sustained the early decision not to restore Japan to economic primacy within the region.

The Cold War and Japan's Economic Restoration

By 1948, with America feeling menaced rather than omnipotent, our policy shifted sharply. The Japanese, like the Germans, gained leverage from the Cold War. With the increasing hostility of Russia, the deterioration of Nationalist China, growing leftist strength within Japan, and the mounting costs of the Occupation, American policy hastened to restore the Japanese economy.

Restoring Japan's economy meant, first and foremost, restoring her position as a trading power. Only with access to foreign markets could insular and crowded Japan regain prosperity and, incidentally, relieve the United States of some of the burdens of occupation.[11] Export expansion would spark recovery. The United States would grant the initial financing for imports of raw materials. Overseas sales of the finished goods would earn new dollars for new raw materials and the economy would thus generate its own growth.

Conflict with Britain and Europe

With the shift in policy, the Anglo-American consensus over Japan dissolved. Instead, we found ourselves in a neverending quarrel with Britain and the rest of Europe over Japan's place in the postwar economic order.

For Britain, Japan's economic restoration not only presaged a renewed hegemonic threat to Southeast Asia, but also immediately imperiled the Commonwealth trade and currency systems upon which Britain's own precarious recovery depended. The British remembered bitterly Japan's dumping of textiles in the thirties and the heavy consequences for Lancashire. And quite apart from her own particular interests, Britain could not pretend to speak for the Commonwealth without reflecting the powerful anti-Japanese sentiment among many of its other members. The influential *Melbourne Age* summed up in 1948 the popular Commonwealth view, a view which spoke, of course, more to Britain's economic interest than to Australia's:

> It was determined by the Great Powers at Yalta, and later, in the British Commonwealth discussions at Canberra, that in a military sense, Japan should not be allowed to menace the peace of the world again. Corresponding safeguards will now be necessary to insure against a revival of Japanese export trade of a kind that could again threaten the soundly conducted industries of Britain by ruinous competition from inferior Japanese products dumped at a fraction of their cost of production under improper standards. To this extent military and economic security are interrelated and Australia, no less than Britain, must continue to exercise strict vigilance against the dangers inherent in the resumption of large-scale trade with Japan.[12]

As usual, America's liberal dogmatism exacerbated the situation's already formidable inherent difficulties. We began in 1949 a long and tortuous campaign to have Japan admitted to the GATT, and with all the privileges of most-favored-nation trade.[13] Beneath the usual rhetoric, our particular commercial interests were rather obvious. Japan was perforce in the dollar bloc. Most of Japan's imports came from the United States. Rather than absorb their exports in return, we preferred Japan to earn dollars from trade with Europe or the Commonwealth. But with the dollar desperately scarce in both places, and with our wellknown antipathy to the Commonwealth system, America's liberal rhetoric inflamed rather than soothed British opposition.

Chiang Kai-shek's fall and the Korean War further intensified the Anglo-American conflict over Japan. Britain, eager for more trade and keenly aware of Hong Kong's vulnerability, had no desire to quarrel unnecessarily with Communist China and hence extended *de jure* recognition in January 1950. Moreover, if Japan had to export somewhere, Britain much preferred China to be the recipient rather than the Commonwealth. American policy moved inexorably in the opposite direction. The Korean War led Congress, in November 1951, to pass a law which threatened to cut off aid to countries carrying on "strategic" trade with the enemy.[14] Thus, not only Britain but Japan was to be excluded from the Chinese market. Earlier, the American government, fearing a Japanese flirtation with communism, had dismantled many of the Occupation's remaining economic controls and pressed for a peace treaty. Japan was to be restored to sovereignty and admitted as a full partner into America's political and economic community of allies. At the same time, we sought to put our military and political protectorate on a more normal and stable basis. We forced through a Japanese peace treaty in September 1951, while a bilateral Japanese-American military agreement cemented Japan to America's political and military hegemony. We continued to press for Japanese membership in the GATT. In effect, our formula was to give Japan commercial compensation for political dependence, but it seemed that our Atlantic allies in general and Britain in particular were to pay the price.

As the *Economist* argued in 1951, British fears were "far from groundless":

> American policy might require Japan virtually to cut off trade with Communist China on the grounds that the capital goods which China most wants to buy from Japan are essentially strategic and that dependence of Japanese industry on Chinese supplies would give China an economic stranglehold on Japan. Whatever the pros and cons of Japan's trade with China, the restriction of it must divert Japan into other areas in an intensive drive for markets, and the effects of this are bound to be felt by Britain.[15]

As tensions mounted, Britain took decisive action. In July of 1951, the Atlee Government flatly refused to expand most-favored-nation trade to Japan.[16] In September 1951, Britain and the rest of the sterling area entered into an Anglo-Japanese Payments Union.[17] Both agreed not to demand dollars or gold for accumulated balances of each other's currencies. Thus the British guarded both their commercial and financial flanks against resurgent Japan.

Meanwhile, the United States pressed its campaign to get the Japanese into the GATT, in this way entitling them to general most-favored-nation privileges.[18] Britain organized a European coalition in opposition. Not until 1955 was Japan admitted; most Europeans simultaneously invoked Article 35, thereby renouncing the obligation to extend Japan MFN status. Japanese membership thus gave America the form of a pan-oceanic community with Japan, but little of the substance.

From America's world-wide view, integrating Japan and Europe into a "pan-Atlantic" community seemed farsighted and logical.[19] But except when convenient to their own safety and recovery, Britain and continental Europe did not share these global perspectives. Had the United States been less obdurate and powerful, Europe's continuing opposition might have been more instructive about the shortcomings of a dog-matic liberal policy. Britain's fears were entirely understand-able and her behavior quite reasonable. Britain could not dis-agree that Japan had a right to recovery, nor that Japanese recovery would aid in bringing prosperity to Asia generally. Limited and negotiated arrangements, like the Anglo-Japanese Payments Union, could be mutually beneficial. But the full scope of the American design, encompassing as it did the cur-tailment of the China trade, the relative displacement of Brit-ish economic activity in South and East Asia, and an early re-turn to convertibility, was more than the British interest could bear.

The rest of Europe's reservations were similar to Britain's. There was the same heritage of ill will from the 1930's and after, and the same preoccupation with domestic recovery. Above all, neither Britain nor Europe shared cultural horizons with Japan which, had they existed, might have inspired co-operation and justified sacrifice.

In short, in the continuing European-American quarrel over Japan, the lines were clearly visible by the early 1950's. Perhaps less visible at the time was the powerful resistance by the Japanese themselves to membership in a Western economic community except on their own terms. Japan proved quite unwilling to give up its own unique system.

Japanese Resistance to Liberalization

The Occupation had pressed forward with structural economic reforms. Before it left, SCAP (Supreme Commander for the Allied Powers) had endowed Japan with a uniform code governing foreign capital investment and a revised and liberalized tariff structure.[20] The peace treaty obliged Japan to extend most-favored-nation treatment to all countries willing to reciprocate.

The Japanese, however, had deep reservations about this liberal direction. Their reasons were both economic and cultural. American policy seems to have understood the former, but gravely underestimated the force of the latter.

Like the European countries, Japan was acutely conscious of the fragility of her recovery and therefore loath to deny herself the instruments of self-protection. SCAP, recognizing that the Japanese would need an extended period of close control and regulation before being strong enough to enter into a more ideal liberal order, endeavored to leave a system which, even if meant to be open, nevertheless permitted a high measure of governmental control over economic affairs. Validated foreign investments, for example, were guaranteed repatriation of profits, but the Ministry of Finance determined which investments to validate.[21] By the mid-1950's, however, the Japanese had installed a new set of controls over trade, exchange and investments. The new Japanese order, as it emerged, appeared the very antithesis of the liberal system America desired. To Westerners, the intent of the new system was clear: to deny foreigners access to the Japanese economy.[22] Moreover, to many Western observers, Japan's export policies began increasingly to resemble the notorious practices of the 1930's.[23]

Until the 1960's, American officials were uneasy but forbearing. For all its apparent success, the stability of the Japanese recovery was still fragile and, for a time, required active export promotion and strict domestic controls, as outbreaks of excess-demand inflation in 1953 and 1957 seemed to confirm. But once recovery was consolidated, American policy expected Japan, like Europe, to join in our grand design for a pan-Atlantic liberal economic community.

American officials might have been less optimistic were it not for their abstract way of looking at international economic issues and divorcing them from the politics and culture of other nations. Japan could not easily join the community we promoted without far-reaching internal changes. The internal liberalization which we expected had no base in modern Japanese life and society.

Unlike the liberal West, Japan had never permitted economic enterprise to be separate and independent from the overall structure of social and political life. The Japanese have never accepted the idea that economics is an autonomous sphere where decisions are determined by the undirected rules of a free market. From the onset of the Meiji Restoration in 1868, the threat of Western penetration produced a system for economic growth based not upon separation of public from private spheres of activity, but upon consolidation and cooperation among them.[24] As the century wore on, Japan became more sure of herself and her unique solutions. An early infatuation with liberal British institutions gave way to an increasing interest in the mercantilist Germany of Bismarck and List.

To be sure, a certain tension remained in Japan between

liberal and mercantilist perspectives. Even during the 1930's, as Japan was actively consolidating her "Greater East Asia Co-Prosperity Sphere," our ambassador, John Grew, hoped that liberal forces would seize control.[25] But to most students, any economic liberalism in Japan was never more than superficial.

Some Western observers and officials occasionally seem to find Japan's traditions a perverse affront to the rest of the world. Those who view Japan with sympathy tend to see her corporatism as the indispensable formula holding together an ancient society and culture through the trauma of rapid modernization. There is, after all, no good reason to equate "economic development" with a Western liberal, social, political or even economic system. The obviousness of such truths when stated baldly in no way prevents otherwise intelligent observers from overlooking them in practice, from tacitly equating Westernization with progress and tirelessly seeking the signs of inexorable convergence among all "advanced" nations.

But the Japanese economic system is not like the Western and, in particular, not like that of the United States. For a start, business enterprise interpenetrates with the rest of the political and social system to a degree unknown in any Western country. In Japan, the relations between business and government, between businesses and their employees, and among the businesses themselves all differ markedly from the Western pattern. Whether business dominates bureaucracy or bureaucracy business has been the subject of a continuing if somewhat futile debate.[26] The closeness of the relationship is, however, beyond doubt. Big business, acting through powerful industrial associations, probably played the determining role in forming the dominant Liberal-Democratic Party. The offer or withdrawal of big business support has decided the fate of more than one postwar prime minister.[27]

On the other hand, governmental control over industry, as vested in the Ministry of Finance and the Ministry of Trade and Industry, is no less certain.[28] Such mutual influence is not without its Western parallels, especially in Europe. Japan, however, is distinguished by almost complete absence of any adversary relationship between government and industry. As Herman Kahn observes: "Probably more than 50 percent of Japanese officials devote their time to improving the prospects of business. However, one would conjecture that in the United States more than 50 per cent of all government officials devote their time to almost the opposite task . . ."[29]

The general absence of conflict between business and labor is another striking difference between Japan and the West. Traditional respect for authority and an evident preference for stable hierarchial structures no doubt help explain a comparatively docile labor force. But as with business and government, the ties are reciprocal. Much of Japanese labor is almost entirely insulated from the vagaries of the market place. Japanese workers enjoy a degree of security which probably has no Western parallel. Although salaries have been low by Western standards, benefits are extensive and dismissal is rare. The corporate system is therefore also a kind of welfare system. Rapidly rising wages and an impending labor shortage will doubtless put the system to some strain, but it seems premature to anticipate a rapid shift to Western conditions.[30]

The relationship among industries is also unique. Although there is no shortage of domestic competition, Japanese industry has never been comfortable in a "free market" economy. Occupation policy dismantled the prewar oligopolistic holding companies—the *zaibatsu*. A new form of business organization now performs the same function. Theoretically autonomous companies join in industrial groupings whose major policy affairs are governed by a *zaikai*, or president's club.[31] Competition is intense among the industrial groupings, but within any group an individual company can find a safe harbor when in need. In hard times, intergroup competition may be modified as well. Competing companies form "depression cartels," in which each agrees to reduce its output by a determined amount.

The Japanese political economy, in short, is a remarkable organism, where both within and among the major sectors of the society, consensus prevails over competition to an exceptionally high degree, and governance is exercised by an informal hierarchy of deferential cooperation. Thus Japan, galvanized into action a century ago by a mortal external threat to her culture, has adapted her traditional corporate patterns to a modern industrial society. It should not be surprising that the whole structure may occasionally show signs of great tension and fragility, nor indeed, that those who have created this unique organism desire to preserve its consensual quality. Under the circumstances, the American clamor for access, not merely for trade, but more alarmingly, for direct investment as well, cannot help but seem a dangerous threat to Japanese stability and self-determination.[32]

The American Reaction

As masterful in dissembling as the Americans are in self-deception, the Japanese have rebuilt their economy and penetrated deeply into the American market, with few of those concessions to alien ways which our policy deemed essential.[33]

By the end of the 1950's, however, American patience already showed signs of wearing thin. In 1958, the Europeans had marked an official end to their economic convalescence by returning to convertibility. Japan, to America's annoyance, showed no inclination to follow suit.

Pressures mounted. After two years of hard bargaining, 1960 saw the end to Japanese discrimination against the dollar. Japan announced a new "Plan for Trade and Exchange Liberalization." In further concessions, she bound herself to GATT and IMF rules; and in 1964, partly as a reward for good behavior, Japan gained membership in the OECD. Again the forms of community brought little substance.[34] As time went on, Japanese concessions revealed themselves as more apparent than real. By the late sixties and early seventies, imports were still largely limited to essentials and exports continued to receive substantial official and quasi-official subsidies.[35] Discretionary and hence unpredictable government regulations continued to hobble foreign investors. Companies which did establish a beachhead faced thinly veiled official and private hostility.

In short, America's attempts to open up the Japanese economy to the West were no more successful than America's attempts to open up the European economy to the Japanese. Thus, by the late sixties, America's grand design for incorporating Japan into a sort of Atlantic and Pacific Community had come to very little. Neither Europe nor Japan itself would accept the domestic disruption that such a scheme entailed.

TABLE 8–1

U.S.–Japanese Trade
(millions of U.S. dollars)

	U.S. Exports to Japan	Japan Exports to U.S.
1964	2,000	1,870
1965	2,070	2,510
1966	2,350	3,010
1967	2,670	3,050
1968	2,930	4,130
1969	3,460	5,020
1970	4,610	6,020

Sources: For 1964-65, *U.N. Statistical Yearbook 1968*, New York, 1969, pp. 398–405; 1966–67, *U.N. Monthly Bulletin of Statistics*, June 1969, pp. xiii–xiv; 1968–1970, *U.N. Monthly Bulletin of Statistics*, June 1971, pp. xiii–xiv.

By the same token, American leaders became less and less willing or able to sustain the economic burdens of their Japanese protectorate. The pressure of Japanese competition was felt ever more keenly in the domestic American market. As a result, since 1957, when textile imports were first restricted, America herself has taken an increasingly illiberal stance toward her trade with Japan.[36] By 1971, restrictive "voluntary" agreements covered an estimated 34 percent of Japan's trade with the United States.[37]

Restrictions notwithstanding, the bilateral trade balance continued to deteriorate.

By 1971, some experts were predicting a $2.4 billion bilateral deficit on goods and services.[38] Accordingly, after the dollar's fall in August 1971, the Japanese suffered extraordinary American pressure and, under great duress, finally revalued the yen by a substantial 16.88 percent against the dollar. Some observers hoped that the collapse of the dollar would presage an American policy more realistic in general and in particular toward Japan. Nevertheless, after the dust had settled from the year-end round of realignments, the substance of American economic policy toward Japan appeared to have changed very little. A greater Atlantic economic community was still promoted as the solution for Japan's economic place in the world. Europe therefore was pressed to take a higher percentage of Japanese trade and Japan to become more open, especially to United States investments. In other words, after twenty-five years of indifferent success the old pan-Atlantic policy was triumphantly reaffirmed. It was not clear, however, that the old objections and obstacles had diminished significantly. Indeed, America's policy of pan-Atlantic integration retained the dubious distinction of being unacceptable to all three of the major "partners"—Europe, Japan and the United States itself. What then were the future prospects for their "community"?

New Prospects for Japan?

Europe and Japanese Trade

European, and especially the EC countries, still distrust Japanese methods and fear Japanese competition. Although

TABLE 8–2

Japanese–European Trade
(millions of U.S. dollars)

	Japan Exports To Europe[1]	% Total	To EEC	% Total	To EFTA	% Total	To Britain Alone	% Total
1958	325	11.2	125	4.3	170	5.9	105	3.6
1962	690	14.0	270	5.5	320	6.5	190	3.9
1967	1,440	13.8	550	5.3	730	7.0	295	2.8
1968	1,670	12.9	690	5.3	760	5.9	365	2.8
1969	2,070	12.9	970	6.1	720	4.5	350	2.2
1970	2,920	15.1	1,300	6.7	1,060	5.5	480	2.5

	Europe Exports To Japan	% Total	From EEC	% External Trade	From EFTA	% External Trade	From Britain	% Total
1958	240	.6	140	.9	90	.7	55	.7
1962	530	.9	315	1.5	205	1.3	125	1.3
1967	1,060	1.2	580	1.8	410	1.9	225	1.9
1968	1,110	1.1	640	1.8	425	1.8	225	1.7
1969	1,340	1.1	740	1.9	550	2.0	295	2.0
1970	1,710	1.2	990	2.2	650	2.1	355	2.1

1. Europe includes Yugoslavia and Turkey.

Sources for figures: 1958–1965 *U.N. Statistical Yearbook 1968*, N.Y. 1969, pp. 398–405; 1966–1967 *U.N. Monthly Bulletin of Statistics*, June 1969, pp. xiii–xiv; 1968–1970 *U.N. Monthly Bulletin of Statistics*, June 1971, pp. xiii–xiv.

Japan's absolute level of trade with the EC has increased nearly tenfold since 1958, the 1970 level still constituted only 6.7 percent of total Japanese exports and 5.9 percent of Japanese imports.

Japanese trade with the EC is hampered by a maze of bilateral treaties. Since 1962, the Commission has sought a general trade agreement. But Europeans cannot even agree among themselves about Japan, let alone with the Japanese. EC-Japanese talks in the summer of 1971 broke down after only two days of negotiation.[39] With the EC absorbing Britain into full membership, and expecting more competition from a devalued dollar, prospects are not brilliant for a significant trade agreement to promote Japanese goods in Europe.

Europeans profess to see only limited prospects for trade with Japan, even with a liberal trade agreement. The real barriers, they argue, are natural rather than political. An official Common Market statement observes:

> Japanese firms and Community firms both concentrate in many of the same industries and produce many of the same products, such as consumer electronics, small automobiles and textiles. The result is much heavier competition for Japanese products in Europe. Japanese goods may be competitive in the United States against American products or even against European products. Yet in Europe, the domestically produced product has the competitive edge, including the advantage of quicker deliveries and better service networks.
>
> Another limitation on Japanese exports to Europe is the natural barrier of distance. Separating the American market from Japan is one ocean. Separating the European market from Japan are two ocean [sic]. The additional transportation cost, above and beyond the high competition, makes the European market much less attractive for Japan.[40]

Other estimates are less negative. Certainly a significant increase in Japanese trade with Europe is conceivable, if only because the present levels are so unnaturally low. The Japanese, it is said, are planning a major campaign. With the EC, however, they may well confront a mercantilism as determined as their own.[41]

The United States and Japanese Trade

Even if Europe opened her gates wide to Japan, Japanese goods still might weigh heavily on the American market. Indeed, there is no reason to assume a static conception of Japan's exporting sector. Japan might well increase her exports to Europe, partly at our expense, and still continue to export at the same level to the United States.

Whatever Japan's prospects in Europe, American protectionism toward Japanese products seems unlikely to abate. Although official American policy seems intent on preserving the close links which tie Japan to the United States, and for this connection close trading relations are still believed crucial, particular American interests grow daily more restive against all imports.[42] As migrating corporations add further to the swell of goods from abroad, American labor, once a mainstay of the free-trade forces, grows more vehemently protectionist. Currency realignments may check further capital outflows and, in time, check imports as well. But should dollar depreciation succeed in ending the balance-of-payments deficit, it will be at the expense of America's trading partners, and the ties between America, Japan and Europe will scarcely grow stronger. As we have already argued, for Europe, with her own large trade deficit with the United States, rising protectionism is the likely response to a falling dollar. But such an evolution scarcely bodes well for a pan-Atlantic economic community, or Japanese membership in it.

The Japanese Interest

Preserving the Status quo

Ironically, the Japanese themselves may, in the end, strive the hardest to preserve what there is of an economic pan-Atlantica. Economically, they probably have the most to gain from keeping the status quo. Japan is far less likely to become "inward-looking" in trade than the United States or even Europe. Despite the surprisingly low percentage of her GNP which enters into exports (11.2 percent in 1970), Japan continues to depend heavily on the outside world for crucial imports.[43] Official plans, moreover, still look forward to a real GNP in 1975 which is more than 60 percent higher than the 1970 level. To sustain such growth, the necessary annual increase in exports is calculated at 14.7 percent, nearly double the growth of world trade as a whole.[44] With such an immediate program before her, Japan still counts heavily on Western economic ties. Their significance in the longer run will depend, not only on the price demanded by the West for those ties but on Japan's alternatives to them.

The Asian Alternative

If Japan is gradually frozen out of Western markets, what are the prospects that she will once again seek to form an Asian bloc (a mercantilist coprosperity sphere) to promote her own grand design? As time heals the wounds, and the rest of the world grows less open, the old economic logic may reassert itself.[45] And recent developments may encourage it. With Britain entering the Common Market, Japan may lose trade with Europe but further improve her position with the Australasian Commonwealth countries.[46] Relaxation in Sino-American tensions, while perhaps signalling the end of America's protectorate and hence tolerance for Japanese imports, may also legitimize for Japan a greatly increased economic intercourse with China and without compelling a break with the United States.

A Japanese bloc policy would nevertheless have serious drawbacks. Postwar Japanese exports, which emphasize advanced products like television sets, desk calculators, and automobiles, are unlikely to find China or Southeast Asia a sufficiently active market. Although Southeast Asia is potentially a rich supplier of raw materials, development costs make these potential sources less economic than existing sources elsewhere, at least for some time to come. Japan has, in fact, found lower prices and better prospects for raw materials either from the developed economies—the United States, Canada, Australia and South Africa—or from the developing economies of Latin America. And, indeed, diversification of her sources of supply has been a conscious Japanese policy. In consequence, Southeast Asian countries now run a chronic and increasing trade deficit with Japan.[47] Any progress toward closer Japanese economic relations with those countries will have to find compensation for those deficits. Japan does promise to give as much as $4 billion in foreign aid by 1975, much of it to be concentrated in Asia. Japanese direct investments are also spreading throughout the region. For obvious reasons, increasing direct Japanese economic activity risks arousing old memories and offending new nationalisms. Japanese corporations will have to learn to tread warily. Mutual profit, however, is a great inducement to tolerance.

Chinese trade has special problems. While the market is colossal, China is apparently successful as an autarchy, and interdependence is not her way. While substantial trade is perhaps possible, the Chinese are not desperate and may well insist on an end to Japan's close ties not only with Taiwan but also with South Korea.[48] The political and economic price may finally be too high.

In summary, while Asia remains full of opportunity for Japan, the opportunities carry economic costs and the politics are treacherous.[49] While alternatives remain, Japan will resist committing her fate to an Asian solution. She is unlikely, therefore, to precipitate a break with her major Western trading partners.

Prospects for Japanese Liberalism

In the face of increasing Western belligerence, Japan will

most probably make concessions. In fact, since June 1971, and Prime Minister Sato's "Eight Points" to cover foreign grievances, the pace of Japanese concessions has apparently already increased considerably.[50]

Some find the concessions so impressive that they foresee a reformed Japan, confident in her economic strength, taking the liberal lead among the world's industrialized nations. Certainly Japan has a good deal to bargain away on trade concessions. For the United States, however, a liberal pan-Atlantic economic community is increasingly defined as a free hand for multinational companies. Foreign capital is now freer to enter Japan than at any time since the War. Nevertheless, in the overwhelming majority of such investments, corporate control remains firmly in Japanese hands. Japanese liberalization must go a long way before it meets American expectations. It is unlikely to do so.[51]

Japan's policy could change. Japanese corporations themselves are beginning to invest heavily abroad. Domestic labor is scarcer and dearer. While the industrial system protects new and growing industries, it can be ruthless with those whose decline seems inevitable. Many such firms may be encouraged to migrate to cheaper labor elsewhere in Asia or perhaps Latin America. Japanese firms, like American, are expected to move directly into the European market.[52] To improve their leverage, Japanese industry may press to allow foreign corporations some reciprocal concessions in Japan. But the unique and fragile nature of modern Japanese society will very likely continue to limit strongly foreign incursions of capital, although much more could doubtless be yielded in form without seriously affecting internal cohesion.[53] But in Japan, as everywhere else, government control over corporations will very likely increase rather than diminish.

Many signs now suggest, moreover, an increasing disinclination to sacrifice domestic values for growth. Environmental degradation and social unrest have reached serious levels and

regional preoccupations, there seems little incentive to concert national policies under American leadership. On the other hand, there seems every reason to strengthen national political control over domestic economies. In short, we are returning to a normal plural world. With our habit of abstracting the world of economics from the world of politics, we will doubtless continue to resist the economic implications. But economic pluralism will almost inevitably accompany political pluralism. Pan-Atlantica will fade. But, as we have argued all along, a more plural economic system need not be illiberal and closed. While the particular American formula for Japan will be even less viable in the future than in the past, the larger and wiser policy of making room for Japan is now entirely feasible. With prudence and mutual restraint on all sides, the Japanese should fit well enough into a plural world economy.

To be sure, Japan is still one of the thornier political problems for a plural system. Japan could not find a satisfactory place for herself in the past, a failure which was, after all, a major cause for the last world war. Ever since, America has simply kept Japan in political tutelage and hoped economic prosperity would be adequate compensation. But the solution is, at best, temporary. Quite apart from America's own restiveness, Japan is too great a center of vitality to remain forever an American political and military ward. Like Germany, Japan will have to be turned loose as a grownup nation. We cannot keep her a political child forever. She will have to come to terms with her own destiny. For Germany, we can hope that a European Community will provide, at last, the larger frame both to satisfy and to contain her vitality. But there is no parallel federalist solution for Japan. Japan is larger and more singular than Germany. Japan will follow a more lonely course not too closely aligned with anyone. In the end, like any great nation, she will have to accept responsibility for her own fate, including whatever means she needs to defend herself.

In any event, pan-Atlantica is not the answer. Japan will not be the model state who submitted herself to permanent American direction. Instead, she may serve as a model for something more realistic and hence more important. To take an optimistic but not altogether improbable view, Japan, more than the United States or Europe, will grow ever more suited for life in a plural world. Japan is a great industrial power, but heavily dependent on the outside world. She has no military ambitions or engagements, and will, we can hope, not be so foolish as to accept them as gifts from the Americans. She will continue to diversify her markets, her aid and her investments. Hence she will avoid dominating or depending excessively on any country or region. More sensitive to the dangers as well as the benefits of foreign incursion, she can do much to help the Third World. As she grows in confidence and prosperity she will turn her energies increasingly to her own internal health and thus restrain her alarming growth and that frantic competitiveness which has accompanied it.

In short, in an age which will increasingly be characterized by economic as well as political pluralism, Japan may come to stand out as the leading example of a great mercantilist state which can live contentedly in a liberal plural world. Others, not least the United States, would then do well to study her example.

CHAPTER NINE

The Atlantic Community and the Third World

Reluctant Interdependence

Our study focuses on the "developed" world—or rather on that part of it where capitalism holds sway. But all of our so-called Atlantic Community, even with Japan and Australasia thrown in, harbors no more than some 700 million people—one-fifth of the world's population. Another 300 million share a high state of development in the Soviet bloc. Vast China, with her own unique system, supports 700 million more. But over half the world's people—some 1.8 billion—belong to none of these groupings. They dwell instead in that "Third World" of new and old countries hoping to achieve economic modernity.[1] These states and peoples—each struggling to master its own destiny—were once tributary but vital elements in the Western economic system. Today, in many instances, their future relation to the West is uncertain. While these states share a determination to become modern, developed societies, the methods of becoming so and the kinds of relationship they wish to have with the West both remain questions of furious contention among themselves. Nor is there among the Atlantic States any broad unanimity on these Third-World matters. Rather, they appear to be of diminishing interest, particularly in the United States.

This present American mood contrasts sharply with that of a decade ago. At the start of the 1960's, ambitious schemes for "developing" the Third World attracted great public attention and enthusiasm. The "development gap"—the chasm in the general standard of living between developed and undeveloped countries—piqued the public conscience and aroused fear for the ultimate stability of so unequal a world society. A "development decade" was to narrow that gap.[2] Accordingly, enthusiasts of the Atlantic Community felt constrained to show how their ideal liberal system could prompt rapid development, and ultimately allow Third-World countries a full sharing in pan-Atlantic prosperity.

Today, rich and poor countries alike are inclined to view the prospects for their potential interdependence with a more skeptical eye. And to Americans now, the soaring rhetoric of the Alliance for Progress seems the artless idealism of a more innocent age. As many see it, our aid seldom wins friends, but often subsidizes corrupt, elitist regimes whose very existence is at once a moral embarrassment and a political liability.[3] Disillusioned idealism tends to give way to calculating realism. And with the Cold War receding, realism suggests to Americans a lessened self-interest in the Third World's economic and political stability.[4]

Skepticism about the advantages of intimacy between the Atlantic and Third Worlds is hardly less common among spokesmen for the Third World itself. To be sure, Western technology brings the Third World an economic growth almost certainly unattainable in isolation. In those many countries where Malthus' predictions on population are more than metaphor, the ability to achieve growth is often the *sine qua non* of political legitimacy. As long as there is rapid growth, people may be inclined to forgive their governments a multitude of other sins, as the Brazilian case suggests.[5] Still, undirected growth is no more an unmixed blessing in the Third World than elsewhere. For a start, Westernization brings not only growth, but also fantastic increases in population that make the labors of the Third World the labors of Sisyphus.[6] Moreover, some forms of growth appear to demand too high a social and political price for too little general benefit. Foreign firms may create "enclave economies" which, while they exploit the country's natural resources, bring little to the general population, and rob the native governments and elites of their self-determination.

The need not only to grow, but to impart direction and coherence to growth inclines Third-World countries toward authoritarian nationalist governments, either of the left or the right. Schumpeter's "creative destruction"—the need to destroy the old order before creating the new—appears to demand nationalism and the nation-state to legitimize and focus change and prevent it from degenerating into anarchy.[7] But nationalism, if almost inevitable in a modernizing society, often makes its government and people extremely sensitive and particular about the type and level of foreign economic penetration permitted within the national boundaries. And, increasingly, groups of strong-minded Third-World states concert forces to revise the ground rules of the international economic system. Hence, for example, the joint investment code of the Andean Pact, the common stand of countries in OPEC, or the various initiatives of UNCTAD and the "Group of 77."[8] Increasingly, the countries of the Third World grow disinclined to accept those traditional rules and relationships which appear contrary to their urgent needs for development.

Thus, America's growing indifference toward the Third World coincides with and confronts the Third World's own mounting revisionism toward the West. How are the "Atlantic" countries to react? In the world of the future, what is to be the economic relationship between those few rich countries which are developed and the many poor countries which hope to modernize?

Obviously, the vast subject of "development" in that bewildering heterogeneity called the Third World can hardly be entered into seriously in a few pages. We focus here on the economic relation between the Third World and the developed countries primarily to show the harmful influence on American policy of those same guiding ideas which have distorted our view of the developed world itself.

The Logical Alternatives

Both official American perspectives and those of the Third World tend to conceive of the relationship in terms of grand interstate systems. American enthusiasts for a pan-Atlantic economic community hope to extend the Atlantic Community's putative interdependence to the Third World in general. Europeans, by contrast, often prefer more limited bloc arrangements between themselves and compatible groups of developing countries. Some in the Third World would prefer to follow the Soviet or Chinese model and develop a primarily autarchic economy independent of developed capitalist nations. Since few countries approach China's vast scale, partisans of autarchy have often become promoters of some regional bloc of Third-World countries which they hope can collectively achieve economic independence. But neither autarchy nor regionalism has had much success in the Third World. For most countries, Western markets and investments seem inescapable requirements for development.[9]

These alternative possibilities for economic and especially trading relationships seem to fall within three logical options:

First, the relationship between the pan-Atlantic countries and the Third World can be either of mutual interdependence or of mutual insulation. In other words, the two sets of countries can be *open* or *closed* to each other.

Second, whatever interdependent relations exist can be in a *regional* or *universal* system. Regional systems mean distinct blocs linking particular countries in special preferential arrangements. A universal system would be open on equal terms to all developed and underdeveloped countries.

Third, the substantive nature of the Third World's relationships with the West can be *competitive* or *complementary*. Third-World industrial products can enter into the markets of the developed countries in direct competition with local industries, or the Third World can export primarily those products not produced in the developed countries.

The Alternatives Considered Historically

These alternative trading systems are to be found not only in theory but in the long historical relationship between the Third World and the West. And naturally, these trading systems are closely related to the general economic and political systems discussed in the first chapter.

For several centuries, interdependence and complementarity were the governing principles for economic relations between the metropole and its colonies. Together they formed an imperial bloc. Early Spanish and British empires were organized in this fashion. Theirs was complementarity of a rather thoroughgoing kind.[10] Colonies were discouraged not only from exporting competing goods, but from producing them at all.[11]

The transition from eighteenth-century mercantilism to nineteenth-century liberalism often left economic complementarity and interdependence intact as, indeed, the architects of liberalism intended. Even after direct political control ceased, trade continued to consist predominantly of finished goods exchanged for raw materials. And although cyclical movements in prices were not uncommon and caused distress, the system appeared to operate to the benefit of nearly all. In general, trade in primary commodities provided a satisfactory "engine of growth" for the countries of the Third World.[12] Primary exports frequently grew faster than manufactured imports.[13]

Export earnings coupled with liberal inflows of capital, much of it invested in government bonds, provided ample foreign exchange.[14] Within the Third World, therefore, there was little incentive to industrialize. The arrangement was particularly satisfactory, of course, for Third-World countries ruled by a traditional agrarian elite. Whereas industrialization might, as in England, raise up a rival elite, an economy which acquired its manufactures from trade would not unduly threaten its agrarian ruling class. Hence Latin American countries and the Southern states of the American Union fitted comfortably into a liberal complementary pattern. Agrarian elites in both were happy to see their primary products go to Great Britain and to buy British manufactures in return.[15]

The First World War gave the liberal complementary system a mortal blow, although it limped on for another decade or so. Autarchic wartime policies left the industrialized countries a legacy of agricultural over-production which flooded markets and forced down prices. When international commerce resumed in the twenties, the terms of trade had thus turned sharply against the Third World's producers of primary products. The consequent decline in the Third World's foreign exchange earnings also meant a decline in export sales from the Western metropole.[16] The liberal system was clearly breaking down. The Great Depression completed what the War began.[17]

The search for recovery produced three rival principles to supplant the traditional interdependence and complementarity. At one extreme lay autarchy. Countries at a loss for alternatives began producing the manufactures at home which they no longer had the foreign exchange to buy from abroad. Even if autarchy was adopted with reluctance, there seemed no alternative. Trading blocs provided another kind of solution. During the 1930's, Germany, England, France and Japan all tried to bind to themselves a particular group of countries in the Third World. Behind these policies lay the presumption that while economic relations between the producers of primary products and the industrialized countries could no longer be left to an undirected world market, certain groups of countries, linked by special affinities, could strike and administer a mutually profitable bargain guaranteeing each other steady supplies and outlets.[18] Trading and monetary mechanisms for these blocs varied, but generally included some arrangements for preferential access and prices. In short, administered preferences were to restore and sustain the traditional complementary relationship which had once grown naturally from market forces.

As we know, the United States strongly opposed bloc arrangements and sought instead to turn as rapidly as possible to the open universal trading system of the past. Autarchic and bloc policies were thought to promote wars and perpetuate colonial relations, whereas free trade was thought to promote interdependence and liberty. Economically, the greater volume and efficiency of an open system was supposed to compensate, and more, for the guaranteed higher prices of the closed preferential systems.

While the Second World War removed the German and Japanese blocs, the British, in spite of Hull's untiring exertions, persisted in their Commonwealth bloc. The French, moreover, managed to restore their prewar African bloc and attach it to the Common Market. And despite American hostility, the Common Market has gone on extending its association agreements throughout Africa, the Middle East and beyond.

In short, the War did not result in that open liberal trading relationship between the Third World and the West which Hull had so fervently espoused. By the 1960's most of the old forms of relationships and their supporting arguments persisted, albeit with some new actors and structures. The United States continued to be the leading champion of an open system, even though her own protectionist actions began increasingly to belie her liberal words. Key European countries, and the Common Market itself, continued to show a predilection for blocs buttressed by preferences. Autarchic principles continued to inspire both the national policies of some developing countries, particularly those with left-wing governments, and also various schemes for regional common markets among Third-World countries.[19]

The Alternatives Considered Economically

A country seldom determines its preferences from among these alternatives according to strictly economic criteria. Trade continues inextricably bound to politics, in the present as in the past. On the other hand, economic realities, in trade as in other political matters, create constraints and consequences not easily or wisely ignored. For the poor and the small, economic autarchy is not a sound strategy, whatever its political attraction for nationalist governments. But if autarchy is not viable, neither is its liberal opposite compelling. Hence rich and poor countries alike generally espouse middle-ground solutions—strategies which promise more growth than nationalist autarchy and more economic self-determination than unregulated liberal openness. However, the precise balance, and how to achieve it, forms the subject of complex, frustrating and increasingly bitter debate. In recent years, as aid has become scarcer and more beset with constricting conditions, finding a way to raise the Third World's revenues from trade has seemed increasingly desirable and urgent.

Although there is at least a broad *pro forma* agreement that the Third World must expand its trade, a more specific agreement on which countries will make the necessary adjustments or what the final system will resemble remains elusive. A brief survey of the past years of debate on these trade relations reveals, among other things, not only the intractable complexity of the issues, but the ideological and dogmatic character of the American position on them. This latter revelation, needless to say, is not unrelated to general American perspectives on international affairs. Thus many of the same mother errors that affect our overall international economic strategy also hamper our trade policy toward the developing countries. The rest of the chapter seeks to illustrate the point further.

The Debate on Trade Policy I: Generalized Preferences

Trade policy began to assume its present significance for relations between rich and poor countries in the later fifties. In 1958, the influential Haberler Report noted and studied the failure of most Third-World countries to expand their exports in proportion to their growing need for capital goods and other imports essential for modernization.[20] According to the Report, much of the fault lay with the rich nations. All protected their agriculture. Many levied high revenue tariffs on non-competing tropical agricultural products as well. Most imposed higher tariffs on processed and manufactured goods than on primary goods, thereby frustrating in the Third World the otherwise logical development of food-processing and labor-intensive industries.

The international organizations, stung by charges of neglect and pressed by a new militancy among Third-World countries, began actively to promote arrangements designed to hasten development through trade. In 1965, the GATT concluded a new series of articles to guide trade between rich and poor countries.[21] And the IMF, pillar of financial orthodoxy, created new "compensatory" financial credits for Third-World countries whose exports were falling below the levels anticipated in their development plans.[22] It became generally accepted that the Third World's legitimate interests demanded some change in the existing structure of the world market.

Schemes, old and new, pressed for consideration. These tended to fall into two broad categories: the first envisaged a more equitable sharing of benefits from the existing international division of labor; commodity prices would be raised by agreement. The second demanded a radical change in the existing division of labor; the Third World was to industrialize and sell its products in the West. The first course meant that trade would remain essentially complementary. The second, that it would become increasingly competitive.

Those who looked forward to rejuvenated complementarity sought a system of commodity agreements for non-competing products. Ideally, these commodity agreements, guaranteeing markets and prices for selected products, could be framed so as to increase the security and incomes of Third-World producers without adversely affecting the interests of Western producers. Whereas opening Western markets to trade in competitive products from the Third World might pose a mortal challenge to individual domestic producers in the West, the costs of commodity agreements in noncompeting products could be spread widely as a small burden on millions of consumers. Despite their theoretical attractiveness, commodity agreements have faced many problems. The appropriate commodities seemed limited to those produced exclusively or predominantly in the Third World, a restriction which greatly narrows the field. But even for such commodities, prices could not be raised too far without turning consumers toward cheaper substitutes. In short, commodity agreements, even if generally helpful, have seemed insufficient in themselves to meet the Third World's need for increased export earnings.[23]

But even if an adequately profitable income could have been manipulated out of these traditional commodity exports, few Third-World countries would be satisfied with the arrangement. Most have been determined to pull away from the old colonial economies and industrialize. Industrialization, along with the economic changes it pulls in its train and the social changes it is presumed to engender, seems the only pathway to a modern national society. Only industrial development, it has been thought, can break the grip of the ancient land-based social systems, and only industrial exports can earn enough foreign exchange to fuel continuing modernization.[24]

Such a strategy, however, implies a Western trading relationship which is competitive rather than complementary. Western markets would have to open themselves to manufactures from the Third World. Indeed, Third-World countries have demanded not only access to Western markets, but preferential and nonreciprocal access as well. Only thus, it is said, can the Third-World countries ever develop sufficiently, first to achieve their own urgent domestic needs, and ultimately to participate as full and equal members of an interdependent world economic community. Hence, preferential and nonreciprocal access for their competitive industrial products can be presented not only as essential for Third-World development, but also as the first step in building a new international economic community which includes the Third World.[25]

The Debate on Trade Policy II: UNCTAD I

The first United Nations Conference on Trade and Development in 1964 provided the forum for direct confrontation between the West and the Third World over these issues. UNCTAD was interesting as the first major international conference whose format and outcome were essentially dictated by the Third World. It was the largest international conference the world had ever seen. Over twelve weeks, two thousand delegates, representing 120 countries, endured 117 opening addresses—nearly all of which urged concerted action to hasten development.[26]

The debate which followed, however, represented not so much concert as confrontation. Thanks in part to the skill of the Conference's Secretary General, Rául Prebisch, both East and West were put on the defensive. The Third-World countries began casting their votes in a bloc which came to be known as the Group of 77. This automatic majority against the developed countries fed their growing discomfiture. Russia and America were both condemmed as restrictionist developed nations.[27] According to the perspectives of the Third-World majority, both superpowers were culpable. Nor was the United States allowed to blame the Cold War. To the majority, the Cold War seemed an extravagant irrelevance. Their moral self-esteem assaulted, the Americans were rather shaken. The experience of being outvoted and pilloried was perhaps less distressing to the Russians, who were used to it.[28] If nothing else, the Conference articulated and aired the full spectrum of Third-World complaints. And of all the issues, the debate over generalized preferences for Third-World manufactures most clearly exposed the problems inherent in the economic relations between rich and poor countries.

Prebisch developed the case for nonreciprocal preferences with the skill and authority of long experience. Echoing Haberler's concern with trade, Prebisch focussed on the "trade gap" anticipated if Third-World countries attained an average rate of growth of 5 percent without at the same time markedly improving their export performance. By 1970, Prebisch estimated, that trade gap would reach $20 billion. In practical terms, of course, the gap would probably never occur to such an extent because growth would soon decline. Developing countries, shorn of foreign exchange for capital imports and lacking outlets for their new industrial products, would thus not be able to sustain growth and would again stagnate. To preserve growth, Prebisch thus believed, something direct would have to be done to close the trade gap. A general growth of world trade among the developed countries, such as that prompted by the Common Market, was not sufficient. It would favor the Third World's trade, but not enough to prevent the anticipated stagnation.[29]

The solution, Prebisch concluded, was a system granting to all Third-World countries preferential access to rich-country markets. In Prebisch's words:

Unless the developing countries manage to expand their exports by stepping up their [exports'] characteristically slow rate of growth, they will have to continue import-substitution in spite of the obstacles in the way. If they were able to export more goods under a preferential system, they could also import more, and this would enable them to relax the substitution policy and make it more rational.[30]

Developed countries should not find such a preferential system so alarming, Prebisch argued:

It is not a matter of controversy among economists that national protection of infant industries is justifiable wherever such industries might have a long-term prospect of reaching a high level of efficiency . . . The case is thus a logical extension of the infant-industry argument.[31]

Preferences, Prebisch noted, were hardly a novelty. Indeed, rich countries were granting preferences to each other in the Common Market. Prebisch had no objection in principle to the EEC. No general harm would come to the Third World from such a rich-country bloc as long as it remained "outward-looking," that is, maintained a high internal growth rate, a low common external tariff and resisted agricultural protectionism.

Partial preferences, Prebisch noted, had also long existed between the rich and poor countries, as in the Commonwealth and French-African trading systems. These partial preferences benefited only a select group of countries and thereby contravened the multilateral and most-favored-nation principles which were the supposed basis of the postwar trading system. Prebisch held this aberration from liberal orthodoxy regrettable but not serious. More serious, however, these partial preference systems required reciprocity from the Third-World partners. Preferential prices of Third-World primary exports in Western markets demanded reverse preferences for Western industrial products in Third-World markets. Not only did reverse preferences impede industrialization in the poor countries, but they also hampered Third-World countries in forming regional preferential groupings among themselves.[32]

By these arguments, Prebisch, in effect, rejected both the American position, which was opposed to all preferences, as well as the European position, which favored preferences that were reciprocal.

The evolution of Prebisch's own ideas itself constitutes a sort of history of Third-World thinking about development. Many years as Executive Secretary of the Economic Commission for Latin America (ECLA) convinced Prebisch that Third-World commodity producers faced adverse and deteriorating terms of trade. The Third World could avoid stagnation only through industrialization.[33] At first, Prebisch had been an outspoken advocate of import-substitution. Experience with that policy's shortcomings had led him to expand his nationalism to regionalism. Third-World countries could achieve their national social, economic and political development, he came to believe, only by cooperating to build among themselves balanced and relatively self-sufficient regional economies. Further discouraging experience brought further evolution in Prebisch's thinking. Neither nationalist import-substitution nor even regionalist autarchy would succeed, he concluded, without extensive assistance from the industrialized centers. To achieve self-sufficient autonomy, the Third World required help from the rich countries. Hence his famous proposal for preferential and nonreciprocal access.

Prebisch's proposal proved awkward for nearly all the rich countries at the Conference. While many rich countries could contemplate commodity schemes, few were ready to grant preferential access to Third-World manufactures. But how then was the notorious trade gap to be closed? Their greatest service, many Western representatives asserted, lay in maintaining the West's own high growth and low unemployment rates. This accomplishment, more than any mechanical scheme, would assure the growing market which the Third World's exports needed. Of the major developed countries, only Britain favored the general preferential treatment of Third-World manufactures. Others thought the proposal should be studied, or dropped, or applied only in a selective, negotiated fashion among particular countries.[34]

The Debate on Trade Policy III: The American Position

Prebisch's demands were especially awkward for the Americans. The preference question seemed to epitomize the dilemmas of America's postwar trade policy. Our first reaction was to oppose. To concede on preferences would breach the most-favored-nation principle, the foundation of our long-standing commercial policy. No one could say what abyss would thereby open up before us.[35] On the other hand, as we realized, without some decisive American move, the French and Common-Market bloc systems would continue to extend and consolidate.

The fear of Europe's further consolidating into an "inward looking" bloc proved more decisive than the fear of breaching the abstract principle of MFN. The policy that Europe finally adopted on preferences in the Third World, like the policy that Europe finally adopted toward agricultural protection, would be, we believed, a decisive turning either toward or away from our ideal of a liberal Atlantic Community. A Europe which persisted in agricultural protectionism and bloc building with the Third World would be a Europe whose "inward looking" forces were in the ascendency. As Under Secretary of State George Ball candidly explained, America had encouraged European unity so that Europe could help America to exercise "world responsibilities," meaning "responsibilities unrelated to specific national interests." But Europe had been laggard: ". . . in the general pattern of their relationships with the Third World, the principal Western nations have tended to direct their efforts more to the advancement of specific national interests than to the discharge of generalized world responsibilities." Europe's pursuit of specific national interests at the expense of a sound general system aroused misgivings in America and a "brooding fear of what is loosely called 'neo-colonialism' " in the Third World. An open system

> would not, of course, preclude special bonds of friendship and intimacy between individual and developing countries, nor even some distribution of tasks among industrial nations on a geographical basis. But there is a major difference between ties based on cultural friendship or military necessity and ties predicated on special financial or commercial regimes that are discriminatory in character. Discriminatory regimes tend not only to result in a poor use of world resources, but they also limit the possibilities for effective cooperation among nations, both North and South.[36]

The American position, as it evolved, mirrored our essential concern with maintaining a liberal Atlantic Community and curbing Europe's contrary-minded "inward looking" predilections. Thus the United States came to support, in principle, a system of generalized preferences for Third-World industrial products, but only if Europeans agreed to cancel their pre-existing preferential arrangements with the Third World. Just as the United States had once agreed to special privileges for a recovering Europe, we reasoned, so it would now consent to special arrangements for a developing Third World. But now, as then, we would insist that the essential liberal principles be honored, even in their breaching. No permanent mercantilist blocs were to be countenanced under the camouflage of development. If the needs of development precluded for a time a unified most-favored-nation system, we would replace it with a "two-tier" most-favored-nation system.[37] Ball's successor, Under Secretary Eugene V. Rostow, spelled out the politics of our position at UNCTAD II in 1968. If certain Third-World countries would not cease granting preferences to Europe, America would not include them in any preferential system in which the United States participated. Was it reasonable,

Rostow asked, "that the United States should give preferred position in the American market to the products of countries which discriminate against American goods? I believe the question answers itself."[38]

The attempt to end the European blocs was a failure. Europe gradually consented to generalized preferences after UNCTAD I, but nevertheless insisted on retaining the old partial preferences as well. Thus, the Associated African States continued to receive special preference in European markets, while European goods received special preference in Africa. Although the commercial significance of these arrangements was minor, the Common Market proved as obdurate in hanging on to them as the United States was insistent that they be ended. No doubt, larger issues were at stake. The EC has continued to show a strong drive to incorporate its Mediterranean, Near Eastern and African neighbors into a special trading system. The same tendency has led toward special reciprocal arrangements with European neutrals, and perhaps, in the end, with Eastern Europe as well. With Britain joining the EC, the old Commonwealth ties offer Europe's preferential system a new target of opportunity.[39] In short, if the troubled ghost of Cordell Hull had returned to possess George Ball, there was some cause. In any event, the difficulties persisted through UNCTAD II in 1968. By October of 1969, President Nixon was threatening a special United States-Latin American preferential system to retaliate against the Common Market's Eur-African construction. The threat was not very successful. Not only were the Europeans unmoved, but the Latin Americans, after a polite interval, declined the offer.[40]

By late 1970, Americans and Europeans reached an agreement of sorts. America would grant preferences to all the Third World, but with the understanding that Europe's partial preferences, while they would continue for the time being, would be dismantled within a reasonable period.[41] By the early summer of 1971, the EC and Japan had granted roughly equivalent generalized preferences for the Third World. By January 1972, Britain followed.

Despite its promise, the United States did nothing. In March 1972, less than a month before the third UNCTAD meeting in Santiago, Under Secretary of State John Irwin announced that the Administration would regretfully suspend its commitment to generalized preferences until the American domestic political climate changed enough to give the measure "a real chance of passage without crippling amendments." Irwin then lashed out against foreign expropriations of American companies. If the United States aid were to continue, he told his audience of Latin Americans, other nations would have to preserve:

> An investment climate in which investors . . . can count on investment protection and fulfillment of contractual obligation. . . . I cannot overemphasize how important it is for all of us who are interested in the common development goals for the hemisphere to come to an understanding on this issue.[42]

Irwin's speech gave voice to an increasing preoccupation among American policy makers. In January 1972, Nixon himself declared it was time to "get tough" with those who failed to respect American property rights overseas.[43] This preoccupation with investment showed signs of generating a new condition for American participation in any preference scheme for the Third World. We hoped, it appeared, to bargain with our agreement to generalized preferences in order both to eradicate European blocs and to gain concessions and guarantees from Third-World countries for American direct investments.

Nixon's emphasis on the importance of private corporate investment for development only continued themes common in preceding Administrations. Before Irwin, both Under Secretaries Ball and Rostow emphasizing the beneficent role of direct foreign investment in hastening development, had counseled developing countries, in their own self-interest, to provide an environment favorable to such investment.[44] And over the years, successive Administrations have promoted international conventions to protect foreign investments, so far with scant success.[45]

The Shortcomings of American Policy

The American response to the generalized preferences scheme has revealed, as in a sort of kaleidoscope, the shifting preoccupations of our liberal international economic policy. From an initial reaction of hostility to generalized preferences, because they violated the MFN principle, we passed to conditional acceptance. Our conditions—first the end of Europe's trading blocs and then access and protection for our multinational corporations—fitted the grander pattern of our liberal economic policy.

It is not difficult to find fault with America's whole response to the preferences issue. In the end, our strategy for the Third World will probably prove no more successful than the rest of the Pan-Atlantic Grand Design which it so clearly parallels. The policy on generalized preferences, and the goals which we have sought in that policy, would appear to commit three miscalculations, any one of them probably serious enough to make the whole policy fail. First, contrary to our strong pressure, Europe has not and very likely will not eliminate her own preference system. As the United States, from a position of overweening strength, had once before failed to uncouple Europeans from their preferential systems, a new failure, from a position of relative weakness, should surprise no one.

Secondly, in our insistence on investment guarantees and freer access for multinational corporations, we appear to overestimate the price the Third World is itself willing to pay for preferences. If gaining preferences means conceding autonomy to alien economic bodies, many in the Third World will strongly resist the bargain. And those regimes which accept our terms are not likely, in many cases, to sustain their commitments.

Thirdly, the policy would appear to overestimate the tolerance of domestic American interests for cheap imported manufactures. In the end, as with the Kennedy Round, we will ourselves be unable to adhere to the principles which we hope to force on others. General industrial preferences, even if qualified by "safeguards" and outright prohibitions, are not likely to be supported by an increasingly protectionist Congress.[46]

In short, American policy on Third-World preferences is finally unacceptable to Europe, to the Third World, and to our own Congress! Without questioning the sincerity of those who have formulated this policy, the preferences issue furnishes yet another example of the extraordinary combination of dogmatism and self-deception which unfortunately is not altogether uncharacteristic of American foreign policy in the last decade.

The Roots of American Policy

American policy toward the Third World has not been haphazard or unself-conscious. On the contrary, it flows from cherished and long-standing principles. Like the Grand Design for the Atlantic Community, which it closely resembles, the official American view on economic development reflects a number of fundamental "liberal" principles deeply rooted in the American political imagination.

From the outset, the United States has viewed the generalized preference system as part of a broader issue—the building of that Wilsonian open economic and political world system which has been a constant theme in American policy since the end of World War II. In our policy in the sixties, generalized preferences became a sort of complement to the Grand Design of the Kennedy Round. The basic American political and economic policy has been well summarized by George Ball, who once observed:

The United States has been the leading proponent of the

open system. Under the onslaught of a tidal wave, the war-weakened European powers were forced to retreat first from one and then another overseas possession. To fill the vacuums thus created and to prevent them from being filled by communist power, the United States progressively extended its responsibilities.

In moving to assist and defend these countries, we were not moved by considerations of specific national interest, since we carried no baggage of colonial history. We were simply the only free-world power capable of providing the strength and resources that were urgently required. In most of these situations we operated on a postulate of general responsibility for stability and peace.[47]

To fill the "vacuum" left by retreating European colonialism, the United States had progressively to extend its "responsibilities." For Ball, as for Hull and, indeed, Wilson before him, our principal responsibility lies in keeping the world open. Political and economic systems become evil when closed off from the world at large. In practical terms, this means access to other people's economies for American goods and investments. What Mr. Ball calls "openness," of course, others describe as penetration—the world's economic colossus practicing an updated version of that liberal imperialism which was once Britain's policy. In short, our view of the ideal relationship for the Third World, like our view of the Atlantic Community, sees a liberal economy open to foreign goods and investments essential to promoting peaceful growth and prosperity. Both our Atlantic and Third-World views are thus pervaded by a marked antipathy toward nationalism. Both tend, therefore, to underestimate the central role of the nation-state in promoting and regulating the successful modern economy.

There is no need to question the good faith of those who apply America's principles to the Third World, or to dismiss their theories merely as a sanctimonious defense of the status quo. On the contrary, the official view consciously accepts the need for a radical transformation of developing economies which will profoundly alter their traditional society and culture. All the same, even in its radicalism, American policy characteristically proceeds from certain fundamental liberal premises. It is the adequacy of these premises which is properly at issue.

In its fundamentals, the official view on development, as it has revealed itself over the years, stresses both the primacy of economics over politics and the primacy of universalism over nationalism. The implications of these assumptions should perhaps be explored at greater length.

For development to occur, it is believed, economic values must assert their benign and rationalizing influence over political values. Economics postulates a value-system which rewards production. Politics, in contrast, rewards power. Power in the Third World still lies on the side of repression and monopoly. Thus, if power alone is served, the traditional poor remain suppressed by the traditional rich. To succeed, development must therefore transfer power from the economically non-functional to the economically functional—in other words from politics to business.[48] As England broke the political monopoly of her landed gentry by establishing the primacy of enlightened economic principles, so the Third World must free itself from bondage to its traditional patterns by adopting the ideal of economic efficiency.

There is an important corollary to this principle, however. In the official American view, not only must economic values displace political, but the displacement must not abruptly tear the social fabric. Violent social revolution, in short, is not in the official American conception the centerpiece of development, as it is in the Marxist. In the American view, growth can replace revolution. Growth, by permitting the old elites to be displaced gently, relatively and without abrupt extinction, can make political revolution obsolete and avoid the customary excesses of violent upheaval. Mollified by a growth which distributes new wealth without confiscating the old, the existing

power structure absorbs new interests and peacefully trans-
forms itself. The system acquires from its new elements greater
efficiency as well as stability.

Such a view of development has rather striking similarities
with the classic Madisonian vision for developing the infant
United States. In Madison's analysis, an enlarged sphere provided space for contentious energies to fulfill themselves without being trapped together in a definitive contest for domination. With the sphere constantly extending itself territorially,
as the American commonwealth did throughout the last
century, expansion to an ever-receding frontier can become in
itself the means for resolving domestic tensions.[49] In the updated version, economic expansion no longer needs to depend
on absorbing fresh territory or conquering new peoples. Economic growth, in effect, creates its own frontier. Modern
technology and organization mean that a rationally managed
society can expand indefinitely within its own sphere.

It can continue to grow, that is, if a liberal world system
allows a continuing rationalization of production. Hence the
great importance given to the second premise of American
policy—the primacy of universalism over nationalism. In this
view, nationalism breeds mercantilism and autarchy, which
prevent the rational allocation of factors internally and internationally; hence nationalism stunts growth, and with it the
prospects for peaceful political change.

Ironically, those liberal biases, however well-meaning, in
fact serve to exacerbate rather than resolve the fundamental
problems in both the Atlantic sphere and the Third World.
In the Atlantic Community, where the chief problem lies in
the peaceful adjustment to Europe's new power, liberalism
has tended to become the ideology of a continuing American
hegemony. In the Third World, where the absence of effective
political integration and authority hobbles economic development fully as much as the absence of markets or capital,
American liberal policy appears to set itself against that na-

tionalist integration which would seem the essential base for achieving a modern economy.

Minimal States: The Latin American Example

While no one can deny the critical importance of growth for societies in which large portions of the population exist on the Malthusian margin, neither should anyone overlook the vital role that must be played by the state in achieving and directing that growth. For as we noted at the outset, the strain of modernization demands nationalism as a focus for legitimacy and community. Otherwise, growth without direction easily degenerates into exploitation, which all too frequently has few even indirect benefits for the general population or even the national economy as a whole. In the end, economic development seems inextricably tied to political development.

Historically, however, the liberal free-trade system of the last century actually seemed to inhibit political development in many parts of the Third World. Liberalism often perpetuated the domestic social and political structures of colonialism. Hence few countries in the Third World have yet become genuinely integrated nation-states. They remain "minimal states," typical of former colonial areas in a liberal international system. In this regard, it is worth considering the case of nineteenth-century Latin America.

Obviously, each country and each region has many unique characteristics. Yet Latin America demonstrates a certain general pattern not uncommon in many other states of the Third World. Ostensibly, the Latin Americans have been the most modern and Western of the Third-World countries. Yet despite their trappings of national statehood, few of their countries have become modern nation-states. The struggles for independence in Latin America have been no less bloody or heroic than in most other countries. But after the Spanish imperial tie was cast off, the corresponding economic adjustments to independence were far too facile and, as a result, stopped well short of creating the economic and social integration which modern statehood implies. For the Latin Americans were born into a liberal international order. Indeed, their emergence as states was in large part stimulated by that order, that is to say, by the military and economic dominance of Britain over the non-European world.[50] Once the political links with Spain were cut, Latin American states found it relatively easy to sustain ostensible political independence without the development of national economies. Nineteenth-century liberal free trade not only made economic nationalism unfashionable, it also made it unnecessary. As a result, Latin America became a continent of minimal states.

Several reasons are commonly advanced for the failure of national consolidation in Latin America—reasons by no means exclusively economic. In most of the large countries, no one region was ever sufficiently strong to dominate the whole and establish genuine control. The areas which might have been the logical centers for national or regional consolidation—the vice-regal capitals—were frequently the last redoubts for imperial Spain, and not disposed to mobilize themselves for a new role. In addition, the large and unabsorbed Indian and *mestizo* populations made the *criollo* elites reluctant to sustain a thorough-going nationalist policy. For the dominant *criollo* minorities, decentralization and even anarchy were less threatening than an integrated national political society.[51] And finally, national consolidation failed because it was economically superfluous. There was no overriding necessity to build a national economy because liberal free trade offered an alternative. Production for the liberal international market simply reinforced the colonial economic structures. In the colonial economic system, commercial agriculture, where it existed at all, had been concentrated in diffuse, autonomous units—the haciendas. Whatever commerce there was turned outward, to the ports and the sea.[52] Thus a subnational system of production fed into a world system of consumption. There was need for neither a national market nor a national mercantilist state. And neither developed.[53] A program of economic nationalism, such as was followed by the continental Europeans, might have striven to redirect economic activity away from an international to a national focus. But Germany had already developed strong mercantilist states which had integrated their military and commercial elites into the political infrastructure. The Latin American elites, gliding easily from colonialism to liberal imperialism, never built a national state. Even if it had been economically possible there was certainly no mandate for it. The same landlords who benefited from the economic system also controlled politics.

Import-substitution policies came to Latin America in force only after the depression wrecked the international liberal order. But far from breaking radically with the past, import substitution, at least initially, was designed to preserve rather than disrupt the role, including the consumption patterns, of the traditional elites.[54] As a result, countries sought to industrialize, but without those political and social changes which would create a democratic mass market for the products of new industry. Hence, after satisfying the demand of small domestic markets, foreign trade was the principal outlet for these manufactures. Radical nationalists have tended to believe that a more thoroughgoing policy of economic self-sufficiency, if coupled with income redistribution and state planning, could transform Latin American societies to create mass domestic markets and thus end their industrial sector's abject dependence on foreign trade and investment.[55]

The progress of this line of reasoning, of course, does something to explain the diminishing enthusiasm for import substitution among Latin American elites, who began instead to search for some variation of the old liberal system that might avoid these revolutionary implications of economic nationalism. But even as a sobered Prebisch was pressing to re-establish economic ties with the Atlantic Community, a more radical school was attempting to press the nationalist strategy through to its logical conclusions. Advocates of a more comprehensive economic nationalism have seemed to gain ground steadily in several countries. They will doubtless continue to do so unless the developed countries do open their markets to the Third World's sprouting industry.

Whether a nationalist strategy of self-sufficiency can succeed in any given country will obviously depend on innumerable particular factors. At a minimum, however, success would seem to require not only a strong government capable of leading its people and managing the economy, but also a sufficient base of resources to achieve relative independence from foreign markets. In other words, economic nationalism cannot succeed in a minimal state.

The implications of this line of reasoning for many parts of the world are obviously revolutionary—not only domestically but internationally. To have any chance of success, economic nationalism demands an economy sufficiently large to achieve the requisite degree of self-sufficiency for nationalist economic, social and political integration. A great many states in the Third World are quite clearly minimal, not simply because they have never integrated a large portion of their population but because—even if they had done so—they lack the economic resources adequate for anything other than highly dependent existence.[56]

In some parts of the world, the Caribbean islands for example, because of the paucity of resources, the base for a self-determining nationalist economic and political integration is never likely to exist. Such states will probably always remain economically minimal and hence dependent. Other regions may follow the Common Market in achieving an adequate and self-sufficient economic base through regional cooperation among existing states.[57] Closely interdependent regional groupings of independent political states may become an increasingly common form of political organism in the modern world.

But if the past is any guide to the future, nation-building will frequently be a bloody business—not only within states but among them. The consolidation of peoples into viable political and economic communities has seldom been peaceful. In many parts of the world the present boundaries between states are clearly artificial, as indeed are several of the states themselves. Yet however insubstantial an existing political entity may be, its ruling elites will struggle to maintain it. And, of course, if they struggle long enough and with success, they may create a genuine state thereby—as the history of such Western countries as Holland and Switzerland suggests. In any event, the transformation—or death—of minimal states is unlikely to be peaceful.

Minimal States and Nonaggression

These considerations lead to a fundamental criticism of another major element in America's Wilsonian vision for the Third World. Not only does this vision imagine the Third-World countries automatically "open," thus serving to frustrate that economic and political integration necessary for modernization in a mercantilist world, but it also opposes all aggression among states. In many parts of the Third World, to oppose aggression or impose peaceful change—in the name of peace-keeping, the indivisibility of peace or the economic interdependence of the world economy—is, in effect, to perpetuate regimes politically and economically incapable of self-determination. Thus we make ourselves protectors of a status quo profoundly antipathetic to the powerful forces in the Third World seeking to master their political and economic fate by creating self-determining national states.

To be sure, most Third-World states cannot transform themselves to modern political and economic communities in isolation from the developed world. The need for Western capital and markets is probably essential for development in most parts of the world. Moreover, even if not essential, Western help will make the agonizing process of change less protracted, perhaps less brutal and uncompromising, in short, mean less suffering for the societies which must endure it. In the Third World, as in the Atlantic, the old liberal ideals retain a large measure of their economic validity, especially for states whose slender resources provide a small margin for maneuver. But as we have argued at length, these liberal principles become self-defeating, both economically and politically, when they become an antinationalist ideology.

The principles which inform liberal developmentalism are not so very different from those that inform the liberal vision of the Atlantic Community itself. Both see a liberal economy, open to foreign goods and investments as essential to promoting peaceful growth and prosperity. Both are pervaded with a marked antipathy toward the nation-state. Thus, both are afflicted with the same blindness to the central role of the nation-state in promoting and regulating the successful modern economy. Ironically, these liberal biases, however well-meaning, in fact serve to exacerbate rather than resolve the fundamental problems in both the Atlantic sphere and the Third World. In the Atlantic Community, where the chief problem lies in the peaceful adjustment to Europe's new power, liberalism has become the idealism of a continuing American hegemony. In the Third World, where the absence of effective political integration and authority hobbles economic development, liberal developmentalism sets itself against that nationalist integration which alone can provide the political base for a modern economy.

Thus the Wilsonian solution for world order, running from Wilson to Hull to George Ball, confronts many in the Third World with a paradox of far-reaching proportions: they can achieve growth only at the cost of community. Every state in a liberal system faces the same dilemma. But for developed states—more certain in their traditions or rich in their resources —the dilemma is not so acute. For the minimal states of the Third World, however, the dilemma becomes a self-defeating contradiction. The liberalism which sustains their nominal independence, and promises them resources for growth, denies them that internal consolidation of economic and political forces which forms the essential basis of any successful modern community.

To say this is only to make a point, not provide a comprehensive alternative. No one can pretend to any simple formula for resolving the multitudinous problems faced by societies transforming themselves into modern economic and political communities. The very term, Third World, belies the copious variety of these countries and their problems and prospects. In view of the tumultuous social and political history of Western states in their modernizing era, the prospects for a peaceful, steady and nonrevolutionary transformation of countries in the Third World are not bright. Still, those who would make theories and policies should take some care not to add further difficulties to what is already a heartbreaking and bloody task. In this respect, American policy leaves much to be desired.

CHAPTER TEN

The True Basis of a Liberal World Economic System

Certain emerging general themes stated in particular contexts in this study need now to be discussed in their larger geopolitical and philosophical settings.

America's postwar international economic policy has been dominated by the ideal of "interdependence," especially "Atlantic" interdependence between ourselves and Europe. In practical terms, interdependence has meant the perpetuation of America's postwar economic and political predominance over Europe and Japan. Thus, while the international economic system we have sponsored has been liberal, it has also been imperial. But American imperial dominance, natural and beneficial in the postwar season, is now breaking down. In the political sphere, it becomes increasingly fashionable, and indeed appropriate, to speak of five or so great centers of world power—Western Europe, Japan and China added to the old Soviet-American duopoly.

But if this is happening to the world's political system, what consequences follow for the world's economic system? In particular, should not the United States abandon that ideal of a closely integrated pan-Atlantic economy which has informed so much of America's postwar economic policy? So far there appears little adaptation in American thinking. While the

United States has exerted impressive energy patching up a decaying liberal structure, little imagination has gone into transforming our liberal economic ideals and policies to suit a plural world. As a result, a general breakdown of any liberal international economic system among the developed capitalist nations is now more and more likely. Some believe the collapse inevitable no matter what the United States may do. A liberal economic system cannot survive, it is said, without a dominant hegemonic power.

We have argued that a liberal plural system is possible, but only if the interpenetration of national economies does not entail the domination of a single hegemonic economy over the others, and does not seriously impede the national political authority from exercising intelligent control over the national economic environment. Unfortunately, the present system fails on both counts. Thus the present version of interdependence between the United States, Western Europe and Japan grows increasingly unworkable.

What sort of ideal might be the most appropriate guide for a new order? We suggest abandoning the vision of a single and closely integrated world economic system centered upon the developed countries. We suggest instead a more loosely related series of national and regional systems. While we can imagine Western European states cooperating successfully in managing a high degree of mutual economic interpenetration, we believe the attempt to extend such close economic interpenetration and joint political management on a pan-Atlantic scale invites either a serious breakdown of the international economic system or else an even more serious retrogression of man's rational control over his economic environment.

Behind our view of the world political economy lies a philosophical judgment about the relation between politics and economics. We reject the economist's notion that the nation-state is a fundamental obstacle to a more reasonable world. On the contrary, we believe the democratic nation-state remains the highest form of rational organization man has yet developed, or will develop in the foreseeable future. We admit that there has grown up in the international field a dangerous tension between the ideals of politics and the ideals of liberal economics. But we reject the common view that national politics should somehow "catch up" with the "realities" of world economics. That view, taking for granted the primacy of economic over political values, we believe pernicious. It continues to influence American policy strongly and is, as a result, a serious obstacle to America's adjusting its external economic policy to a plural world.

In short, we believe the pure science of economics is, at best, a limited guide to understanding the economic relations among states, or within them. Obviously, economic theory constitutes a towering intellectual edifice. But its characteristic strengths are also its weaknesses. Abstracting the manifold phenomena of economic life out of the full stream of human affairs inevitably distorts the significance of these phenomena. Economic theory, when heedless of the political dimension, tends to be either irrelevant or else a self-serving ideology of power. "Pure" economics is thus a dangerous guide for public policy, a proposition which, of course, has long been accepted in domestic affairs.

But the enlightenment of economic theory by politics is far more advanced in the domestic than in the international sphere. Domestic liberal economics of the nineteenth century, attacked and refined by a broader political humanism, transformed itself from an apology for laissez-faire into the theory of the modern welfare state. The liberal vision of the world economic order badly needs comparable enlightenment and transformation. Above all, international liberal economics, like domestic, needs to come to terms with the nation-state.

The nation-state is not a concept that a pure economics can easily grasp. For the concept of a political community springs from a more complete view of man and society than that of economics. The economist has a tendency to see the state as merely a limited or imperfect market. But to quote from Burke's classic distinction:

> . . . the state ought not to be considered as nothing better than a partnership agreement in a trade of pepper and coffee, calico, or tobacco, or some other such low concern, to be taken up for a little temporary interest, and to be dissolved by the fancy of the parties. It is to be looked on with other reverence, because it is not a partnership in things subservient only to the gross animal existence of a temporary and perishable nature. It is a partnership in science; a partnership in all art; a partnership in every virtue and in all perfection. As the ends of such a partnership cannot be obtained in many generations, it becomes a partnership not only between those who are living, but between those who are living, those who are dead, and those who are not yet born.[1]

What is needed to form Burke's state? A state needs to be able to maintain its security against outside control. It certainly needs an economy capable of providing an acceptable standard of living for its people. It also needs a nation with a living culture. Nearly all modern states are built on nations. In general, only a shared national culture has proved to be a sufficiently cohesive foundation for that political consensus and mutual identity necessary for an effective state, above all for a democratic state. Multinational states have generally either deteriorated from partnership to imperialism, or else come apart into their national elements.[2]

In today's world, economics, too, remains essentially national. For economic life now is more than ever closely interwoven with political power. Hence, what is called the world economy is more a congeries of national economies, each one thoroughly transformed by the policy of its national government.

In this respect, we live in a mercantilist world. In the broader sense, every modern state is mercantilist in that it accepts the responsibility for managing the national economy for the general welfare. Every political system defines that welfare in broad social, political and cultural as well as economic terms. The state, drawing on its authority as the historic and legitimate expression of general interest, tries to shape the national economic environment. It guides, mediates, encourages, and occasionally punishes the multifarious dynamic elements that make up the social economy. Of course, a state —even the most despotic—is only a sort of conductor over the economic, political and cultural forces striving to express themselves. With a society in a stable or at least nonrevolutionary condition, these elements of national life reach a certain equilibrium, uneasy but bearable. This reconciliation of elements into a relatively coherent, persistent and distinctive balance— guarded by certain rules, tolerances and loyalties—forms the particular character or constitution of the national political organism.

In a dynamic society, the reconciliation of forces is tentative and fragile. From this fragility follows an essential principle: the national organism has only a limited tolerance for destabilizing intrusions from the outside. When these intrusions threaten the cohesion and distinctive character of a state, they trigger a reaction. The healthy political organism unites to resist the destabilizing outsider. To be sure, the organism is sometimes overwhelmed for a time, or even destroyed for good. It can lose its self-determination. The national elements may float loose to attach themselves as parasites, servants or sojourners in some other system. But whenever the national organism regains vitality, it will inevitably seek to regain its cohesion.

This self-preserving intolerance seems the fundamental law of the organized political commonwealth. What is true of the commonwealth in general is no less true of its economic aspects. Economics and politics can be abstracted from each other only in theory. The same self-preserving intolerance, or nationalism, covers them both. A view of international economics which does not comprehend this national principle risks becoming the formula for chaos or the ideology for imperialism. An international economic system that does not make sufficient allowance for nationalism is thus doomed to break down.

There are two powerful arguments against the view we have just expressed. The first holds that any differentiation of the "world economy" into economic "blocs" will promote political conflict and lead to a breakdown of international political cooperation. The second holds that, as an open unimpeded world market is essential to growth, national economies cannot function in blocs without unacceptable economic and social costs.

Both are wrong and for much the same reason; neither argument grasps the relation between domestic and international affairs.

The first argument is based on a false analogy with the 1930's. Since Hull's day, the Second World War has been seen as the ineluctable outcome of a world economy broken into blocs. But an equally convincing case can be made that it was the forlorn attempt throughout the twenties to restore the outmoded liberal order of the nineteenth century which produced that social and political breakdown which led to Hitler. Had Hitler's mercantilist policies been practiced earlier in Germany, perhaps the nation might never have succumbed to Nazism.

Economic nationalism does not, in itself, lead to imperialism. What can lead national states to an imperialist struggle for control over external markets is their inability to absorb their own economic product.[3] A national society tends to become imperial when its government is too weak—its political consensus too fragile—to permit a distribution of income and production compatible with national social and economic stability.

The great postwar achievement of the Western nations is not only abundance, but a distribution of that abundance which leads to relative social and political stability. Nations at peace with themselves at home are less of a menace abroad. But domestic stability has never ,been achieved by an un-directed free market. A satisfactory resolution of social prob-lems demands intelligent public intervention in the economy. Thus the planned democratic welfare state offers the greatest opportunity for peace in today's world. For with the social transformation which permits national integration, plus the greatly expanded technical capacity of governments to man-age economic affairs, an affluent modern state, given an intelligent set of national priorities, should be able to absorb its own economic product. Rationally, the war for international markets becomes obsolete among developed nations.

To be sure, such a view presumes the relative abundance now characteristic of advanced capitalist societies. But can abundance be sustained without the constant "growth" char-acteristic of the modern market economy? And does not growth demand an international market?

Among the developed countries, growth is on its way to becoming obsolete. For generations, especially in this country, growth has been seen the panacea for all problems of social justice and equilibrium. As the Madisonian pie grew larger, new shares could be found to satisfy new forces without taking from the old. But the solution has become no longer workable. The earth itself has rebelled against growth. And the problems of pollution are unlikely to be solved by a few new technologi-cal gimmicks added to production. What is now visible is a complete transformation of economics—from a morally auton-omous mechanism based in the unquestioned priority of growth to a system of techniques subservient to the broad human goals of a national commonwealth.

The pollution issue, real enough in itself, is also a metaphor for the moral instability of a society which seeks to substitute growth for justice—of a society which has never come to terms with nature because it cannot come to terms with itself.

The weaning away of economics from growth will not be easy. It will doubtless be resisted to the end. Among other things, a great deal of intellectual capital is in danger.

If this view of the future is correct, what happens to the liberal principle of an open world? We are not suggesting, of course, that it be abandoned. In its broadest meaning, the liberal principle embodies a profound truth about human affairs. To remain good, a society must remain open. No society is likely to sustain an adequate vision of a Good Life if it is closed to the stimulus of new ideas and forces. For the political-economic costs of illiberalism, we need only look at our great rival among the developed nations. Moreover, we have no wish to deny the obvious: that states must act in concert in an increasing number of affairs of common concern. But international concert must be the result of strong stable states acting in rational self-interest. Openness carried to the point of anarchy—to the abdication of any rational control over the social and physical environment—is self-destructive for states and the state system. But there is no need to oscillate from one pathological extreme to its opposite.

Liberty, now as always, requires self-discipline. If we in the West are to retain our liberal heritage, we must regulate particular liberty so that it does not menace general good. No nation or private interest has the automatic right to penetrate and disrupt the social and political organism of its neighbors. In the community of nations, no state should hope to resolve its internal lack of balance by exporting its unbridled forces to other states. It is the destructive penetration of others which truly constitutes "nationalism" and "mercantilism" in their pathological sense. To confuse such a policy with liberalism risks corrupting our Western intellectual heritage beyond redemption.

What finally of the Third World, where the rule is scarcity and not glut? If the developed nations of the Atlantic Community evolve beyond the imperative of growth, and toward a closer regulation of their domestic economies, the consequences for the Third World may well be extremely serious'. Welfare states, regulating their economic life to preserve domestic employment and other priorities, may not be very good markets for outsiders.

Third-World countries, hoping to achieve prosperity by selling manufactures from cheap labor, will become partisans of liberal "openness," albeit of the rather one-sided kind expressed in the nonreciprocal preferences scheme. Similarly those anxious to preserve the Atlantic Community in something like its current form will predictably drape their present conservatism with concern for the developing countries. Nevertheless, the problem will be real. A diminution of growth in the developed countries may well mean a slowing of traditional Third-World exports; moreover a developed economy which does not grow will guard more jealously its existing jobs and industries. A "post-industrial" Atlantic Community must therefore evolve new mechanisms for transferring significant income to the Third World. Doubtless trade will continue to be an important mechanism. But to expect the developed countries to absorb enough trade in competitive manufactures to provide the resources needed for the Third World's development is highly unrealistic, and in the end, undesirable.

Third-World countries and regions must be their own markets. Like the West, they must learn not only how to increase production, but also how to absorb it.

Poor countries should not expect, any more than rich, to export their internal imbalances. New countries, like old, must face up to the problem of building viable national communities. The age of the minimal state should now be over.

NOTES

Chapter Two

1. Ricardo, *Principles,* p. 97.

2. Ricardo's theory of the future of capitalism followed logically from his theory of diminishing returns. Even if production per worker diminished and the price of food increased, workers would still receive an undiminished real wage by the economic laws which bound that wage to the subsistence minimum. Thus, profits, squeezed between rising wages and rising rents, would decline until they became too low to encourage new investments. Society would then reach a stationary state where population and capital could no longer increase because every available surplus had been appropriated by rent. See Heimann. *History of Economic Doctrines.* pp. 105–06.

3. Ricardo, *Principles*, pp. 81–82.

4. As quoted in Amery, *Chamberlain*, Vol. 5, p. 221

5. See Coleridge, "Lay Sermon," in Shedd, ed., *Complete Works of Samuel Taylor Coleridge*, Vol. 6. For a discussion, see Calleo, *Coleridge and the Idea of the Modern State*, pp. 10–20.

6. Blake, *Disraeli*, p. 487

7. Quoted in Monypenny and Buckle, *Life of Benjamin Disraeli*, Vol. 2, p. 387.

8. Marx and Engels, *Manifesto*, p. 12.

9. Such a view was, of course, central to Ricardo's theories. As he wrote in 1815: "The interest of the landlord is always opposed to the

interest of every other class in the community. His situation is never so prosperous as when food is scarce and dear: whereas all other classes are greatly benefited by procuring cheap food." Quoted in Halévy, *Philosophical Radicalism*, p. 330.

10. Thus, in Ricardo's words: " . . . this freedom of commerce, which undoubtedly promotes the freedom of the whole, promotes also that of each particular country; and that narrow policy adopted in the countries of Europe respecting their colonies is not less injurious to the mother countries themselves than to the countries whose interests are sacrificed." *Principles*. p. 227.

11. As quoted in Julian Amery, *Chamberlain*, Vol. 5, p. 203. Cobden's enthusiasm for free trade was boundless: "I see in the Free Trade Principle that which shall act on the moral world as the principle of gravitation on the universe, drawing men together, thrusting aside the antagonism of race and creed and language, and uniting us in the bonds of eternal peace." As quoted in Bosanquet. *Free Trade*. p. 2.

12. Bernard Semmel in his *Rise of Free Trade Imperialism* discusses early nineteenth-century mercantilist schemes and relates them to a thread of heterodox economic theory, stemming from Malthus and the Physiocrats, which concerned itself with the problem of glut—too many goods, capital and people. An Anglo-Saxon Empire, inhabited by Britain's surplus people, developed by Britain's surplus capital, and buying Britain's surplus goods was believed by many to be the only viable solution for an increasingly overspecialized and overextended British home economy. For contemporary sources see the writings of Edward Gibbon Wakefield, especially *England and America*. New York, 1834; and Robert Torrens. *The Budget*. London, 1844. Torrens actually proposed an imperial *Zollverein*. For a discussion of J. S. Mill's ambivalent views, see Semmel, pp. 95 ff.

13. In the West Indies, a number of factors combined to bring economic ruin. The end of the lucrative slave trade in 1807 and the freeing of the slaves in 1833 made labor scarce and raised costs. Subsidized beet-sugar production gave growing competition. See Knowles. *Overseas Empire*, Vol. 1. pp. 98–128. The Canadian case is less clear, thanks to the Canadian-American Reciprocity Agreement of 1855. See Officer and Smith, "Canadian-American Reciprocity Agreement." On India, see note p. 265.

14. See Woodham-Smith, *The Great Hunger*, passim.

15. See Semmel, *Free Trade Imperialism*, p. 179.

16. Although the mid-nineteenth century came to be a highwater-mark of economic liberalism on the continent, continental powers shared little of Britain's enthusiasm for free trade, but were drawn into the system out of political expediency. Thus, the Anglo-French Commercial Treaty of 1860 was, in effect, Britain's compensation for France's annexation of Nice and Savoy. Gladstone is reported to have said: "the choice lay between the Cobden Treaty and not the certainty, but the high probability of war with France." Bismarck, undoctrinaire in trade matters, signed a liberal tariff agreement with France in 1865, mostly as a political move against Austria. Austria, remaining protectionist, attempted a commercial rapprochement with Italy, but was foiled by a commercial treaty between Italy and the *Zollverein* in 1869. See Bosanquet, *Free Trade*, pp. 71–112.

17. See Bosanquet, *Free Trade*, pp. 94–101.

18. List, *National System*, p. 133.

19. In 1790, Alexander Hamilton argued in his *Report on Manufactures* that the United States should not depend on Europe for its manufactures but should aim at developing "all the essentials of national supply." Semmel. *Free Trade Imperialism.* pp. 177–78.

20. List, *National System*, p. 259. List continues: "The school (of laissez-faire) does not discern that the merchant may be accomplishing his purpose . . . at the expense of the agriculturalist and manufacturer, at the expense of the nation's productive powers, and indeed of its independence" (p. 259).

21. The Marxist critique of international commerce was, in many respects, similar to List's nationalist critique. Free trade would leave the poorer country forever the hewer of wood and the drawer of water. But whereas List saw the possibility of peaceful and profitable relations among comparably industrialized countries, Marxist-Leninism saw only heightened conflict.

22. Bismarck's initial dependence on the Liberal party for his *Reichstag* majority impeded a move toward state socialism. By 1880, the Liberal alliance over, Bismarck began to build his famous social welfare program which placed Germany well in advance of any other European government in the field. See Burnie, *Economic History*, pp. 226ff. For Bismarck's motives see Dahrendorf, *Society and Democracy*, pp. 40ff.

Comparative Trends 1870–1913

	Annual Compound Rate of Growth of Tot. Output	Pop. Growth, Compound Annual % Change	Output Per Cap. Compound Annual % Change	Productivity: Annual Av. Growth of Output Per Man-Hour
Belgium	2.7%	1.0%	1.7%	2.0%
France	1.6	0.2	1.4	1.8
Germany	2.9	1.1	1.8	2.1
Italy	1.4	0.7	0.7	1.2
Netherlands	2.2	1.3	0.8	1.1
Britain	2.2	0.9	1.3	1.5
U.S.	4.3	2.1	2.2	2.4

23. Figures in Angus Maddison's excellent survey, *Economic Growth of the West*. pp. 28–30, 37, show the rapid growth of Germany and the United States as compared with Britain and the rest of continental Europe.

24. For the period 1876/80–1911/13, primary-producing countries offered the largest and most dynamic market for British exports. Liberal outflows of British capital compensated for the large export surplus Britain enjoyed with some of these countries, notably Australia, Brazil and India. After 1890, the trade surpluses grew more and more necessary to offset Britain's growing deficits in her United States trade. See League of Nations. *Industrialization and Foreign Trade.* Geneva, 1945, pp. 107–08 and Table 15, p. 115.

25. For 1907, a not untypical year, Britain's net foreign investment has been estimated at £133 million, by contrast with a net home investment of £180 million. Cairncross, *Home and Foreign Investment,* pp. 104–06. Figures for 1870–1913 show interest on foreign investment almost always exceeding the net export of capital. *Ibid.* p. 180.

26. Nevertheless, textiles, 72 percent of manufactured exports in 1867, were still 51 percent on the eve of World War I. Capital goods rose from 20 percent to 39 percent of exports for the same period. Hobsbawm, *Industry and Empire,* p. 118.

27. Hobsbawm notes that at no time in the nineteenth century did Britain enjoy an export surplus in goods, despite her industrial monopoly, her export orientation, and her modest domestic consumer market (p. 119). The rise of industrial competitors, which weakened Britain's position in "visible" trade, only reinforced the primacy of her services and especially finance. Until 1875, Britain's "invisible" dealings in shipping, and the City's insurance and brokerage earnings, insured a large British payments surplus. Afterward, as the trade deficit grew, the needed margin came from an increasingly vast income from overseas investments. Hence Britain's international economic position depended increasingly on the British inclination to invest or lend accumulated surpluses abroad (p. 120). British foreign investments did grow by leaps and bounds and were continually fed by the reinvestment of interest and dividends. By 1913 Britain owned £4,000 million abroad as compared to less than £5,500 million for France, Germany, Belgium, Holland, and the United States combined. Hence, until the First World War, the threads of world trade and finance ran through London, and Britain depended on the consequent earnings. See Hobsbawm. *Industry and Empire.* pp. 119 ff.

28. Ibid., p. 122. See also Cairncross, *Home and Foreign Investment,* p. 185.

29. India forms the striking exception to the British policy of laissez-faire in the Empire. The most enthusiastic proponents of laissez-faire in Britain became devoted state planners in India. India became an increasingly vital market for the export of British textiles, particularly after Britain succeeded in destroying the local industry. India's own exports were in surplus, especially because of the opium trade, administered by the British as a state monopoly. These surpluses were siphoned off so successfully by Britain, through various political charges, that before World War I, India financed an estimated two-fifths of Britain's total trade deficit. See Hobsbawm. *Industry and Empire.* p. 123.

30. Garvin, *Life of Joseph Chamberlain,* 3 volumes, and its completion by Julian Amery (vols. 4–6), London, 1969, form the definitive study. Our own interpretation of this general period owes a great debt to Amery. See especially Vol. 5, pp. 196–222, and Vol. 6, pp. 993–1055.

31. Chamberlain drew on the tradition of Wakefield and Torrens rather than Ricardo and Cobden. Torrens, in particular, presaged many aspects of Chamberlain's thinking. Torrens wrote in 1844: "The prosperity of the country cannot be arrested by the hostile tariffs of foreign rivals, if England will establish throughout her widespread empire a British Commercial League—a colonial Zollverein." Torrens. *Budget.* p. 102. See note 12, p. 261.

32. Lord Rosebery, along with H. H. Asquith, organized a most energetic opposition to the Chamberlain scheme. See James. *Rosebery.* pp. 444–45, and Raymond. *Man of Promise: Lord Rosebery.* pp. 213–16.

33. In 1911, half of Britain's investments were in the Empire, with Canada replacing Australasia as the leading attraction for British capital. Europe had sunk to a position of relative unimportance, while investments in America, both North and South, came to well over 50 percent of the total, as compared to 40 percent in 1885 and a smaller proportion in 1870. See Cairncross. *Home and Foreign Investment.* pp. 184–85.

34. Financing the war had forced Britain to liquidate nearly 70 percent of her United States investments. During the 1920's, gross foreign investment ran at about 4.5 percent of national income, the same as the rate prevailing in the 1870's but only half that of the 1910–13 period. Hobsbawm, *Industry and Empire,* p. 126.

The return to the Gold Standard in 1925 at the prewar parity is thought to have encouraged overseas investment above domestic, and thus slowed down domestic industrial development. See Skidelsky, *Politicians and the Slump*, pp. 1–26.

35. Although Jacksonian democracy inaugurated an age of domestic laissez-faire, leading Whigs such as Henry Clay, Edward Everett and others sought to re-establish key ideas of mercantilism, particularly protection of the home market. Their economic policies appealed not only to businessmen in the North but to merchants in the South. North-South ties of this nature persisted until the outbreak of the Civil War. For a discussion of the persistence of protectionism throughout America's era of laissez-faire, see Williams. *Contours*, pp. 227–342.

36. By the 1890's, three decades of poor economic performance and the "end of the frontier" convinced many business, political and intellectual leaders that the era of easy growth was over and the long-predicted "crisis of capitalism" at hand. Some looked increasingly to an imperial foreign policy to solve domestic problems. Others concentrated more on domestic reform. Figures like Theodore Roosevelt and Herbert Hoover both looked overseas and hoped for a domestic system balancing labor, capital and government and avoiding socialism, fascism or bureaucratic domination. For a discussion of the period leading to 1890 which emphasizes the continuity of American expansionism, see van Alstyne, *Rising American Empire*. Williams in *Contours*. pp. 345–439, gives an extended discussion of Hoover's views and his influence on American corporate and labor leaders. Gardner. *Economic Aspects of New Deal Diplomacy*. pp. 7–10, discusses Hoover's fears that the New Deal would be "inward-looking."

37. Halévy, *Philosophical Radicalism*, p. 251.

38. Peek and Moley recommended strict protectionism—through tariff barriers, exchange restrictions and state trading—to accompany domestic recovery policies. Hull finally triumphed. Moley was "exiled" to Hawaii, Peek's office of Foreign Trade Adviser to the President was abolished, and the way cleared for the Trade Expansion Act of 1934. For a concise discussion, see Schlesinger, *Coming of the New Deal*, pp. 256ff.

39. From 1934 to the outbreak of World War II, the United States reached agreements under the Trade Agreements Act with twenty

nations, half of them Latin American. Among the more important were agreements with Canada in 1934 and Britain in 1938. Nevertheless, United States tariffs remained very high, and the trade agreements although theoretically "unconditional"—i.e., extended to third countries "without request or compensation"—rarely moved out of their initial bilateral scope. See Curzon, *Multilateral Commercial Diplomacy*, p. 27.

40. Hull, *Memoirs,* Vol. 1, p. 349.

41. Ibid. Vol. 2, p. 1644.

42. Ibid. Vol. 2, p. 976.

43. Lend-lease Agreements were signed with thirty-three countries; eleven, including the agreements with Russia and China, followed the British "Master Agreement" with its commitment to eliminate discrimination in international commerce. See: Office of the President, *Twentieth Report to Congress on Lend-Lease Operations for the Period Ended June 30, 1945,* Washington, D. C., 1945.

44. Churchill, *Closing the Ring,* p. 713.

45. Attlee's government, unlike Churchill's, was ready to set India loose and close out the formal colonial empire everywhere as rapidly as possible. Labour, moreover, seemed actively hostile to the old financial empire. Labour's first Chancellor of the Exchequer, Hugh Dalton, declared himself generally opposed to the City and all its international activities. See Einzig, *Euro-Bond Market,* p. 50. Labour was, however, greatly interested both in preserving the old preferential trading links to sustain a precarious balance of payments, and in seeing the old colonial system evolve into a new multiracial commonwealth. See Gordon Walker, *Commonwealth,* pp. 128–41, 259–75. Labour thus continued, in its fashion, the traditional British shrinking from Europe and preoccupation with the underdeveloped world.

46. Two reports by Sir William Beveridge—"The Beveridge Report on Social Insurance and Allied Services," (1942), and "Full Employment in a Free Society," (1944), set the tone for Labour economic policy in the early postwar years. The first advocated a "cradle to grave" welfare policy while the second, mindful of the chronic unemployment of the interwar years, urged a stockpile of public investment schemes ready to counter unemployment. See Winch, *Economics and Policy,* pp. 273ff.

47. Certainly United States officials also realized aid was necessary to spark recovery, and full debt repayment probably a futile cause. Hence we contributed massively to the UNRRA and cancelled all but a nominal amount of the Lend-lease debt. But we insisted that aid was no substitute for trade. And, while a balanced trading system was self-sustaining, aid was expensive. America could not ask her citizens to add yet more to the national debt, already mountainous from the war. More debt would prompt inflation in the United States and undermine the last intact economy—a catastrophe for the world.

As the Truman Administration gained its footing, more orthodox business views began to prevail over the advanced internationalist thinking of New Dealers like Morgenthau and Harry Dexter White. For the effect on plans for the Bretton Woods institutions, see Gardner, *Sterling-Dollar Diplomacy*, pp. 257–68. For a Wall Street view of Bretton Woods, see the testimony of W. Randolph Burgess, President, American Bankers Association in House Committee on Banking and Currency: *Bretton Woods Agreements Act. Hearings*, Washington, D.C., 1945. Vol. I, pp. 345–403.

48. The notorious "Morgenthau Plan," whereby Germany was to be deprived of her industrial capacity and turned into a nation of farmers, had as one of its roots the desire to reconcile England with a liberal economic future. Thus, in a discussion with Roosevelt in September 1944, Morgenthau observed: ". . . I realize that this would put eighteen or twenty million people out of work, but if we make an international zone out of it it is just time before Germany will attempt an Anschluss. . . . This will have a tremendous effect on England and Belgium, and ought to guarantee their prosperity for the next twenty years because their principal competition for their coal and steel came from the Ruhr, and this ought to go a long way towards solving the economic future of England." Blum, *Morgenthau Diaries*, p. 353.

49. The United States policy was to regulate Lend-lease in order to keep British reserves no lower than $600 million, nor greater than $1 billion. An outraged Churchill sent the following to Roosevelt in March 1944:

> Will you allow me to say that the suggestion of reducing our dollar balances, which constitute our sole liquid reserve, to one billion dollars would really not be consistent either with equal treatment of Allies or with any conception of equal

sacrifice or pooling of resources? We have not shirked our duty or indulged in any easy way of living. We have already spent practically all our convertible foreign investments in the struggle. We alone of the Allies will emerge from the war with great overseas war debts. I do not know what would happen if we were now asked to disperse our last liquid reserves required to meet pressing needs, or how I could put my case to Parliament without it affecting public sentiment in the most painful manner, and that at a time when British and American blood will be flowing in broad and equal streams and when the shortening of the war by even a month would far exceed the sums under consideration—Churchill, *Closing the Ring*, p. 698.

America's use of Lend-lease to pressure Britain and other allies is a key element in the "revisionist" critiques of American wartime policy. See Kolko, *Politics of War*, pp. 280–313. A more cautious view in an article by George C. Herring, "The United States and British Bankruptcy" (pp. 260–80), nevertheless concludes: "Whether or not the Americans intended to leave Britain impotent and bankrupt, the effect was the same. The termination of Lend-lease (in June 1945) left the Labour government little choice but to accept American demands in return for a loan. Thus what Churchill called the 'most unsordid act' became at least indirectly the means by which Britain was reduced to dependence on her ally" (p. 280).

50. Even so, the loan had a difficult time in Congress. It took the emerging Cold War, used none too subtly by Churchill in his famous "iron curtain" speech in March 1946, to get the loan through Congress in July 1946. See Gardner, *Sterling-Dollar Diplomacy*, pp. 199–254.

51. Ibid., p. 306.

52. Support in Britain for preferences was bipartisan and firm. Churchill, noting the Republican majority in Congress, rightly suspected an ebbing American faithfulness to the liberal vision. While negotiating with the British in Geneva, the United States established a preferential arrangement of her own with the Philippines, and Congress passed a highly restrictive quota on wool imports—a move particularly obnoxious to New Zealand. Fearing a complete breakdown, Will Clayton, chief American negotiator, persuaded Truman to veto the wool quota. The impasse was broken.

Commonwealth preferences were reduced somewhat, but the system remained intact. See Gardner, *Sterling-Dollar Diplomacy.* pp. 348–380.

53. On Dec. 6, 1950, the Administration quietly announced that the President and interested agencies had agreed not to resubmit the proposed Charter to Congress. Gardner, *Sterling-Dollar Diplomacy.* p. 378.

54. Harry Dexter White was called to testify before the House Un-American Activities Committee on August 13, 1948. On July 31, 1948, Elizabeth Bentley, a self-confessed spy for the Soviet Union, had identified White, former Assistant Secretary of the Treasury, as a member of the Silvermaster Group, a core of highly placed government officials allegedly supplying the Soviet Union with secret documents. Later, Whittaker Chambers, claiming extensive contact with White in the 1930's and 1940's, although stressing that White was not a member of the Communist party, testified that White did supply him with secret documents to photograph. White testified at his own request and denied being a Communist, knowing Miss Bentley or Chambers, or helping to obtain information or positions for people engaged in espionage. He admitted knowing Silvermaster well but denied giving him secret information. Three days later White died of a heart attack, which his brother laid to the stress of testifying at length.

Three months afterwards, Chambers produced documents, microfilms, and a secret memorandum of 1938 in White's handwriting. White's brother maintained that they were either forged or stolen.

55.

Europe's Balance of Payments with the U.S. and Other Overseas Countries 1946–1948
(billions of dollars)

| | 1946 | | | 1947 | | | 1948 | | |
	U.S.	Overseas	Total	U.S.	Overseas	Total	U.S.	Overseas	Total
Europe's Imports	4.4	5.0	9.4	6.1	7.6	13.7	4.7	9.6	14.3
Europe's Exports	.9	3.4	4.3	1.0	5.4	6.4	1.3	7.5	8.8
Trade Bal.	−3.5	−1.6	−5.1	−5.1	−2.2	−7.3	−3.4	−2.1	−5.5

Sources: United Nations Economic Commission for Europe, *A Survey of the Economic Situation and Prospects of Europe*, Geneva, 1948. Table 29 p. 54; and ECE *Economic Survey of Europe in 1949*, Geneva, 1950. Table 63, p. 109.

Chapter Three

1. For postwar Britain's lack of enthusiasm for European integration and corresponding predeliction for a loose Atlantic context, see the following: Northedge, *British Foreign Policy*, especially pp. 132–67; Camps, *Britain and the European Community 1955–1963;* Mayne, *The Community of Europe;* Beloff, *The United States and the Unity of Europe;* and Calleo, *Britain's Future*, ch. 3.

2. For a highly qualified endorsement of postwar European trade discrimination, see Patterson, *Discrimination in International Trade*, pp. 60–61.

3. For de Gaulle's early criticism of NATO, see his *Press Conference* December 21, 1951. For a sympathetic discussion of his views, see Calleo, *Europe's Future*, ch. 4 or *Atlantic Fantasy*, ch. 5. For a final summary of his opposition both to NATO and European supranationalism, see de Gaulle, *Memoirs of Hope*, especially pp. 199–200.

4. For the decisive influence of the Cold War on getting Britain's loan through Congress, see Gardner, *Sterling-Dollar Diplomacy*, pp. 237–254.

5. For France's colonial commitments and consequent inability to contribute major forces to NATO, see Osgood, *NATO The Entangling Alliance*, pp. 65, and 90. For French resentment of her minor role, see Beaufre, *NATO and Europe*, pp. 37–38.

6. For an interesting essay on the influence of foreign imperialist ideas on the world view of American elites in the late nineteenth and early twentieth centuries, see May, *American Imperialism*.

7. Henri Bergson's vitalist view of evolution can be found in his *Creative Evolution.*

8. See Henry Adams "The Rule of Phase as Applied to History" and "The Heritage of Henry Adams" (written by his brother Brooks) in Adams, *Degradation of the Democratic Dogma.*

9. For Lodge's fears of the effects of immigration on American society, culture and politics and his general pessimism about the

future of American democratic institutions, see Garraty, *Lodge*, p. 143 passim.

10. For Lodge's enthusiasm for sea power, and the connection betwen his wife's family and Mahan, see Garraty, *Lodge*—in particular a speech quoted on p. 152.

11. Mahan, *Interest*, p. 122.

12. Ibid., pp. 118–19.

13. Ibid., p. 245.

14. Ibid., p. 243.

15. Ibid., p. 119.

16. Samuels, *Henry Adams: The Major Phase*. p. 247. But Henry Adams and John Hay, on the other hand, were diffident about his "Accidency" in power. While Henry Adams continued on intimate terms with the President, his private evaluations of Roosevelt's intellect and character could be devastating. He described him as a "stupid, blundering, bolting bullcalf"—"one of those brainless cephalopods who is not afraid" (p. 251). "In correct expression, his mind is impulse and acts by the instinct of a schoolboy at a second-rate boarding school. Mind, in a technical sense, he has not." "Theodore is blind drunk with self-esteem. He has not a suspicion that we are all watching him as we would watch a monkey up a tree with a chronometer." (p. 253).

Hay wrote Henry Adams in London: "When he was one of us we could sit on him—but who, except you, can sit on a Kaiser? Come home and do it or we are undone." (p. 248).

17. In Brooks Adams' view, economics and geography were the chief determinants of power. Power was inexorably concentrating and the strong were thus fated to confrontation:

> The acceleration of movement, which is thus concentrating the strong, is so rapidly crushing the weak that the moment seems at hand when two great competing systems will be pitted against each other, and the struggle for survival will begin. . . .
> Whether we like it or not, we are forced to compete for the seat of international exchange or, in other words, for the seat of empire. . . . Our adversary (France Germany and Russia) is deadly and determined. . . . If we yield before him, he will stifle us.
> ——Adams, *America's Economic Supremacy*, pp. 80, 104–05.

18. For Lodge's irritation with businessmen more interested in trade than in empire, see Garraty, *Lodge*, pp. 182ff.

19. Mahan, *Interest*, pp. 258–59.

20. Samuels, *Henry Adams: The Major Phase*, p. 575.

21. In an important speech to the Senate on March 2, 1895, which stressed the importance of sea power to America, Lodge also observed:

> This country is the rival and competitor of England for the trade and commerce of the world. . . . Since we parted from England her statesmen have never failed to recognize that in men speaking her language, and of her own race she was to find her most formidable rivals. She has always opposed, thwarted, and sought to injure us. She desires to keep her control of the great pathways of commerce.
>
> ——Garraty, *Lodge*, p. 152.

22. For Henry Adams' view of his father's trials and tribulations as United States Ambassador to Britain during the Civil War, see his *Education of Henry Adams*, especially chapters 7–11.

23. Mahan, *Interest*, p. 116.

24. Tocqueville's American travels in the 1840's prompted the following:

> There are at the present time two great nations in the world, which started from different points, but seem to tend towards the same end. I allude to the Russians and the Americans. Both of them have grown up unnoticed; and while the attention of mankind was directed elsewhere, they have suddenly placed themselves in the front rank among the nations, and the world learned their existence and their greatness at almost the same time.
>
> All other nations seem to have nearly reached their natural limits, and they have only to maintain their power; but these are still in the act of growth. All the others have stopped, or continue to advance with extreme difficulty; these alone are proceeding with ease and celerity along a path to which no limit can be perceived. . . Their starting point is different and their courses are not the same; yet each of them seems marked out by the will of Heaven to sway the destinies of half the globe.
>
> ——de Tocqueville, *Democracy in America,* Vol. I, p. 452.

25. Good general discussions of United States-British relations and apprehensions during this troubled period can be found in Adams, *Great Britain and the American Civil War;* Bailey, *A Diplomatic History of the American People,* chs. 22 and 23; Nevins, *The War for the Union, Vol I;* and Temple, "William H. Seward," in *American Secretaries of State and Their Diplomacy,* pp. 3–115.

26. Gladstone, "Kin Beyond Sea," *North American Review,* Vol. 127, p. 180.

27. Quoted in Monypenny and Buckle, *The Life of Benjamin Disraeli,* Vol. V, p. 196.

28. Fischer's *Germany's Aims in the First World War* and *Krieg der Illusionen* and Meyer's *Mitteleuropa in German Thought and Action 1815-1945* discuss various German schemes to organize continental Europe into an economic and political bloc to hold its own against imperial Britain or the emerging Russian and American superpowers.

One of the best-known advocates of a Central European super-economy and superstate was Friedrich Nauman (1860-1919), a protestant cleric and deputy in the Reichstag. In 1915 he published in Berlin his famous book, *Mitteleuropa,* in which he called for a Central European economic and political bloc as the German and European answer to the continental economies of Russia and the United States.

The Jewish industrialist and politician Walther Rathenau (1867–1922) was an advocate close to the center of power. Influential with Wilhelm II and Imperial Chancellor Bethmann-Hollweg, Rathenau headed the Imperial War Ministry's department for raw materials from August 1914 to March 1915, and was minister for reconstruction and later for foreign affairs in Weimar. As early as 1911, he had proposed that Germany lead in creating a customs union in Central Europe to meet the economic challenge of America. Rathenau's plans heavily influenced Bethmann-Hollweg's September Program of 1914, in which Germany's war aims were officially spelled out. In three memoranda to Bethmann in August and September 1914, Rathenau had argued for the establishment of a continental economic union to unite Europe under German leadership against Britain and the United States on the one side and Russia on the other. He believed economic ties would be sufficient and annexations unnecessary. See: Wilde, *Rathenau,* pp. 83–86.

29. Max Beloff summarizes the essence of the British debate:

> Churchill's final word was that there could be no more fatal policy than for Britain to combine with Japan against the United States. In Lloyd George's view, there was one even more fatal policy, by which Britain would be at the mercy of the United States.
>
> ——Beloff, *Britain's Liberal Empire*, p. 335.

30. Wilson's shipbuilding program, as presented to Congress, drew heavily from Mahan's doctrines about the importance of naval strength to a world trading power. The program was designed in particular to block a British-Japanese alliance that might threaten American policies, and in general to overawe the European allies, especially Britain, into accepting the President's comprehensive plans for arms reduction and world order. See Beloff, *Britain's Liberal Empire*, p. 331.

31. A. J. P. Taylor, discussing the various failures of Britain and France to cooperate effectively with each other, or of either to contain or conciliate Germany, makes the following general point:

> . . . Later on, men blamed the Germans for not accepting the defeat as final. It is futile to suppose that more concessions, or fewer, would have made much difference. The conflict between France and Germany was bound to go on as long as the illusion persisted that Europe was still the center of the world. France would seek to preserve the artificial securities of 1919; Germany would strive to restore the natural order of things. Rival states can be frightened into friendship only by the shadow of some greater danger; neither Soviet Russia nor the United States cast this shadow over the Europe of Streseman and Briand.
>
> ——Taylor, *Origins of the Second World War*, p. 61.

32. Dilke, *Greater Britain*, p. 546.

33. Seeley, *Expansion of England*, p. 297.

34. Levin, *Woodrow Wilson*, p. 45.

An interesting insight into the mind of Colonel Edward M. House, Wilson's close adviser and aide at the Peace Conference, comes from his novel, *Philip Dru: Administrator* (New York, 1912), which speculates at length on the general benefits of an Anglo-American partnership to maintain world peace and commercial freedom.

35. Lodge was hardly an isolationist, but he was an imperialist. Link comments:

> Personally, Lodge had little hope for the success of the League, a profound personal contempt for Wilson, and almost a sardonic scorn for the President's international ideals. The Massachusetts senator was an ardent nationalist, almost a jingoist, no isolationist, but a believer in a strong balance of power. His solution would have been harsh terms, including dismemberment, for Germany, and the formulation of an Anglo-Franco-American alliance as the best insurance for future peace.
>
> ——Link, *Wilson the Diplomatist,* p. 138.

See also Garraty, *Lodge,* pp. 348ff.

36. For the great importance such men as Hoover, Hughes and Stimson attached to overseas economic expansion in maintaining domestic American prosperity, as well as the influence of their ideas on the business community, see Williams, *Tragedy of American Diplomacy,* pp. 116ff.

37. Streit, *Union Now,* p. 31.

38. Ibid., p. 90.

39. Ibid., p. 70.

40. In addition, however, the United States used its foreign aid to compel Western European cooperation with our strategic embargo on exports to communist nations. Congressional action tying aid to trade policies began in March 1948 with a provision in the Foreign Assistance Act of that year and culminated in the Battle Act of 1951, which threatened to cut off United States aid to nations not joining our embargo policy. Europeans, already heavily dependent on United States exports and desperately short of dollars, resented and resisted the dictation for both economic and political reasons—fearing among other things the prolongation of Eastern Europe's seemingly unnatural economic isolation. For a lengthy discussion, see Adler-Karlsson, *Western Economic Warfare,* passim.

41. For an excellent analysis of the continual tension between Europeanist and Atlanticist strands in postwar American policy, and the various compromises, see Cleveland, *The Atlantic Idea and its European Rivals.* See also Calleo, *Atlantic Fantasy.*

42. For an honest and powerful exposition of the Atlanticist view, see Rostow, *Law, Power and the Pursuit of Peace*.

43. President Kennedy, George Ball, McGeorge Bundy, and Robert McNamara were all strong opponents of European national nuclear forces, although the legitimacy of a "federal" European force was occasionally conceded. Secretary McNamara's commencement address at Ann Arbor in June 1962 provides a classic statement. As McNamara put it, weak, independent national nuclear forces (i.e. those of France and Britain) are "dangerous, expensive, prone to obsolescence, and lacking in credibility as a deterrent." Such forces were vulnerable, invitations to pre-emptive attack, and suicidal if used. Moreover, an effective nuclear deterrent could not permit conflicting allied strategies or targets. A nuclear confrontation would have to be based on centralized direction and control, i.e., that of the United States alone. See McNamara, "Remarks," *Department of Defense News Release No. 980–62*. For a full discussion of the American view, see Brown, *Faces of Power*. For a dissenting French strategic view, see Beaufre, *Deterrence and Strategy*. For a survey of the French program and its uses, see Kohl, *French Nuclear Diplomacy*.

44. The IMF, in particular, continued to probe the Sterling Area and Commonwealth preference system. Because of an increasing scarcity of dollars, Britain declared in 1949 that the Sterling Area would restrict its purchases of dollar goods to 25 percent below its 1948 level. The Fund's response was not to recognize the "legal" existence of the Sterling Area—only that of its constituent members. Thus, those countries which did not have to discriminate for balance-of-payments reasons should not be permitted to do so—leaving only India and Pakistan as "legitimate" discriminators. The British reacted with outrage. The Sterling Area was more than a "narrow economic thing," the press declared. The IMF beat a hasty retreat. See Patterson, *Discrimination in International Trade*, pp. 70–73.

Chapter Four

1. Federalism is a broad movement in political philosphy stemming from the Middle Ages. The concept is rather ambiguous, for in history it is sometimes applied to those advocating a devolution of power from the center to the regions—the kind of federalism recommended by Tocqueville—and sometimes to those urging the absorption of power from the regions to the center—the sort of federalism promoted by Alexander Hamilton. In European history most federalists have been men who opposed the power of a centralizing national bureaucracy, and urged instead the preservation or renewal of local liberties and self-government. Hence, historically, federalism has often been identified with the defense of localized rights and privileges in opposition to a centralizing, equalizing monarchy and bureaucracy. Contemporary versions of federalism have found expression in the various schemes in Western Europe for "regionalization" of one sort or another. Another important school of European federalism stresses not only the importance of small-scale government, but of popular participation within it. The French Catholic philosopher, Emmanuel Mounier (1905–1958), drawing in turn from the traditions of French writers like the humanist socialist, Joseph Proudhon (1809–1865), or the corporatist, Felicité Robert de Lamennais (1782–1854), helped found an influential modern movement often styled Personalism. De Gaulle's ill-fated scheme for *participation* drew some inspiration from these ideas and, indeed, they form an important element of "left-wing Gaullism."

The Functionalists form another important school of European federalism. These, drawing from the traditions of Henri de St. Simon (1760–1825) and Auguste Comte (1798–1857), foresee a world where the functions of government are broken up and parcelled out to specialist bureaucrats who can engineer a harmonious and progressive society free from the stupidities and dangers that accompany mass politics within the context of the nation-state. Functionalist ideas have made an important contribution to the ideology and practice of the European Communities.

In the United States federalism naturally continues to be identified with our own constitutional experience and with various schemes in recent decades to link together national states through transnational institutions. In Britain, federalist formulas have sought both to build states out of portions of the Empire and to link them together into a voluntary commonwealth.

2. States' Rights is not a dead issue in the United States, although the demand for regional autonomy may be taking less traditional forms. The feeling has grown in recent years, on both the American Left and Right, that "federal" centralization has been carried to an unhealthy and self-defeating extreme. Thoughtful European visitors occasionally reflect that America's domestic governmental chaos suggests strong reservations against a federal or supranational Europe after the American model.

3. Madison's principle of expanding the sphere of government to "take in a greater variety of parties and interests" is seized on by some historians to explain a main impulse underlying American expansionism. By combining elements from Madisonian federalism and Turner's "frontier thesis," historians such as Van Alstyne *(The Rising American Empire)*, and Williams *(The Contours of American History)*, argue that the American Republic from birth has consciously pursued expansion as the key for domestic stability. Whatever the truth of their arguments, and although the later Madison was a key figure in the Louisiana Purchase, the Madison of the *Federalist Papers* did not advocate constant expansion—only a base large enough at the outset to make it difficult for a single majority faction to form itself and control the state.

4. In contrast to the American experience, the British Empire turned to federalism to guide the devolution of central power, rather than its accretion. Despite the efforts of Lord Halifax to forge a single Commonwealth policy in the postwar era, the desire for independence proved stronger and the Labour Government had little desire to resist it. The independence of India and Pakistan was followed by that of Ceylon, and the withdrawal of Burma and Ireland. By 1960 the Commonwealth, whose earlier cohesion had depended on allegiance to an indivisible crown, became a grouping of sovereign realms and republics. The Crown remained the symbol of association, but without any vestige of sovereignty. Cohesion depended on an act of will to remain within the Commonwealth, based on the links of historical affinity, rather than the unifying force of British military, political or even economic power. For a full discussion, see Gordon Walker, *The Commonwealth*.

5. The Netherlands, among the smallest of European powers, was able to frustrate France's "Fouchet Plan" for a political and military consultative group composed of EEC members exclusively. For an interesting discussion see Couve de Murville, *Une Politique Étrangère*, pp. 347–384. A summary of events and selected relevant documents are found in Parlement Européen, *Le Dossier de l'Union Politique*, January 1964.

6. See Mayne, *Recovery of Europe*, pp. 170–189, 207–210, 227–334.

7. De Gaulle, *Memoirs of Hope*, pp. 183–184.

8. Hence de Gaulle's veto of British entry in 1963. Britain, an alien herself, would also be the conduit for American influence in the councils of the Community, thus undermining prospects for a strong independent Europe. See de Gaulle, Press Conference, January 14, 1963, in *Major Addresses, Statements and Press Conferences*, p. 214. For a full discussion of this view, see Calleo, *Britain's Future*, pp. 78ff.

9. De Gaulle, Press Conference, May 15, 1962, *Major Addresses*, p. 177.

10. Ibid., pp. 214–215.

11. See Levin, *Woodrow Wilson and World Politics*, pp. 45ff.

12. See Coudenhove-Kalergi, *Paneuropa: 1922–1966*, pp. 11–12, 61, 96.

13. For a full discussion see Calleo, *Atlantic Fantasy*, pp. 57–74.

14. On the military consequences of French withdrawal from NATO, see Hunt, "NATO Without France: The Military Implications," *Adelphi Papers No. 32*. See also Calleo, *Atlantic Fantasy*, pp. 56–83.

15. Quoted in Preeg, *Traders and Diplomats*, pp. 285–286. Placing trade within the Cold War arsenal was an old American trick for which Europeans showed little enthusiasm. See Chapter 3 (Geopolitics), note 30.

16. Quoted in Preeg, *Traders and Diplomats*, p. 95.

Chapter Five

1. For a full discussion of the underlying politics of international monetary relationships, see Susan Strange *Sterling and British Policy*, London 1971, especially chapter 1, "The Politics of International Currencies." The author distinguishes four set of political-monetary relationships involving a "master currency," a "diplomatic" or "negotiated currency" (currently the pound and the dollar), a "top currency" (the dollar until the mid-1960's), and "neutral currencies."

2. United States House of Representatives, *Bretton Woods Agreements Act*, Hearings before the House Committee on Currency and Banking, March 1945, Vol. 1, p. 5.

3. Statements during the Bretton Woods hearings by Morgenthau, White and then Assistant Secretary of State Dean Acheson, indicate that they expected the Fund would give debtors the credit to balance their accounts without resorting to restrictive policies. As Morgenthau argued, the Fund "removes the excuse for the tangle of import quotas, discriminatory tariffs, and other desperate measures" of the 1930's. (United States House of Representatives, *Bretton Woods Agreements Act*. Hearings before the House Committee on Currency and Banking. Vol. I. March, 1945, p. 6). White admitted, however, that the adjustment process might well be lengthy. Keynes, remembering the deflationary discomfort of debtor countries in the interwar period, was determined that the burden of adjustment should fall on the creditor countries, particularly the United States. Hence, he fought for the IMF's "Scarce Currency" clause (*Ibid.*, p. 279), whereby the Fund was empowered to declare the currency of a surplus country to be "scarce," thereby rationing its supply, and authorizing any member to discriminate against the exports of that surplus country. Indeed, in Keynes' original formulation, accumulated balances of the surplus countries could be taxed by 1 percent or they might be cancelled altogether.

As the world's major creditor, the United States insisted that the IMF's powers against surplus countries be reduced to recommendations. See Michael Hudson, "Epitaph for Bretton Woods," p. 275.

4. The United States had 70 percent of the world's monetary gold stock in 1947, and still had 59 percent by 1957. Moreover it was long believed our deficits would be short-lived. As holders earned interest on dollars and none on gold, it seemed only sensible to hold the former.

5. At the time of Bretton Woods, some experts advocated a "key currency" standard. The United States and the United Kingdom would agree initially on the sterling-dollar rate and other currencies would be linked to one or the other. By contrast, the actual agreement was meant to represent a "multilateral" solution to manage the postwar system, rather than an Anglo-American "special relationship." The reality, of course, was to be a key currency dollar standard, with the pound as junior partner. See John Williams, *Postwar Monetary Plans and Other Essays*. For contemporary analyses of the proposal, see August Maffry, "Bretton Woods—and Foreign Trade," *Foreign Commerce Weekly*, Oct. 7, 1944. (Reprinted in "Hearings," *Bretton Woods Agreement Act*, p. 313), and Carlyle Morgan, *Bretton Woods: Clue to a Monetary Mystery*.

6. Britain and, to some extent, France form exceptions to this generalization about ample postwar liquidity. Britain's enormous debts, low reserves, and the pound's continuing role as a reserve currency all greatly strained the postwar British economy. Devaluation in 1949 was repeated in 1967, after several years of currency crises and "Stop-Go" stabilization policies which many believe greatly slowed Britain's growth. See Calleo, *Britain's Future*, especially pp. 14–40.

France, burdened with the Indo-Chinese and later the Algerian wars, devalued in 1948 and 1949. DeGaulle devalued by 17.55 percent in 1958 and attempted a stringent stabilization policy, reinforced by Giscard d'Estaing's stabilization plan in 1963. Inflationary wage increases after the May-June events of 1968 led ultimately to another austerity program followed by an 11.1 percent devaluation in 1969. For the early period, see Willis, *France, Germany, and the New Europe*, pp. 274–78. For the effects of the May-June events on the French economy and the franc, see Hanrieder, *The Stable Crisis*, 1970.

7. For the classic exposition of this "Triffin Paradox," see Triffin, *Gold and the Dollar Crisis*, and *The World Money Maze*.

8.

U.S. External Balances
(billions of dollars)

Year	Goods and Services	Official Settlements	Liquidity Balance	Reserves	Short-Term Indebtedness
1950	1,892		− 3.489	24.27	7.12
1960	4,126	− 3,403	− 3.665	19.36	18.01
1965	7,130	− 1.289	− 2.493	15.45	24.75
1969	2.011	+ 2.702	− 6.084	16.96	39.36
1970	3.592	− 9.821	− 3.852	14.49	41.29

Sources: (1) 1950–1960 goods and services, liquidity, *Economic Report of the President*. Feb. 1971. Table C-87; (2) 1960–70 goods and services, official settlements, liquidity, U.S. Dept. of Commerce *Survey Current Business,* June 1971, p. 30; (3) Reserves 1950–1970 and short term indebtedness, IMF *International Financial Statistics* 1971 Supplement, pp. 276–277.

9. "Roosa bonds," denominating American obligations in foreign currencies, reassured nervous creditors. Proliferating swap and re-cycling arrangements marshalled the funds of cooperating central banks against speculative runs. Most ingenious of all was the "two-tier "gold market, born in the dollar crisis of 1968, which separated the official fixed dollar price for gold from the fluctuations of the private market. Establishing the two-tier system, as Jacques Rueff observed, effectively ended dollar convertibility into gold. By agreeing not to buy or sell on the private gold market, central bankers could only convert their dollars through the United States government, increasing its ability to exert pressure. Rueff argues the dollar became effectively inconvertible for any country under United States military protection. See Rueff, *Monetary Sin of the West,* pp. 184–189.

10. For an early awareness of the unlikelihood of any improvement in the United States payments balance see Stevens, "Wishful Thinking on the Balance of Payments," also Calleo, *Britain's Future,* pp. 110ff.

11. The first serious break in the dollar's facade followed the British devaluation of November, 1967. Between November 1967 and March 1968, when the two-tier gold market was established (see note 9), over $3 billion of official gold, mostly American, passed into private hands. The new gold market quieted specula-

tion, but only temporarily. The "May events" in France added to the confusion. Between May and November 1968 France lost $4.5 billion in reserves, mostly to Germany, and finally devalued in August, 1969 by 11.1 percent. In October 1969, heavy selling of dollars and francs for marks forced the German *Bundesbank* to revalue the mark by 8.5 percent. In 1970, sales of expatriate dollars for other currencies brought the American official settlements deficit to a record $9.8 billion (modest only in comparison to the monumental $29.6 billion figure recorded for 1971). By early 1971, no drastic improvement in the American balance-of-payments deficit seemed probable. In an election year, Nixon was retreating from his deflationary domestic policy. Declining American interest rates and the Federal Reserve's massive increase in the money supply accelerated the outflow of short-term capital. (See Cleveland, "How the Dollar Standard Died," p. 45). Early reports made the first annual United States trade deficit since 1893 seem inevitable. In May, the dollar crisis began anew. On May 3 and 4, the German *Bundesbank* was forced to buy $2 billion in dollars to defend the parity of the mark, and an additional $1 billion during the first 40 minutes of trading on May 5, after which the mark was allowed to float upward. Switzerland, Austria, the Netherlands and Belgium followed. But the rush to sell dollars continued. European and other central banks began to demand that the United States settle her debts. Despite swaps and other measures, the United States paid out $3.1 billion to foreign official dollar holders in the first 8 months of 1971 (most of that during July and August), including $864 million in gold, $394 million in foreign currencies, $480 million in SDR and $362 million against United States reserves in the IMF. In addition, $600 million of United States securities denominated in foreign currency was issued, bringing the total of such instruments to $2.1 billion. (See Charles A. Coombes, "Treasury and Federal Reserve Foreign Exchange Operations.")

12. After two days of talks with President Pompidou in the Azores, President Nixon announced on Dec. 15, 1971 that the United States was prepared to devalue the dollar in return for a European pledge to revalue their currencies upwards. After two days of bargaining at the Smithsonian in Washington, D. C. (Dec. 17 & 18, 1971), Finance Ministers of the Group of Ten reached agreement on a new pattern of currency rates, including an 8.5 percent devaluation of the dollar (by raising the price of gold from $35 to

$38 per ounce) and removal of the 10 percent import surcharge. Dollar convertibility was not restored.

13. Europeans have invested heavily in the United States although, as the figures reveal, almost two-thirds of European long-term investment in the United States is portfolio, whereas over 80 percent of United States investments in Europe are direct.

Private Long-Term Investment Position
of W. Europe and the U.S.
(millions of dollars)

	1958	1969
W. Europe investments in U.S.		
Long-term total	11,389	27,452
Direct	4,070	8,510
Corporate stocks	6,030	12,106
Corporate state and municipal bonds	136	3,770
Other	973	3,012
U.S. investments in Europe		
Long-term total	6,905	26,721
Direct	4,573	21,554
Foreign dollar bonds	244	583
Other foreign securities	974	2,840
Other	1,114	1,290

Sources: (1) For 1958 figures see Sidney Rolfe and Walter Darum, Editors *The Multinational Corporation in the World Economy*, New York 1970, p. 15; (2) For 1969 figures David Devlin and George Kruer, "The International Investment Position of the U.S. Developments in 1969," *Survey of Current Business*, October 1970, p. 23.

14. See Walter Salant, "Does the International Monetary System Need Reform?", p. 26.

The notion that savers should revalue is part of the "benign neglect" theory articulated by Gottfried Haberler and Lawrence Krause. Haberler argues that since the dollar is the standard worldwide unit of account and an international reserve currency, a few surplus countries should revalue rather than cause a reduction of the gold value of not only the dollar but also of the great majority of other currencies that would devalue with it. See Hobart Rowan, Understanding the Functions of Benign-Neglect Policy," *Washington Post*, May 23, 1971.

As Krause explained in 1971: "Because of the basic nature of the dollar standard, the United States cannot change the value of its currency and it need not do so to maintain the equilibrium of the system . . . If all other countries adjust their dollar exchange rates, then the United States need not exercise any control . . . Obviously the economic consequences will be much the same no matter who takes the initiative as long as the same exchange parity is established. But United States action destabilizes reserve holdings, since a United States devaluation involves an increase in the price of gold, or special drawing rights (SDRs), or both. If the exchange rate mechanism is going to be improved, governments will have to get over their psychological hangups about initiating a change, although the United States may still play a useful role." Lawrence B. Krause, "A Passive Balance of Payments Strategy," pp. 347–348.

Many experts argued that a floating dollar would not decline seriously, i.e., be less attractive to foreigners. A leading figure on the Joint Economic Committee, Congressman Henry Reuss, impressed with the fundamental strength of the American economy, observed in 1967: "I should think the dollar would be a very desirable currency to hold, and it's quite likely that the dollar might even appreciate in value." (See Joint Economic Committee meeting, Jan. 7, 1967, relevant extracts of which appear in *The Banker*, March 1967. For contemporary criticism of this view see Calleo, *Britain's Future*, pp. 121–28.)

15. France has generally opposed the existence of national reserve currencies since the Genoa Conference of 1922. See Rueff, *The Monetary Sin of the West*.

16. In de Gaulle's view, gold was the only objective basis for an international monetary system: "Yes, gold, which does not change in nature, which can be made into bars, ingots, or coins, which has no nationality, which is considered in all places and at all times, the immutable and fiduciary value par excellence. Furthermore . . . it is a fact that even today no currency has any value except by direct or indirect relation to gold, real or supposed. Doubtless, no one would think of dictating to any country how to manage its domestic affairs. But the supreme law, the golden rule—and indeed it is pertinent to say it—that must be enforced, and honored again in international economic relations, is the duty to balance, from one monetary area to another, by effective inflows and outflows of gold, the balance of payments resulting from their exchanges." Charles de

Gaulle *Press Conference*, Feb. 4, 1965. In his Press Conference of September 23, 1971, President Pompidou repeated the continuing French view that a stable and equitable international monetary system must be based on fixed parities and gold, and elaborated current French ideas on monetary reform: ". . . On this matter, France has some ideas, some principles to which she clings firmly. No international monetary system is valid without fixed parities. There can be fixed parities only in relation to something that is free of manipulation of one and all, that is gold."

"It matters little that for the creation of needed liquidities, use be made of credit or of something like special drawing rights, provided these special drawing rights are backed by gold, at least partially convertible into gold, and issued under the supervision of, and by, the International Monetary Fund, a Monetary Fund free of any unilateral influence."

"Next, all currencies must be convertible—not into gold, of course, that would be a dream—but among themselves, that is, that anyone having dollars, for example, could exchange them at an established and known rate for marks, or yen or francs or pounds, or the other way around. Central banks should accept in their reserves only gold, special drawing rights and to a minor extent fixed parities currencies. Furthermore, they should diversify this last category of their reserves . . . And when all that was accepted, we would still not have succeeded in changing from the present situation to a new system if we did not first settle the past, that is, the problem of those 50 or 60 billion dollars that circulate all over the world under different names." Georges Pompidou, *Presidential Press Conference*, September 23, 1971

17. See, for example, Servan-Schreiber, *The American Challenge* and *The Spirit of May*.

18. The Eurodollar Market provided increasingly dramatic evidence of the perils of interdependence. For example, in the late sixties, tight money, combined with interest rate ceilings at home attracted Americans to the Eurodollar Market, both to borrow and to lend. Dollars circulated from the United States to the Eurodollar Market, to gain high interest rates, and back to the United States through the foreign branches of United States banks to relieve the credit squeeze. In this manner, the liabilities of American banks to their foreign branches jumped in 1969 to some $14 billion (from $1 billion in 1964). These developments, besides contributing to an inter-

national currency crisis, also worked counter to the United States government's deflationary domestic policy.

In Europe, economic policy seemed reduced to reactions to the sudden twists and turns of a system beyond comprehensive understanding or control. The French Plan, based on a government control of credit, was in disarray and in Germany, swamped with dollars, the banking system and government began to lose control of the domestic money supply. Attractive forward rates and other policies failed to stanch the dollar flow. Meanwhile, high German interest rates to check domestic inflation simply attracted more dollars into deutschmarks, thus not only producing new pressure for revaluation, but feeding domestic inflation.

In addition, of course, the Market's abundant short-term credit in itself helped finance the huge speculative movements in or out of one currency after another. See Little, "The Euro-dollar Market."

International corporations, another feature of interdependence, also added significantly to the speculative tides by shifting reserves from one currency to another. See, for example, "Industrial Policy in the Community," Memorandum from the Commission to the Council, Brussels, March, 1970.

19. Since the Community's unit of account for its Common Agricultural Policy was based on the dollar value of gold, France's devaluation would give her farmers more francs for their products and thus stimulate, it was feared, even greater French surpluses. After protracted negotiations, France agreed to restore the predevaluation balance by granting subsidies to Community agricultural imports and levying duties on her own agricultural exports. See Dennis Swann, *The Economics of the Common Market*, Harmondsworth (England), Penguin Books, Ltd. 1970, pp. 94–95.

20. The first stage included a reserve pool for medium-term balance-of-payments support for members (to complement a short-term support system initiated in June 1970), also coordination of national budgets, Community targets for prices, employment and growth, and concerted management of credit, interest, and capital flows by the Committee of Central Bank Governors.

The second stage (subject to agreement at the end of the first stage) envisioned a harmonization of fiscal systems, integration of capital markets, and common central bank policies for intervening in exchange markets. SDR's would be managed jointly and margins between EEC currencies progressively reduced.

The third stage was to see complete monetary integration. Exchange rates among member countries would be completely frozen, reserves would be pooled and a federal central bank would control monetary policy throughout the Community. "Economic and Monetary Union," *European Community*, March 1971, No. 143, pp. 4–5. See also European Community Information Service "European Community Agrees to Start Economic and Monetary Union," EC Press Release, Febuary 25, 1971.

21. Experts differ on the source of funds for the Eurodollar market. According to the 1970 *Economic Report of the President*, European central banks were the major source of Eurodollars (p. 128). Milton Friedman, on the other hand, argues that the foreign central bank dollar holdings—some $5 billion from 1964–1968—are not enough to account for the size of the Eurodollar market, estimated to be from $30 billion to $40 billion in 1969 and roughly $60 billion by 1970. Most of the credit, according to Friedman, is created "by a bookkeeper's pen." Dollar claims held by banks in Europe are used, in the normal banking practice, to create a credit pyramid. See "The Euro-dollar Market: Some First Principles," *Morgan Guaranty Survey*, October 1969, pp. 4–14. For a contrary view, see Fred H. Klopstock, "Money Creation in the Euro-Dollar Market—A note on Professor Friedman's Views," *Federal Reserve Bank of New York, Monthly Review*, January 1970, pp. 12–15.

22. The basic balance measures the current account plus flows of *long-term capital* plus flows of government capital, American and foreign, other than changes in official reserve holdings. This balance is intended to serve as a better indicator of the long-term trends in the United States balance-of-payments than the "reserves-transactions" or "net liquidity" balances, since it is not affected by the volatile and often massive short-term capital flows.

In practice, however, there are numerous deficiencies. For example, although all direct investment transactions are considered long-term, many movements in inter-company accounts are, in fact, short-term and quite volatile. United States stocks held by foreigners are also considered long-term items, but in fact are easily marketable and often behave like short-term flows.

The erratic effects of those can be seen in the basic balance in the 1960's. This balance was near zero in 1964, mounted to a deficit of $3.2 billion in 1967, temporarily recovered in 1968, but deteriorated again to a deficit of about $3.0 billion in 1969 and 1970. See

David T. Devlin, "The United States Balance of Payments: Revised Presentation," *Survey of Current Business*, June 1971, pp. 24–29.

23. Theoretically, a country could have a large and stable overseas debt without excessively volatile short-term capital flow in and out of its currency. Similarly, a country could have such flows even if it had no large external debt. Nevertheless, the larger the country's foreign indebtedness, particularly if its redemption is uncertain, the more unstable the country's currency is likely to appear and hence the more volatile the short-term capital flows are likely to be. The working out of these effects is often rather intricate. For example, fear of the dollar's payments deficit was a major factor inducing Nixon to adopt a tight domestic money policy. That policy, and the deflation it caused, led much American capital to go abroad in search of greater returns (see note 18). Meanwhile, European central banks, fearing an ultimate dollar devaluation, were even less content to sit on their growing dollar reserves and so placed large amounts in the Eurodollar Market, which in turn helped fuel short-term capital flows.

24. Foreign exchange costs of United States defense expenditures abroad are said to be "offset" by sales contracts for American military goods, particularly advanced weapons systems, aircraft and parts, training in the use of such equipment, and sales of other less sophisticated weaponry such as tanks and communication systems. Particular "offset" agreements have made Germany the largest buyer, receiving 30 percent of the shipments between 1960–1970. The United Kingdom has also been a large buyer, accounting for 13 percent of the total in this period. Other Western European countries combined received about 20 percent of the United States military exports, Australia and New Zealand accounting for 8 percent, other Asian and African countries 19 percent, Canada 4 percent, Latin America and Japan 3 percent each. The practice of deducting our foreign military sales from "net" United States external military expenditures appears to presume that no sales would occur without the same level of United States expenditures overseas. Other countries, e.g., France and Britain, make large arms sales to foreigners without maintaining a comparable overseas outlay.

In any event, as the following table shows, these transactions (the credit item subtracted from military expenditures in United States balance-of-payments accounts) totaled about $10 billion from 1960–1970, in contrast to total United States foreign military expenditures of over \$40 billion during this period.

U.S. Military Agency Sales Contracts
(millions of dollars)

	1970	1960–1970
Total	1,480	10,084
U.K.	177	1,324
EEC	270	4,097
Other W. Eur.	152	926
Canada	35	422
Latin America	41	301
Japan	25	276
Australia, New Zealand, S. Africa	168	841
Other Asia and Africa	612	1,846
International Organizations	. .	56

Source: Campbell and Shupe, "Military Transactions," pp. 22–28.

25. *Department of the Treasury News*: "Remarks of the Honorable John B. Connally, Secretary of the Treasury, at the International Banking Conference of the American Bankers Association, Munich, Germany, May 28, 1971.

26. Even as late as 1970, roughly a third of the net exchange cost for our military forces occurred for European defense, and a considerable part of the remainder for Japan. (Campbell and Shupe, "Military Transactions," pp. 22–28.) Despite recurring campaigns and although there have been modest improvements, we have been unable to get even these highly prosperous beneficiaries to pay the military exchange costs of our protection, either directly or through "offset" purchases. See John M. Goshko, "Bonn Offers to Share Costs," *Washington Post*, Nov. 8, 1971; John Newhouse et al., *United States Troops in Europe*, Washington, D.C., 1971, p. 17. See also note 24 above.

27. Restraints on private capital outflows began in 1963 with the Interest Equalization Tax on United States resident income from foreign securities; in 1965 "voluntary" restraints sought to discourage foreign lending by United States banks and direct foreign investments by American businessmen, and in January 1968, direct investment restraints became mandatory. The mandatory measures were meant to be of "temporary but immediate effect" and to reduce the deficit by at least \$1 billion in 1968. (See United States Depart-

ment of the Treasury. *Maintaining the Strength of the United States Dollar in a Strong Free World Economy,* Washington, D.C., Jan., 1968 pp. xii–xiii). Longer-term improvements were to come through an increase in exports, foreign tourism in the United States, and encouragement of foreign direct and portfolio investment in the United States. The Foreign Investors Tax Act of 1966 was to enhance the attractiveness of United States corporate securities by reducing the taxes on income from portfolio investment by foreigners.

The Interest Equalization Tax has successfully reduced both the volume of foreign bond issues placed in the United States ($.5 billion in 1963) and United States purchases of foreign stocks. The American position shifted from an average annual net outflow for portfolio investment of $225 million from 1958–1962 to an annual average net inflow of $200 million per year from 1963–1966.

Voluntary and mandatory curbs on direct investment have turned American investors to capital sources abroad. The amount of borrowing shifted is reckoned at some $2 billion a year, compared to total foreign investment earnings of $8 billion. Although the overall effect of the three programs is hard to quantify, the IET and Voluntary Restraint programs have reduced outflows by an estimated $1–2 billion, and the mandatory program (i.e., since 1968) by another $2 billion.

Critics argue that the income returned and exports to foreign affiliates have more than recouped the balance-of-payments loss from the initial capital outflow. Yet others fear significant relaxation would risk a large surge of capital outflow—partly to refinance the amounts borrowed abroad. For a discussion, see Pizer, "Capital Restraint Programs," *Williams Report,* Papers I. pp. 87–112. Others believe the curbs endanger not only the growth of American foreign subsidiaries, but the preservation of their existing market positions. See Polk, *United States Production Abroad.* pp. 132–36.

Whatever the particular balance-of-payments effects of restrictions, it is worth noting that various tax concessions and other government incentives have continued to encourage foreign investment by American corporations. For further discussion, see Chapter 7.

28. The merchandise trade surplus in 1970 improved to $2.2 billion in 1970, up from $.6 billion in 1969. Exports were $42.0 billion, up $5.6 billion (15 percent) while imports were $39.9 billion, up $4 billion (11 percent). See Evelyn M. Parrish, "The United States Balance of Payments: Fourth Quarter and Year 1970," *Survey of*

Current Business, March 1971, pp. 31–43.

29. Hendrik Houthakker, using trade models developed by the Council of Economic Advisors, predicted that, for 1971 a policy of improving foreign trade by $1 billion through domestic deflation would require a minimum loss of $6 billion in national income and more than 218,000 people unemployed. Houthakker believes the cost intolerable. Houthakker, "United States Balance of Payments," *Williams Report*, Papers I, pp. 31–50.

30. See Chapter 6, Tables 6–5.A and 6–5.B.

31. In his speech to the Finance Ministers of the Group of Ten in London on Sept. 15, 1971, Treasury Secretary Connally demanded a $13 billion improvement in the United States balance of payments within the next two years. According to the Secretary, $5 billion was needed to cover the anticipated deficit on current account for 1972. Of the remaining $8 billion, $6 billion was needed to finance American "responsibilities" in the world: military expenditures, foreign aid, and long-term capital flows; and $2 billion more was required as a margin of safety, a "basic surplus on current and long-term capital accounts."

America's trading partners were asked to help the United States achieve this $13 billion swing by revaluing their currencies upward against the dollar, sharing more of the cost of America's defense burden, and abolishing restrictions to trade, particularly the variable levies of the Common Agricultural Policy and Japan's import controls. For a contemporary account and European reactions see William Keegan, "Six Protest at United States Plan," *Financial Times*, Sept. 16, 1971.

32. Official American estimates reckoned each percentage point revaluation of foreign currencies collectively would add $800 million to our trade balance. But the commercial effects of such parity changes are not only slow to appear, but highly uncertain—since they depend on differing rates of foreign and domestic growth and inflation, comparative income and price elasticities, and other highly unpredictable supply and demand factors, e.g., changes in technology, quality of products and consumer tastes. The Department of Commerce, for example, sees a growing American preference for foreign-made goods as one of the major factors in United States trade deterioration. See Jack L. Bame, "United States Balance of Payments Developments, Fourth Quarter and Year 1971," *Depart-*

ment of Commerce News, Feb. 15, 1972, p. 2. Marginal changes in price thus may not have a corresponding effect on demand.

Some of Houthakker's studies also suggest less optimism about the positive commercial effects to be expected from devaluation. He maintains that as American income rises, the propensity to import rises proportionately faster, whereas as the national income of several major foreign countries rises, their propensity to import American goods shows a relative decline. In his calculations, the United States has an import income elasticity one-and-one-half times greater than her export elasticity. On the price side, the price elasticities for total United States imports and exports are relatively small. This suggests that devaluation (i.e., a lower price for our exports and a higher price for imports) will not alter aggregate trade flows substantially. Houthakker does note, however, that price elasticities are notably higher for particular commodity classes and individual countries. For example, long-run price elasticities are higher for finished manufactures, a category which has grown from about one-seventh of American imports in 1947 to one-half in 1966. In all, however, Houthakker's price and income elasticity trends imply a continuing deterioration of the United States trade balance. See Houthakker and Magee, "Income and Price Elasticities in World Trade," pp. 111–25.

But even if devaluation could restore America's trade balance, it would not thereby end the dollar's weakness. As we argue at length, our deficit in the 1960's stemmed not from trade but from an excess of investment and official expenditures overseas. It is implausible that a devaluation of 8.5 percent will provide a trade surplus sufficient to cover this basic deficit, or that it could do so without provoking foreign retaliation.

33. America's rising trade deficit could, in fact, be traced to a massive deterioration in the balance with Canada, Japan, and to a much lesser extent, Germany. Selective controls might well be the cheapest, most direct and least distorting corrective. America's liberal principles, however, have made it awkward to take selective discriminatory action against these principal sources of trade deterioration, although some negotiations along these lines have been conducted. By contrast, a general dollar devaluation or even a selective change in parities, while preserving the fiction of liberal trade, provokes resistance among those many countries already in trade deficit with the United States, e.g., the EC, or distorts trade

between other trading partners, e.g., France and Germany. Interestingly, Canada rejects United States demands for trade adjustments on the grounds that the Canadian earnings of American corporations more than compensate for United States trade losses. See Chapter 6, Table 6–1.

34. American officials spoke confidently of restoring America's international payments to balance. In July 1965, for example, Secretary of the Treasury Henry Fowler predicted: "The deficit will be reduced by half by the end of 1965 and fully eliminated by the end of 1966." That accomplished, it would be essential to begin "the deliberate creation of a new reserve instrument to replace the additional liquidity arising out of the United States balance-of-payments deficit, which is not expected to continue." Rueff. *Monetary Sin.* p. 200.

35. France and the United States contended sharply over the nature and amount of the SDR. While the United States pressed for a large amount of freely-usable new world liquidity ($3-5 billion per year), the French insisted on a smaller amount and stringent reconstitution obligations. In the French view, the SDR was only to be an extension of credit to be repaid. The 1967 Rio de Janeiro Agreement on SDR left the issues cloudy. The French had won a collective EC veto as well as a vague understanding that activation depended on an end to American deficits. See International Monetary Fund. *Summary Proceedings, Annual Meeting 1967.* p. 67.

The United States however, appears to have got its way, as Henry Fowler contended at the time. The new SDR are, in fact, a freely acceptable international reserve asset, 70 percent of which can be spent without reconstitution. See Cohen. *International Monetary Reform.* p. 147. Moreover, the first allocation of SDR to IMF members in January 1970 was large ($9.5 billion over three years) and took place despite a continuing American payments deficit. The next round is likely to be more difficult for the United States.

36. Here, of course, the Europeans revealed their own naïveté about the American deficit. The degree of domestic deflation necessary to turn around the United States balance of payments was well beyond the political tolerance of the American system (see note 29). It was difficult enough to apply the same remedy in European economies where the high proportion of exports to GNP gave much greater leverage. And, of course, the Europeans would have been

the first to complain if the American export surplus had, in fact, jumped high enough to bring our payments into balance.

37. Giscard d'Estaing gave a clear view in advance of at least the French reaction to a new dollar crisis:

"The era of the floating and of revaluation of all the European currencies is over; it's finished. . . . You have to know that the era of massive purchase of dollars by central banks is over. This is not a preference here; this is a factual finding of a political reaction. . . . And, therefore, what might happen if the present monetary uncertainties were to continue? . . . I am merely making a forecast. I think that we would be faced with restrictive measures which will be adopted at first gradually and individually by the various countries; and then probably on an agreed scale in order to put a brake on the entry of outside capital." Speech by Valéry Giscard d'Estaing at the United States-EC Businessmen's Conference, March 3, 1972, p. 6. Unofficial translation.

38. Harold van B. Cleveland, "How the Dollar Standard Died," p. 46.

39. Giscard d'Estaing has argued that the essential element of European monetary union is not merely a narrowing of bands, but the displacement of the dollar and the use of European currencies as a means of settlement of intra-European balance-of-payments transactions:

> The substance will lie in the continuous and growing use of European currencies—when I speak of Europe, obviously, I am speaking of the expanded Economic Community—the growing use then of European currencies, as instruments of settlement, without these currencies even attempting to be reserve currencies. (p. 3).

In Giscard's view, the objective of monetary reform "should then be a progressive substitution of objective liquidities, such as SDR's, Special Drawing Rights, for the present use of reserve currencies" (p. 11). Speech by Valery Giscard d'Estaing at the United States-EC Businessmen's Conference, March 3, 1972. Unofficial translation.

40. Monetary expert Robert Triffin sees IMF reserve accounts the appropriate basic instruments for international settlements and reserve accumulations. These reserve accounts, carrying interest and exchange rate guarantees, would grow proportionately to world

trade and production. The IMF itself would be a clearing house for the system.

To encourage national discipline and "adjustment," he would limit strictly the use of national currencies (5 percent of imports or 15 percent of global reserves). Excess balances of national currency would be promptly converted into IMF reserve accounts, thereby depriving former reserve currency countries of the "exorbitant privilege" of financing their own deficits through an involuntary foreign accumulation of their IOUs. See Robert Triffin, "Toward a Viable Monetary System," *N. Y. Times*, January 23, 1972, Section III, p. 16.

41. The American government would, of course, prefer to convert its dollar debt without paying any compensation. Such an arrangement would constitute a rather spectacular form of nationalization in reverse. Americans would continue to hold the foreign assets they had bought, but the United States would be absolved of any particular obligations to honor the dollars used to pay for assets. Such a system appears to have been contemplated by J. Fred Bergston, who proposes a simple substitution of dollar and other reserve assets by SDR. See Bergston, "The New Economics and United States Foreign Policy," *Foreign Affairs*, Jan 1972, pp.199–222. Triffin, on the other hand, would hold the United States responsible for its past deficits. In his view, new SDR or their equivalent would be backed by outstanding dollar deficits, funded as long-term investments or "consols," and subject to gradual amortization. See Robert Triffin, "Toward a Viable Monetary System," *New York Times*, Jan. 23, 1972, Section III, p. 16.

42.

Exports and Imports of the EEC in 1970
(millions of dollars)
(Continued on page 300)

	Exports (f.o.b.)	Imports (c.i.f.)
Total Trade of Present Six EC Countries:	88,679	88,618
Total Trade of Three Expected EC Members:		
Denmark	3,288	4,384
Ireland	1,034	1,569
United Kingdom	19,351	21,724
Total Trade of Six EC and Three Expected Members:	112,352	116,295
Intra EC Trade of Present Six EC Countries:	43,283	42,805
EC Trade of Three Expected Members:		
Denmark	2,006	1,336
Ireland	911	998
United Kingdom	5,132	5,599
Total Intra EC Trade of Present Six EC Members and Three Expected Members:	51,332	50,738
EC Trade of Expected Commercial Associates:		
Austria	2,072	1,078
Finland	677	592
Sweden	2,251	2,000
Switzerland	4,029	1,981
	9,029	5,651
Total Intra-Community Trade	51,332	50,738

Exports and Imports of the EEC in 1970
(millions of dollars)

Intra-Community Trade as Percent of Total Community Trade:

$$\frac{60{,}361}{112{,}352} = 54\%$$

$$\frac{56{,}389}{116{,}295} = 46\%$$

Source: International Monetary Fund, *Direction of Trade, 1966–70*; European Free Trade Association, *EFTA Reporter, 1970*.

42. In 1958, the first year of the Common Market, intra-Community trade accounted for 30 percent of the total imports and almost 30 percent of the total exports of the EEC countries. By 1970, intra-EEC trade accounted for 40 percent of total imports and 49 percent of total exports. As the following table shows, enlargement of the Six to Nine plus the expected associations will raise intra-EC exports to 54 percent of total exports, and intra-Community imports to approximately 46 percent of total imports.

43. For an indication of the increasing self-sufficiency of the European Communities, see note 20. Ronald McKinnon presents the economic arguments for two corresponding currency zones. Since in commodity trade the United States and EC each form within themselves distinct and highly integrated markets, not closely related to each other, a floating dollar-EC currency rate, which continually changed the price of externally imported goods would be preferable to a single transatlantic currency system of fixed rates. Changes in the transatlantic rate would not, McKinnon argues, significantly affect average domestic price levels in either the United States or the EC. But the high elasticity of response of the small foreign trade sector connecting the two areas would make changing exchange rates an efficient control device for maintaining equilibrium.

By contrast, McKinnon finds the present unitary system of fixed rates unsound. The small American trade sector with its small direct connection with Europe should not be allowed to influence overall American monetary and fiscal policy. In the American economy, the gains in the value of output from the restoration of full employment are much greater than the dollar value of the foreign trade sector, and even this sector need suffer only minor inconvenience from a floating rate. Since the United States and the EC are not highly integrated with each other, the two areas are likely to experience greater dissimilarities in prevailing inflationary or deflationary trends than are the highly integrated countries of the EC. In short, the two regional economies are not sufficiently integrated to justify the high costs, in domestic goals, of the attempt to maintain fixed exchange rates between them. Ronald McKinnon, "Optimum World Monetary Arrangements and the Dual Currency System," pp. 366–96. For the same point, stressing also its political and historical implications, see Cleveland, "How the Dollar Standard Died."

44. See, for example, Cooper, *Economics of Interdependence*, especially pp. 177–193.

45. Such is often the story of backward regions in all countries. People migrate or vegetate. The United States offers several classic illustrations of permanent regional depression. In the United States such inequalities may—as in Appalachia—be countered by the federal government's diverting trade and investment to the stricken area, but the flow is seldom adequate.

46. In theory, decentralization of our central banking system into twelve regional Federal Reserve banks permits varied policies suited to the particular needs and interests of a region, alongside nation-wide banking and credit policies. Changes in reserve requirements do apply to all members of the system equally, but open market operations and changes in the discount rate can vary according to regional financial conditions. In recent years, however, the high degree of integration of American commercial and financial markets and the increasing mobility of credit funds have tended toward uniform discount rates. For a detailed discussion, see: United States Board of Governors of the Federal Reserve System, *The Federal Reserve System: Purposes and Functions*, Washington, D.C., 1963.

47. Hints by the United States in the fall of 1971 that the 10 percent import surcharge might be lifted selectively—for countries that revalued—were seen as a crude American attempt to pry apart any European consensus, and as such provoked sharp European reactions. When Treasury Secretary John Connally announced that he was ready to consider a selective removal of the surcharge for Germany, because it had allowed the mark "to float upwards to a realistic new parity with the dollar," German Economics Minister Karl Schiller hotly denied German interest in any such bilateral deal. French Foreign Minister Maurice Schumann rather hopefully saw Connally's maneuver as only strengthening the Six's resolve to maintain a common front *(New York Times,* Oct. 19, 1971).

48. Ralf Dahrendorf, member of the EC Commission in charge of foreign trade, has publicly criticized the official American position which looks to trade to correct our balance of payments. The United States deficit, he observes, comes mainly from excessive military spending abroad, particularly in Vietnam, and the outflow of American capital to foreign shores. Similarly, he denies that American trade suffers from European protectionism and other discriminatory practices. Community imports from the United States, he notes, have risen from $6.3 billion in 1968 to $9 billion in 1970. The EC had a trade deficit with the United States of $2.4 billion for 1970; a $2.5 billion deficit was projected for 1971. See "U.S. Economic Measures Alarm EC," *European Community*, Sept. 1971, pp.12–14.

Chapter Six

1. See, for example, Dean G. Acheson. *Present at the Creation*, pp. 9–13.

2. See Note 42 p. 313.

3. The Kennedy Round cut the average *ad valorem* rate on American imports to an historic low of 8 percent. The remaining significant impediments to further liberalization are therefore not tariffs at all, but infinitely more troublesome "non-tariff barriers." For a description as well as possible negotiating techniques, see Committee on Economic Development, *Non-Tariff Distortions of Trade*; also, Malmgren, *Trade Wars or Trade Negotiations?*

4. Depending on the method of calculation, the American trade deficit for 1971 was the first since 1888—for a calendar year on the census basis—or since 1935—on the balance-of-payments basis. *Survey of Current Business*, March 1972, p. 38.

Unlike most other countries, the United States and Canada report their imports f.o.b. rather than c.i.f., thus understating the comparative total costs of our imports. To compensate, the IMF's world tables in its *Direction of Trade*, adjust American and Canadian import data upwards by 10 percent except for American imports from Canada and Mexico and Canadian imports from the United States. *Direction of Trade Annual 5, 1963–1967*. p.v.

Interestingly, by this IMF calculation, similar to that used by most other countries, the United States has had substantial trade deficits since 1968.

Year	Exports	Imports	Balance
1966	30,450	28,193	2,257
1967	31,634	29,586	2,048
1968	34,635	36,551	− 1,916
1969	37,988	39,672	− 1,684
1970	43,228	43,960	− 732

Source: IMF, *Direction of Trade Annual, 1966–1970*, p. 3.

5. A recent official State Department analysis summed up our trading problems thus: "The decline on our trading surplus was not general, but was due entirely to our trade with only three countries—

Canada, Germany and Japan. Our export surplus with all the other countries of the world in 1969 was $4.4 billion, virtually unchanged from 1965." Department of State, "United States Trade and Investment Policy in an Interdependent World," *Williams Report*, Papers I, p. 7. See also *Monetary* ch. note 11, 12 p. 284 and Table 6–1.

6. See, for example, Welch. "U.S.-Canada Automotive Trade Agreements," *Williams Report*, Papers II, 239–253.

7. See the Federal Reserve study by F. Gerard Adams and Helen B. Junz, "Effects of the Business Cycle on Trade Flows of the Industrialized Countries," *Journal of Finance*, May 1971. By their estimates, the incomes and price effects of inflation between 1963 and 1969 may have been responsible for excess imports into the United States of some $2 billion annually.

8. The Smithsonian settlement of 18 December 1971 constituted an effective overall devaluation of the dollar of about 10 percent. This, Washington officials estimated, would yield a balance-of-payments improvement of about $8 billion and an increase in American employment of about 750,000. The full effects of these adjustments, however, are not expected to show until after about two years. See *N.Y. Times*, 21 January 1972, p. 52. The overall actual devaluation effect may at times be even greater than 10 percent, as currencies fluctuate within their new broader bands. Morgan Guaranty Trust Co. calculated the trade-weighted average depreciation of the dollar from pre-May 1970 parties to have been as much as 11.4 percent on 9 March 1972. See *Journal of Commerce*, 20 April 1972. See also *Monetary Chapter*, Note 32, and Note 33.

9. See Houthakker and Magee, "Income and Price Elasticities in World Trade," *The Review of Economics and Statistics*, May 1969, pp. 111–125; also Houthakker, "The United States Balance of Payments—A Look Ahead," *Williams Report*, Papers I, pp. 31–50. See also Monetary Chapter Note 32.

10. The so-called Burke-Hartke Bill—the Foreign Trade and Investment Act of 1972 (S2592)—submitted to Congress in September 1971, called for a ceiling on imported goods in every category not exceeding the average annual quantity entering the United States during 1965–1969. In current dollar terms, this implied a 40 percent cutback from 3rd quarter 1971 levels. The Bill also proposed removing tax incentives for overseas investments and recommended

prohibiting the export of advanced technology where it could be shown that such exports would lead to a decline in domestic employment. For the Bill, see *Congressional Record*, September 28, 1971 (S15142), Vol. 117, No. 142.

11. See Krause, "The Balance of Payments of the United States and Other Countries: An Equilibrium View," *Williams Report*, Papers I, pp. 51–70.

12. Adjustment assistance programs, theoretically in effect since the passage of the Trade Expansion Act of 1962, offered government assistance to companies and employees displaced by the effects of Kennedy Round tariff cuts. For contending views, see Metzger, "Adjustment Assistance," *Williams Report*, Papers I, pp. 319–342, and Fooks, "Trade Adjustment Assistance," ibid., pp. 343–366.

13. Cf., however, Bergsten, "Crisis in United States Trade Policy," *Foreign Affairs*, July 1971, pp. 619–635, and Krause, "Trade Policy for the Seventies," *Columbia Journal of World Business*, Jan./Feb. 1971, pp. 5–14. Krause and Bergsten argue that since the declining traditional manufacturing industries are well organized, while new high-technology and service sectors are not, the protectionists have gained an influence which is out of proportion with their contribution to the national economy.

14. In the usage of some politicians and writers the concept of an "Atlantic Community" is often expanded to include Japan or even South Africa, Australia and New Zealand. The United Nations, more appropriately, refers to this group of countries as the world's "developed market economies." Occasionally, "Atlantic Community" is meant to comprise all the members of NATO or of the OECD. As used in this chapter, the "Atlantic Trading Community" comprises the developed market economies in Western Europe and North America, as indicated in the table below:

I. Developed Market Economies in North America
    (1) Canada
    (2) United States
II. Developed Market Economies in Western Europe
    A. Original EEC
        (3) Belgium
        (4) France
        (5) Federal Republic of Germany

   (6) Italy
   (7) Luxemburg
   (8) Netherlands
  B. Original EFTA
   (9) Austria
   (10) Denmark
   (11) Norway
   (12) Portugal
   (13) Sweden
   (14) Switzerland
   (15) United Kingdom
  C. Other Developed Market Economies in Western Europe
   (16) Finland
   (17) Iceland*
   (18) Ireland
   (19) Greece
   (20) Spain
   (21) Turkey
   (22) Yugoslavia

  * (Iceland joined EFTA in 1970 as a full member.)

Both sets of figures also include minor sums for the overseas departments of member states and other overseas territories associated with the EEC.

15. If Japan is included, this "Atlantic" trading community's share of free world exports rose from 63.0 percent to 77.5 percent over the same period, while its share of free world imports increased from 63.3 percent to 77.3 percent (See Tables 6–2 and 6–3).

16. With the inclusion of Japan, the figures would be 62.4 percent and 74.0 percent respectively (see Table 6–4).

17. For a general discussion of the political issues surrounding Britain's bid for entry into the Common Market, see Cleveland, *The Atlantic Idea and its European Rivals*, pp. 124–170; and Calleo, *Britain's Future*, pp. 66–91. For a fuller description of the earlier years, see Camps, *Britain and the European Community*, passim.

18. Although the United States enjoyed a substantial trade surplus with the EEC countries—some $1.17 billion in 1963 by American calculations—both the Common External Tariff and the prospective Common Agricultural Policy made the future uncertain. Since the United States enjoyed a surplus going into the negotia-

tions, "the neutral assumption," according to Treasury Secretary Dillon, "would be that exports and imports would rise by the same percentage. As a result, the American trade surplus would become larger." Cited in Preeg, *Traders and Diplomats*, p. 51. Others disagreed; see Patterson, *Discrimination in International Trade*, pp. 176–177. Kennedy's statement about trade liberalization aiding the American payments balance did not represent the government's real expectations, it is said, but was designed to encourage Congressional support.

19. See Chapter 4.

20. Under the general provisions of the Trade Expansion Act, American negotiators were allowed to offer 50 percent across-the-board tariff cuts. For goods where the United States and the EEC together accounted for 80 percent of free world trade, however, the "dominant supplier" authority permitted reductions to zero. Without British membership in the EEC, the offer was insignificant. See Patterson, *Discrimination in International Trade*, p. 227n.

21. Preeg, *Traders and Diplomats*, p. 95.

22. As a case in point, American negotiations in the Kennedy Round agreed to abolish the American Selling Price system of valuation, which adjusts the duty on some imports—chiefly benzenoid chemicals—to eliminate any price differential between comparable foreign and American products. Congress refused to act, thereby invalidating concessions on imports valued at $325 million annually. For a brief discussion, see Dam, *The GATT: Law and International Organization*, pp. 189–192.

23. While liberalization proceeded according to schedule, the adjustment assistance meant to mollify displaced industries was rarely available. See Metzger, "Adjustment Assistance," *Williams Report*, Papers I, pp. 319–342.

24. John F. Kennedy, "Special Message to the Congress on Foreign Trade Policy," 25 January 1962.

25. Preeg, *Traders and Diplomats*, p. 82.

26. The elements of the struggle were complex. The German government was unenthusiastic over any Common Agricultural Policy, a view shared by the British and Americans in the wings. The Commission, counting on France's eagerness for an agricultural settle-

ment, sought to tie the settlement to institutional changes giving over Community finances to itself and the European Parliament. Various governments supported the proposal for various reasons. France, however, not only rejected the Commission's proposal, but made clear it would not accept decisions reached in the Council by weighted majorities—an arrangement scheduled to begin on 1 January 1966. Despite mounting pressures from French agricultural groups and Centrist parties, the Gaullist government held out. As it appeared that no agreement would be reached, the French, starting in July 1965, ceased participating in the Council meetings and withdrew their permanent representatives from Brussels. Buttressed by his electoral success in December, de Gaulle sent Couve de Murville back to Luxemburg in mid-January with orders to insist on a veto and a timetable for agreement on various key issues. At the second Luxemburg meeting of 28–29 January 1966, the Six agreed to disagree on the issue of majority voting. In effect, the French had their way, at least for the time. The Commission's powers were curbed—clearly not only on French insistance—and within six months the main outlines of the CAP were established. Partisans of supranationalism hoped enough of an institutional nucleus remained for a supranational renewal whenever France's Gaullist regime came to an end.

For France's internal politics, see Williams, *French Politicians and Elections, 1951–1969*, pp. 177–203; for an account of farm pressure on de Gaulle, see Muth, *French Agriculture and the Political Integration of Western Europe;* for the compromise reached at the meeting of 28–29 January 1966, see Commission of the EEC, *Ninth General Report on the Activities of the Community: 1 April 1965–31 March 1966* (Brussels, 1966), Chapter 1; for an account of the crisis, see Camps, *European Unification*, and Couve de Murville, *Une Politique Étrangère*, Chapter 8, especially pp. 329–339.

27. Economists list four sets of "distortions" which commonly interfere with the market's capacity to achieve absolute economic efficiency. First, monopolistic or monopsonistic conditions within the economy may prevent perfect competition within a national market. (Not only can a monopoly producer influence supply and demand within the national market as a whole, but transport costs, imperfect knowledge, or small real or imagined differences between products may cause the fragmentation of the large national market

into several regional markets in which regional monopolies or monopsonies can use their power to distort prices and to prevent competitive market forces from equalizing marginal costs and values.) Secondly, external economies and diseconomies may exist, in which case the differences between marginal social and marginal private costs and values may make it more—or less—beneficial for a particular producer to employ additional productive capacity than it would be for society as a whole. Thirdly, governments and other institutions may intervene to prevent market forces from operating beyond certain limits. And finally, subsidies and taxes may affect prices and cause divergences between marginal social costs and values. See Meade, *Theory of International Economic Policy*, Vol. II, pp. 10–26.

Most economists, nevertheless, have tended to assume that even with some particular conditions not optimally satisfied, it is desirable to fulfill other marginal conditions. Since the mid-1950s, however, the so-called "second-best theorem" criticizes this assumption and justifies, instead, forgoing the absolute satisfaction of particular conditions and focusing on moving the economy as a whole as close as possible to the absolute optimum. See Meade, *Theory*, pp. 102ff.; and Nath, *Reappraisal of Welfare Economies*, pp. 48–55.

28. If unlimited substitutability between the two factors of production is assumed, the production possibility curve could be drawn as a straight line. In this case, the costs of producing either good would not change as a result of any change in the proportionate allocation of productive factors to their production. By the same token, of course, the main reason and incentive for specialization would be absent.

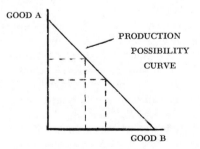

GOOD A

PRODUCTION
POSSIBILITY
CURVE

GOOD B

29. A consumption indifference curve is actually only one curve in

an infinite schedule of such curves, each of which corresponds to a different level of total consumption. A consumer would prefer any position on a higher indifference curve over a position on a lower one, but is presumed to be indifferent as to various positions on one particular curve.

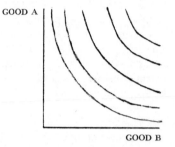

30. As economists point out, moving from an individual to a collective consumption indifference curve requires the generous assumption that everyone's "marginal subjective rate of substitution" is the same. The obvious logical and practical objections to such an assumption generally give way before its convenience.

31. This point is frequently referred to as the "overall Paretian optimum," defined as the point where the marginal rate of technical transformation between the two goods equals the community's marginal rate of subjective substitution. For a detailed discussion of the Paretian optimum and its assumptions, see Nath, *Reappraisal of Welfare Economics*, pp. 8–43.

32. As the optimization of trade within the national economy is one of the four marginal conditions for the achievement of utopian efficiency in the national economy, so international free trade is an additional marginal condition for the attainment of utopian world efficiency. It has been pointed out, however, that three basic arguments can be made against the complete freeing of international trade, and these constitute the so-called "second-best arguments for trade control." First, if any other marginal conditions for utopian efficiency are not satisfied in the trading countries, the freeing of trade may not increase, but actually decrease, efficiency in the world. Secondly, intervention in international trade may be needed in order to improve the world's economic structure. And thirdly, trade intervention may be desirable for reasons of economic equity.

See, Meade, *Theory of International Economic Policy*, Vol. 2, pp. 140ff.

33. See Galbraith, *New Industrial State*, pp. 221–34 and passim.

34. To one dedicated free-trader, Irving Kravis, the economic case against protection is "simple and irrefutable":

> The gain from our trade with the rest of the world consists not of the things we export, but of the things we import. We are not made better off by giving up goods; we are made better off by receiving them. Public policies that limit our ability to obtain goods from abroad freely and cheaply reduce the real income of the nation. Of course, restriction of imports may help particular groups in the economy, just as any restriction of supply may. . . . Why not then spread these beneficial effects to everybody? . . . The answer is, of course, that every one of these restrictions benefits the individuals concerned at the expense of the rest of the people. . . . Every current claim for protection, no matter what its guise, is a claim for special preference at the general expense.

———Irving Kravis, "The Current Case for Import Limitations," *Williams Report*, Papers I, pp. 141–142.

35. Industrial Imports from OECD Countries
Subject to Quantitative Restrictions:

Country Imposing Restrictions	1963	1970	Additional Restrictions Applied to Imports of Japanese Industrial Goods
Canada	2	7	8
United Kingdom	10	28	21
United States	7	67	1
EEC	76	65	73
Japan	132	81	—

The comparisons are in terms of the Brussels Tariff Nomenclature categories subject to restrictions. They do not account for (1) the varying importance of the products in international trade, (2) the degree of restrictiveness of the particular quotas applied, and (3) various other impediments. *Williams Report*, Compendium p. 373, Chart 36.

36. With increasing product differentiation and the growing importance of technology in the production process, specialization in

broad industrial sectors ("inter-industry specialization") in response to comparative advantages becomes less necessary and less practical. However, these same forces, product differentiation and technological innovation, vastly improve the possibilities for so-called "intra-industry specialization," i.e., the specialization on particular products *within* broad product groups. See, for example, Robert Hettlage, *Die Veränderungen in den Handelsbilanzen der EWG-Länder zwischen 1958 und 1967* (Munich, 1969), pp. 315–338.

In an investigation of the European Coal and Steel Community between 1952 and 1966, Michael Adler found no indications of inter-industry specialization—as the traditional theory of customs unions would have it. Instead, there was a marked increase in intra-industry trade based at least partly on a clear, though less distinct, increase in intra-industry specialization. Based on his findings, Adler discounts the significance of comparative advantage *per se* and attributes the tendency toward intra-industry trade and specialization mainly to technological differences and innovations. Michael Adler, "Specialization in the European Coal and Steel Community," in *Journal of Common Market Studies*, Vol. VIII, No. 3, March 1970, pp. 197–191. See also, E. A. G. Robinson, ed., *Economic Consequences of the Size of Nations*, pp. 415–438.

37. See Staffan Burenstam Linder, *An Essay on Trade and Transformation*, New York, 1961.

38. Tibor Scitovsky distinguishes "economic efficiency" from "technological efficiency." The market size needed for economic efficiency, which he defines as production according to the community's wishes, may be larger, he says, than the size needed for mere technological efficiency, which he defines as the greatest possible output with the smallest possible input. In other words, a smaller market, of say 50 million consumers, may be large enough for specialization to take place, but a market of perhaps 100 million, may be needed to introduce sufficient competition to induce firms to operate in an "economically efficient" manner. The argument implies that size, or free trade, induces a competition that responds to the community's wishes. The behavior of the American automobile industry, forced to produce smaller cars only in the face of foreign competition, seems a supporting illustration. Scitovsky's distinction points to a potentially serious deficiency in a closed market system, possibly to be remedied by enlightened state intervention or the proliferation of "public interest" advocates like Ralph Nader. See Scitovsky,

Welfare and Competition, pp. 148–188, 373–450.

39. See, Jean Jacques Rousseau. *The Social Contract.* Book I, Ch. VII. For a provocative essay dealing, in part, with the role of commerce in Rousseau's ideal state, see, Stanley Hoffman, "Rousseau on War and Peace," in Hoffman, *The State of War,* pp. 54–87.

40. Edmund Burke, *Works,* Boston, 1865, Vol. III, p. 359.

41. For a good, nontechnical survey of the various issues, see, Kindleberger, *Foreign Trade and the National Economy.*

42. The "virtuous circle" argument is developed in Andrew Shonfield, *Modern Capitalism,* pp. 19–38. The argument is usually developed by demonstrating the relationship between the growth of national product and the growth of imports. Thus, for example, from 1960 to 1970, the American GNP grew 94 percent (in current dollars), spurring a growth of imports of goods and services of 153 percent. During periods of rapid GNP growth, however, rapid export growth is more problematical. Where rapid GNP growth feeds inflation, exports become less competitive. Where it strains an economy's capacity for meeting domestic demand, fewer products are available for export.

Chapter Seven

1. Ricardo. *Principles of Poltical Economy*, pp. 81–83.

2. Hobsbawm notes that nineteenth-century Britain never ran an export surplus in goods, despite her industrial pre-eminence, export orientation and modest domestic consumer market. Hobsbawm, *Industry and Empire*, pp. 110–126. See also Cairncross, *Home and Foreign Investment*, p. 180 (table 40).

3. The analogy is not exact. Until 1971 (or 1968 by IMF statistics) America ran a surplus on merchandise trade. Still, as the surplus has disappeared, earnings on foreign investments have been increasingly important to our balance of payments, and are expected by many to become more so. See Krause, "The Balance of Payments of the United States," *Williams Report*, Papers I, pp. 51–70.
Interestingly, the American ratio of foreign investments to GNP has not changed much since before World War I. In 1914, as in 1970, foreign investments represented approximately 7 percent of our GNP. See Wilkins, *Emergence of Multinational Enterprise*. Gross comparisons, of course, miss critical differences in the composition, location, or overall economic and political significance of foreign investments.

4. *Survey of Current Business,* October 1971, pp. 28–29, Table 3, and *Fortune,* December 1971, p. 54.

5. Judd Polk, cited in *Fortune,* December 1971, p. 57. Polk uses as a rule of thumb a ratio of 2:1 between the value of American production abroad and the book value of its foreign investments at the end of the preceding year. His formula yields an estimate of $140 billion for output of foreign affiliates of the United States in 1970, as compared to American merchandise exported (adjusted to the balance-of-payments basis and excluding military grants and transfers under military sales contracts) of $41,980 million for the same year. Even with allowances for trade among American corporations, United States foreign-based production was still over three times greater than United States exports. See Polk, *United States Production Abroad;* also Sidney Rolfe: "The International Corporation in Perspective," Conference Working Paper No. 1, The Atlantic Council of the United States, February 1969, mimeographed, p. 4.

6. Foreign Operations of U.S. Corporations

	FOREIGN OPERATIONS AS A % OF	
	Sales	*Earnings*
American Smelting Refining	65	73
American Standard	36	33
Bausch and Lomb	23	35
Boeing	35	40
Burroughs	35	45
Colgate Palmolive	55	55
CPC International	50	51
Dow Chemical	44	44
Ferro	46	62
Firestone Tire and Rubber	30	35
W. R. Grace	30	39
H. J. Heinz	44	44
Hoover	59	35
I.B.M.	39	48
International Flavors and Fragrances	59	54
I.T.T.	40	35
McDonnel Douglas	40	40
Otis Elevators	53	35
Perkin-Elmer	32	39
Pfizer	45	55
Proctor and Gamble	25	25
Sperry Rand	34	45
Squibb	27	63
Sterling Drug	37	37
Sybion	27	46
Technicon	31	76
Timkin	30	35
Uniroyal	27	75
Upjohn	33	55
F. W. Woolworth	26	61

Source: Standard and Poor's *Outlook,* as quoted in *Newsweek,* January 3, 1972, p. 40.

7. Experts differ over whether American or European corporations are more international and why. For contrasting views, compare Hellmann, *Challenge to U.S. Dominance,* with Rolfe, *The International Corporation,* p. 24; and "The International Corporation in Perspective," in The Atlantic Council, *The Multinational Corporation in the World Economy,* pp. 17–20. In 1964, Rolfe found an equal or greater number of European companies with a significant

foreign content. Six Hundred and Twenty European and only Five Hundred and Nineteen American companies owned between six and nineteen foreign subsidiaries and eighty European and eighty-six American firms owned twenty or more, according to the *Yearbook of International Organization,* 12th edition, 1969. But in 1967, Raymond Vernon classified only thirty European but some two hundred American companies as multinational. (Vernon, "Multinational Enterprise and National Sovereignty," *Harvard Business Review,* March/April 1967.) In 1971, the Office of Business Economics of the Department of Commerce estimated that about 3,400 American companies have foreign affiliates. (*Survey of Current Business,* August 1971, p. 14.) Problems of definition, of course, are critical and complex. For the O.B.E. definition of American investments abroad see Office of Business Economics, *U.S. Direct Investments Abroad 1966, Part I,* pp. 1–5.

8. *Survey of Current Business,* October 1971, pp. 28–29, Table 3.

9. Over the five years 1966–1970, of the $51.2 billion total investments in plant and equipment by foreign affiliates of American companies, $25.2 billion (49.2 percent) went to manufactures; $16.2 billion (31.6 percent) to petroleum (including tankers); and $5.2 billion (10.2 percent) to mining and smelting. For 1971 and 1972 the projected percentages are 46.7 percent in manufacturing, 30.2 percent in petroleum, and 12.7 percent in mining and smelting. (*Survey of Current Business,* Sept. 1971, p. 28.)

10. Even as the United States government moved to discourage capital outflows for overseas direct investments during the 1960's, in particular through the use of "voluntary" and then "mandatory" restrictions, other special inducements, including tax concessions and investment insurance, continued to favor overseas investing. On government restrictions, see Chapter 5, Note 27.

11. At the end of 1950, total book value of American direct investments in the six future EEC members was $637 million—5.4 percent of American direct investments abroad. By the end of 1957, the last pre-Common Market year, the percentage was only 6.6 percent. But by 1965, it was 12.7 percent and by 1970, 14.9 percent.

12. According to its early promoters, the Common Market, by greatly stimulating general economic growth, would also expand trade more than enough to offset any diversionary effects of a new

tariff differential. For corporate planners, however, the diversion was certain while the expansion was hopeful. And whatever their original spirit, the Communities, once established, might later turn protectionist.

13. The Kennedy Administration's Grand Design seemed influenced by such a view of American corporate motivation. As Kennedy stated to Congress: "if we can lower the external tariff wall of the Common Market through negotiation our manufacturers will be under less pressure to locate their plants behind that wall in order to sell in the European market, thus reducing the export of capital funds to Europe." John F. Kennedy, "Special Message to Congress on Foreign Trade Policy," Jan. 25, 1962.

14. Polk et al, *U.S. Production Abroad,* pp. 59–61, 133–135.

15. For further discussion of the motives of United States industrialists in Europe, see Layton, *Transatlantic Investments,* pp. 19–24; Kindleberger, *The International Corporation;* Rolfe, *The International Corporation,* pp. 61ff; Polk, *U.S. Production Abroad,* pp. 41–76; Aharoni, *The Foreign Investment Decision Process;* Cooper, *The Economics of Interdependence,* pp. 88–91; Balekjian, *Legal Aspects of Foreign Investment in the European Economic Communities,* pp. 304–308.

16. As Judd Polk observes: "The probing of company motivation produced little to suggest that a differential profit rate is sufficient to induce a company to establish producing facilities abroad, and even less to suggest that a committed company would, because of a decline or the disappearance of this differential, discontinue the investment support required for the maintenance of its market position. Even a continuing decline in total earnings in a market may provoke rather than discourage further investment depending on the company's opinion of what is required to safeguard its longer-range financial interests." Polk et al., *U.S. Production Abroad,* p. 61.

17. See, for example, Dunning and Rowan, "Inter-firm Efficiency Comparisons: U.S. and U.K. Manufacturing Enterprises in Britain," in Dunning, *Studies in International Investment,* pp. 345–400. But, as Dunning observes elsewhere in the same work: "because of the increasing volume of intra-group transactions of multinational enterprise the profitability measure of performance for any part of

an international organization is becoming more and more suspect,"
p. 262, note 1.

18. Rolfe, *International Corporation*, pp. 49–50. Zbigniew Brzezinski notes that although Western Europe registers annually slightly
more patents than the United States, the industrial application of
patents is roughly eight times higher in the United States. Brzezinski, *Between Two Ages*. pp. 27–28.

19. These "product cycle" theories to explain the migration of cor-
porate activity are explored in Hirsch, *Location of Industry and
International Competitiveness*. For an interesting application see,
Abbegglen, "Dynamics of Japanese Competition," *Williams Report*,
Papers II, pp. 153–181.

20. For a good general analysis of international corporate investment from Marxist perspectives see Magdoff, *The Age of Imperialism*.

21. J. A. Hobson early developed the idea that income redistribution could solve the over-saving/under-consumption "crisis" of
capitalism and thereby render imperialism unnecessary: "There is
no necessity to open up new foreign markets; the home markets
are capable of indefinite expansion. Whatever is produced in
England can be consumed in England provided that the 'income,'
or power to demand commodities, is properly distributed." Hobson,
Imperialism, pp. 88–89.

22. The classic statement is Lenin's *Imperialism: The Highest
Stage of Capitalism*. Interestingly, Karl Kautsky, Lenin's rival
theorist, argued that international finance might not lead to perpetual confrontations among the imperialist powers, but mutual
accommodation: "the joint exploitation of the world by internationally united finance capital in place of mutual rivalries of national
finance capital . . . is at any rate conceivable." Kautsky in Lichtheim,
Imperialism, pp. 105–106.

23. For a discussion of the economic role of militarism see Kolko,
Roots of American Foreign Policy. Kolko argues: "The relationship
between the objectives of foreign economic policy and direct political and military intervention . . . has been a continuous and intimate
one—indeed, very often identical." (p. 81).

24. See especially, Galbraith, *New Industrial State*. Of course Galbraith is only one of the more recent analysts of the role of the

corporation in the American political economy. Earlier members of this school ranged from Theodore Roosevelt, Herbert Croly and Thorstein Veblen at the turn of the century, through Herbert Hoover and the New Deal reformers of the 1930's. See especially, Adolph Berle and Gardiner C. Means, *The Modern Corporation and Private Property* (1934). For further discussion of their ideas, see Williams, *Contours;* and Gilbert, *Designing the Industrial State.*

25. This tendency is no doubt intensified when the home government has a free trade and anti-trust mentality. Where free trade brings international competition to the domestic market, corporations can guard their profits by going international themselves, thus both escaping exclusive dependence on one national environment and challenging foreign rivals in their own domestic markets. Companies may also seek to circumvent domestic antitrust policies by gaining strength from growth abroad to face their competition at home.

26. Repatriated Income of United States Direct Investment Abroad (billions of dollars)

	1970	1971
Direct investment fees and royalties	$1,880	$2,041
Direct investment interest, dividends, and branch earnings	6,026	7,256
Total repatriated income from direct investment abroad	$7,906	$9,297

Source: *Survey of Current Business,* March 1972, p. 44, Table 2.

27. See Rolfe, *The International Corporation,* pp. 77ff; and Barber, *The American Corporation,* pp. 279ff.

28. On occasion, United States jurisdiction has been extended, under the so-called "effects" doctrine, to cover the non-United States activities of foreign-owned corporations or cartels seeking a share of the American market. See Rolfe, *International Corporation,* pp. 78–84.

29. See Hymer and Rowthorn, "Multinational Corporations and International Oligopoly," and Vernon, "Future of the Multinational Enterprise," in Kindleberger, ed., *The International Corporation.*

30. Counter-arguments hold that without American investments abroad, United States corporations would not so much increase

their exports from the United States as lose much of the foreign market to foreign competition. Foreign investment by the United States preempts investments by foreigners. The preemption argument, based on conditional analysis, is difficult to prove or disprove, at least as long as the large outflow of American capital, technology and entrepreneurial skill continues.

More recent arguments to counter the highly protectionist Burke-Hartke Bill (See *Trade* Chapter, note 10 p. 304), maintain that multinational corporate activity enhances rather than inhibits American exports and employment. See, for example, Department of Commerce, *Policy Aspects of Foreign Investment by U.S. Multinational Corporations*, Jan. 1972; also Department of Commerce, *U.S. Multinational Enterprises and the U.S. Economy*, Jan. 1972. The latter summarizes a report prepared for the Department of Commerce at the Harvard Business School.

For a brief critique of these arguments see Stanley H. Ruttenberg, "Trade Data, Conclusions May Differ," *Washington Post*, March 26, 1972. For a discussion of these issues in Britain, see Reddaway. *Effects of U.K. Direct Investment Overseas: Final Report.*

31. For a skeptical view of whether size and diversity contribute to corporate efficiency, see Bernard Nossiter's review of Galbraith's *New Industrial State, Washington Post*, Nov. 2, 1971.

32. Britain faced a corresponding dilemma in the early nineteenth century over whether to export only the final products or also the "technology," i.e., machines and machine tools as well. The prevailing view emphasized Britain's unique strength and invulnerability to foreign competition. As one report to the Board of Trade concluded: "These circumstances (of Britain's uniqueness) when taken together, give such a decided superiority to our people, that no injurious rivalry either in the construction of machinery or the manufacture of commodities can be expected." *Report on Machinery*, submitted to the Board of Trade, London, 1825, as quoted in Clairmonte, *Economic Liberalism and Underdevelopment*, p. 17. See also the *Reddaway Report*, Note 36; and Cairncross, *Home and Foreign Investment*, pp. 232–234.

33. If the United States sloughs off its old industries, what will replace them? The "old" industries now appear to include automobiles, steel, television, etc. Experts argue that technology is a function of 1) the size and wealth of a consumer market, and

2) the concentration of capital and scientific entrepreneurial talent. Optimistic protagonists of the theory see the United States as pre-eminent in these characteristics and hence as the economy most likely to develop and exploit the major technological breakthroughs of the future. See Brzezinski, *Between Two Ages*, pp. 24–35.

34. See Lawrence Lessing, "Why the United States Lags in Technology," *Fortune*, April 1972, pp. 69ff. Despite some $27 billion per year spent on Research and Development, Lessing observes, the United States has developed no new technology of major industrial importance in recent years.

35. Galbraith, *Affluent Society*. See especially, Chapter 18, "The Theory of Social Balance."

36.

U.S. Gross Private Saving
(in billions of dollars)

	1967	1968	1969	1970
Personal Savings	40.4	39.8	37.9	54.1
Business Savings	93.0	95.4	95.6	99.3

Source: *Survey of Current Business*, July 1971, p. 33, Table 5.1.

37. See OECD, *Gaps in Technology*, pp. 19–20.

38. As quoted in Servan-Schreiber, *American Challenge*, pp. 16–17.

39. See Balassa, "Whither French Planning?" and Cohen, *Modern Capitalist Planning: The French Model*, pp. 176–187.

40. The EC Commission, by contrast, has been trying to promote "European" corporations. See, for example, Commission of the European Communities, *Proposed Statute for the European Company*. The Preamble states: ". . . the only solution capable of effecting both economic and legal unity of the European undertaking is . . . to permit the formation, side by side with companies governed by one or another national law, of companies subject only to a specific legal system that is directly applicable to all member states, thereby freeing this form of company from any legal tie to this or that particular country" (p. 7). Such a European company would be termed "S.E." (Societas Europa) rather than "S.A." (Societé Anonyme) and would fall under the judicial control of the EC's Court of Justice.

41. The notion of a "European Company" so fits the theoretical models of integrationist scholars that many perhaps incline to overemphasize its significance. In any event, although some direct investment among European countries has occurred, most "European" companies in this transnational sense are American. Thus total direct investment among Community members in 1965–1968 was some $1.7 billion, much of it in sales and warehouse facilities, compared to a direct investment inflow from third countries—mainly the United States—of about $5 billion.

By contrast, national mergers, often with government blessing and capital, especially in France and Britain, have achieved striking consolidation of firms on a national scale. But governments have not generally encouraged transnational mergers. Endorsements in principle are frequently followed by interference in practice. For further discussion, see Friedrich, *Europe*, pp. 47–68; Tugendhat, *The Multinationals*, pp. 57–92; Manser, "U.K. and the EEC: The Prospects for Finance," p. 48; and Siekman, "Europe's Love Affair with Bigness," *Fortune*, March 1970, pp. 95ff.

Whether the present pattern will persist is uncertain. A common view sees transnational mergers as primarily a function of size. Thus the larger national units emerging in Europe are expected both to go international and to merge among themselves across national boundaries (Manser, pp. 48–49). Many prominent Europeans seem persuaded by this logic. (See Milo Feranti, "Electrical Machinery Firms Urged to Push for Multinational Integration," *Journal of Commerce*, April 12, 1972). The issue is complex and not always well defined. Many European national firms, of course, already have large international investments. But only a few, like Unilever, are multinational in their ownership and control. It is conceivable that European national firms will make large direct investments in distribution facilities within other states of the Communities, but will nevertheless remain essentially national and not "European" in their ownership and control. A certain growing skepticism about the advantages of big corporations may also, in time, dampen the enthusiasm for even national mergers.

42. For the degree of involvement of European states in local enterprise see Allen and MacLennon, *Regional Problems and Poli-*

cies in Italy and France; McArthur and Scott, *Industrial Planning in France;* and Pryke, *Public Enterprise in Practice.*

43. President Theodore Roosevelt and his intellectual adviser, Herbert Croly, were notable exceptions to the laissez-faire tradition. Candidly aware of the "real and grave evils" of the corporation system, and of the "arrogant stupidity" of some of its leaders, Roosevelt sought to supervise and control the giant corporations in the interests of public welfare. For a discussion of Roosevelt's trust-busting activities, see Williams, *Contours,* especially pp. 390–412.

44. See Polanyi, *The Great Transformation,* especially pp. 66–76.

45. Kindleberger, *American Business Abroad,* p. 207.

46. For a clear statement of this viewpoint, see Ball, "Cosmocorp," pp. 163–170.

47. Gene E. Bradley, ed. *American-European Market,* p. xiv.

48. Bradley, *American-European Market,* p. viii.

49. For a critical view of corporate internationalism, its philosophical and cultural as well as economic roots, see Gilpin, "The Politics of Transnational Economic Relations, pp. 398–419.

50. Judd Polk, "New World Economy," p. 9.

51. In Bradley, *American-European Market,* pp. xv–xvi.

52. For a critique of the "collective obsession" with scientific discovery and technological invention which has "misdirected man's energies" since the sixteenth century, see Mumford, *Pentagon of Power.*

Chapter Eight

1. During the 70 years preceding World War II, Japan's economy grew some 3–5 percent annually. (OECD, *Economic Survey, Japan,* Paris, 1964, p. 4). In the War, some 30 percent of Japan's industrial capacity, 80 percent of her shipping and 30 percent of her thermal power capacity were destroyed. From 1946 to 1953, GNP grew at 10.9 percent annually, and 9.4 percent for 1953–1962. During the sixties, growth continued to accelerate, averaging 11.1 percent for 1963–1968, and peaking at an extraordinary 14.3 percent for 1968 itself. By mid-1970, however, Japan entered into a "recession." (OECD, *Economic Survey, Japan,* Paris June 1971). From a level of 12 percent in 1970, GNP growth fell to a mere 5.9 percent in 1971. (*Japan Economic Journal,* March 28, 1972).

2. See Kahn, *Japanese Superstate,* pp. 100–103.

3. The *New Long Range Economic Plan of Japan, 1961–1970,* aimed at doubling real national income (from its 1960 level) by 1970. The goal was exceeded by 1966.

National Income
(Billions of Yen)

1960	11,474
1970	56,460

Source: United Nations, Monthly Bulletin of Statistics, New York, January 1972, p. 185.

The succeeding plan, although dated by the "recession" and yen revaluation, projected a yearly growth rate of 10.6 percent through 1975. See Economic Planning Agency, Government of Japan, *New Economic and Social Development Plan,* May 1970, p. 102 (Table 3).

4. Kahn, *Japanese Superstate,* p. 2, Cf, however, Henry Rosovsky, "The Economic Position of Japan," *Williams Report,* Papers II, pp. 111–128.

5. For a broad Asian view of World War II, see Iriye, *Across the*

Pacific, pp. 111ff. Compare with Hull's view, *Memoirs,* Vol. II, pp. 1000–1105.

6. For Hull, the Co-prosperity Sphere posed an "impossible situation" for other nations interested in the region: "It meant that they would be frozen out of the Pacific area and could not enter it except under such arbitrary terms and exactions as Japan might impose," *Memoirs,* Vol. I, p. 282.

7. Thus, an "unknown" cabinet member is quoted as saying: "The Japanese are still fighting the war, only now instead of a shooting war, it is an economic war. Their immediate intention is to try to dominate the Pacific and then perhaps the world" *Time,* May 10, 1971, as quoted in Brzezinski, *Fragile Blossom,* p. 69.

8. *Report on Japanese Reparations to the President of the United States,* Washington, D.C., November 1945–April 1946, pp. 6–7, as cited in Cohen, *Japan's Economy in War,* p. 420.

9. *New Year's Message to the Japanese People,* January 1, 1948, as cited in Cohen, *Japan's Economy in War,* p. 427.

10. Supreme Command Allied Powers (SCAP) *Official Statement,* January 31, 1947, as cited in Cohen, *Japan's Economy in War,* p. 432n.

11. The "Draper Report," which recommended restoring Japan to its 1930–1934 standard of living, providing the official American endorsement for Japanese economic recovery. *Report on the Economic Position and Prospects of Japan and Korea and the Measures Required to Improve Them,* Washington, D.C., April 26, 1948. The Dodge Stabilization Plan, initiated in 1949, curtailed inflation and left Japan with a strong currency. Finally, massive United States expenditures related to the Korean War—some $315 million for 1950–1951, provided the necessary demand to set Japan on its way to recovery. See Cohen, *Japan's Postwar Economy,* pp. 85–91.

12. *Melbourne Age,* February 25, 1948, as cited in Cohen, *Japan's Economy in War,* p. 496.

The ANZUS (Australia, New Zealand, United States) Treaty of September 1951 was seen widely as a move to assuage Australia's fears and gain her signature on the Japanese Peace Treaty. Britain was excluded both from the deliberations and the ANZUS

Treaty itself—a slight widely noted at the time. See Grattan, *United States and the Southwest Pacific*, pp. 217–222; also Starke, *The ANZUS Treaty Alliance*, especially Chapter 4.

13. See *N.Y. Times*, June 17, 1949, p. 17; November 7, 1950, p. 10. British-led opposition kept the Japanese question off the GATT agenda.

14. The trade embargo against Communist China, in fact, antedated the Battle Act by six months, in compliance with a United Nations resolution of May 18, 1951. Even earlier, however, strong American pressure had been building up to force Britain and the Sterling Area to terminate their China trade. See *N. Y. Times*, May 4, 1951, p. 6. The sanctions clause of the Battle Act, like the later "Hickenlooper Amendment" designed to cut off aid to unruly developing countries, proved difficult to invoke. See "President's Letter to Congress Reporting the Continuance of Aid to the United Kingdom, France, and Italy," in *Mutual Assistance Defense Control Act of 1951 (The Battle Act), Problems of Economic Defense*, Second Report to Congress, Washington, D.C., January 1953, pp. 75–86. For a critical review of United States economic warfare during the Cold War, see Adler-Karlsson, *Western Economic Warfare*.

15. *Economist*, July 21, 1951, p. 145.

16. See *The Times*, July 14 and 15, 1951. Article 12 of her peace treaty committed Japan to extend reciprocal most-favored-nation trading privileges for four years afterwards. In March 1951, an uneasy British Government, through Harold Wilson, then President of the Board of Trade, announced that Britain, presently extending MFN privileges to Japan, was not bound on principle to continue (*The Times*, March 19, 1951). Revival of trade between Japan and China would have greatly assuaged British commercial fears. Britain, in fact, agreed to the American draft of the peace treaty on the assumption that Japan would be free to recognize either of the two Chinas. Subsequent publication of the "Yoshida letter," implying heavy American pressure all along to recognize Nationalist China, suggested duplicity. See Epstein, *Britain—Uneasy Ally*, pp. 227–229.

17. For a discussion of the Anglo-Japanese Payments Union see *Economist*, September 8, 1951, pp. 577–579.

18. The United States even helped negotiate the Anglo-Japanese Payments Agreement, presumably believing that a more secure Britain would permit Japanese membership in the GATT. Britain, however, apparently feared that Japan's membership in the liberal GATT would undermine the discriminatory aspects of the payments agreement. The single best study of Japan's fight to win GATT membership, which draws on confidential GATT files, is Patterson, *Discrimination in International Trade*. For a British view, see James E. Meade, "Japan and the General Agreements of Tariffs and Trade," *Three Banks Review*, London, June 1957.

19. Japanese threats to deal with Russia and China lent urgency to the American plans. It was "absolutely mandatory to us, and to our safety," President Eisenhower declared in the spring of 1954, that the Japanese nation "did not fall under the domination of the Kremlin" (*N. Y. Times*, 22 February 1955). United States-Japanese trade negotiations, announced in February 1955, were part of a final campaign to gain Japanese membership in the GATT. To gain European cooperation, the United States proposed "triangular" trade concessions. If Europe would grant concessions to Japan, America would grant equivalent concessions to the Europeans, and be compensated by further concessions from the Japanese. By June 1955 American negotiators conceded the scheme's small success (*N. Y. Times*, 8 June 1955).

20. See Hunsberger, *Japan and the United States in World Trade*, pp. 21–24, 88–94.

21. Hunsberger, *Japan and the United States*, pp. 89ff.

22. For details on this complex subject, see Hunsberger, *Japan and the United States*, pp. 88–94, 127–140; OECD, *Liberalization of International Capital: Japan*; Chitoshi Yanaga, *Big Business in Japanese Politics*, New Haven, 1968. Nothing, perhaps, symbolizes so well the reassertion of Japanese control as the increase in power of the Ministry of International Trade and Industry (MITI), and the concurrent decline of the Occupation agency for enforcing anti-trust, the Fair Trade Commission. See Yanaga, *Big Business*, pp. 152–176. MITI, in coordination with the Ministry for Foreign Affairs, exercised power through "administrative guidance"—a euphemism for discretionary bureaucratic control. Together, Westeners argued, their practices minimized foreign access to the Japanese economy.

23. During three months in 1950, the *Economist* noted, Japan had exported nearly 200,000 dozen shirts to the United States at an average landed cost of only $1.19 per dozen; British f.o.b. export prices during the same three months averaged £7/13/4 per dozen. The difference was sufficiently fantastic not to be explained by lower quality or higher industrial efficiency (*Economist*, 4 November 1950, pp. 707–708).

While cheap labor explained much of Japan's general export advantage, the notorious "linkages" system, which gave Japanese exporters control over import permits, allowed an exporter to recover no more than his foreign exchange costs in his export price, and find his profits by selling his quota of import permits at a premium. With IMF pressure, the practice was formally discontinued in 1954. See S.J. Wells, *British Export Performance: A Comparative Study*, Cambridge (England), 1964, p. 95.

24. For the Japanese integration of economics with traditional non-economic values and structures, See Sansom, *Western World and Japan*, especially pp. 437–441.

25. See Waldo H. Heinrichs, Jr., *American Ambassador Joseph C. Grew and the Development of the United States' Diplomatic Tradition*, Boston, 1966, pp. 227–230.

26. For a typical view, see Lockwood, " 'The Socialist Society': India and Japan," p. 127.

27. The "Big Four" industrial organizations, acknowledged to play a determining role in politics, are The Federation of Economic Organizations (Keidanren), said to be the most powerful; the Federation of Employers' Associations, specializing in labor-management relations; the Japanese Chamber of Commerce and Industry; and the Japan Management Association, representing small and medium industries. See Yanaga, *Japanese People and Politics*, p. 96ff. For a detailed study of the pervasive business influence in the political system, see Yanaga, *Big Business and Politics*.

28. The high prestige of bureaucrats is generally acknowledged, although perhaps no longer to the extent suggested by the pre-World War I saying: "one is not a human being unless he is a government official." Still, it remains much more common for a high bureaucrat to become a businessman than vice versa, suggesting the greater prestige of the former. The move from bureauc-

racy to business is termed, "the descent from heaven." Yanaga, *Big Business in Japanese Politics,* p. 97, 108.

29. Kahn, *Japanese Superstate,* p. 88.

30. This system, while it is generally kind to those employed in the advanced, or, as they are sometimes known, the "rising sun" industries, can be brutally cruel to the "setting sun" industries—the small, labor-intensive firms responsible for much of Japan's export recovery during the 1950's. Abegglen, "Dynamics of Japanese Competition," *Williams Report,* Paper II.

31. See Yanaga, *Big Business.* For a detailed account of business reorganization in the post-occupation period see Iwao Hoshi, *Japan's Business Concentration,* Philadelphia, 1969.

32. For the dangers of further exacerbations from the liberalization issue, and the view that a friendly Japan is more important than commercial concessions, see Adams and Kobayashi, *World of Japanese Business,* p. 217.

33. It is interesting to recall, by way of contrast, the beneficent domestic effects which Hull, according to his theories, expected from free trade. Hull accepted the constant competition of interests characteristic of Madison's federal system but, as a populist, feared the concentrated power of big business to dominate the whole. Free trade, extending the orbit of competition to include the contending business forces from abroad, would prevent domination by native big business and preserve the Republic from the rule of its major faction. Thus, for Hull, free trade and federal equilibrium were complementary forces, whereas in Japan, free trade threatened an internal order that was not federal and competitive, but consensual and cooperative.

34. For Japan's various steps toward liberalization in the earlier sixties see OECD, *Liberalization of International Capital Movements: Japan,* p. 61.

35. See, for example, Trezise, "U.S.-Japan Economic Relations," *Williams Report,* Papers II, 186–188.

36. That textiles should be the first Japanese industry to provoke American protectionism was not without its irony. SCAP, fearing a revival of warmaking capacity had concentrated on the recovery of textiles as the one "safe" industry whose products would

be in high demand in foreign markets and yield an export surplus to pay for needed food imports. See Cohen, *Japan's Economy in War*, p. 479.

37. Trezise, "U.S.-Japan Economic Relations," *Williams Report*, Papers II, p. 188.

38. In mid-1971, Secretary of State Rogers announced an anticipated American trade deficit with Japan at twice the 1970 level of $1.2 billion (*N. Y. Times*, July 1971, p. 74). The final figure was $3.2 billion, well above the most dire predictions.

39. For Japan's unwillingness to agree to a common "safeguard" clause, and the consequences, see *European Community*, September 1971, p. 6. For expectations of a more tractable Japanese position, see *Japan Economic Journal*, 22 February 1972.

40. European Communities Press Release, "A Review of the Commercial and Monetary Relations between the United States and the European Community," Washington, 21 October, 1971.

41. The semi-official Japan Economic Research Center projects the following balance and distribution for Japanese trade by 1980:

Japan's Trading Partners

	SHARE IN JAPAN'S EXPORTS (%)		SHARE IN JAPAN'S IMPORTS (%)		JAPAN'S TRADE BALANCE BY REGION ($ MILLIONS)	
	1970	1980	1970	1980	1970	1980
North America	34.1	32.4	34.5	31.4	1,180	6,190
Western Europe	15.1	19.2	10.9	15.5	1,210	6,004
Australia, New Zealand, South Africa	5.5	5.6	10.4	9.5	555	2,000
Developing countries	39.9	34.2	38.9	33.8	1,380	5,570
Centrally planned economies	5.4	8.6	4.9	9.7	280	612

Source: *Japan Economic Journal, International Weekly,* January 18, 1972.

42. By the spring of 1972, for example, the United States was arguing that unless the price of Japanese exports to her reflected the full 16.88 percent yen revaluation, Japan should expect a strict application of American anti-dumping laws (*Japan Economic Journal*, April 18, 1972).

43. In 1970, imports accounted for over 99 percent of Japanese oil, 85 percent of iron ore, 73 percent of copper, and 72 percent of coking coal, *Williams Report*, compendium, p. 216.

44.

Principal Economic Indicators
Average Annual Rate of Increase in %

F.Y. 1970–1975

GNP	
Real	10.6
Nominal	14.7
Consumer Prices	4.4
Wholesale Prices	1.0
Labor Force	1.1
Exports	14.7
Imports	15.3
Mining, Manufacturing Production	12.4

Source: Economic Planning Agency. *New Economic and Social Development Plan*. May 1970, p. 102 (Table 3).

45. At a March 1972 meeting of the United Nations Economic Commission on Asia and the Far East (ECAFE), Japan proposed a special "Asian Currency Union" to promote mutual trade through the collective settlement of trade accounts, *Journal of Commerce*, March 14, 1972.

46. Japan is Australia's biggest market. In 1969–70, Japan took 25 percent of Australia's exports, compared to 13.5 percent for the United States and 11.9 percent for Britain. Japan took about half of Australia's mineral exports. Fears of becoming Japan's Canada, some observers note, may provoke an anti-Japanese backlash. See Brzezinski, *Fragile Blossom*, p. 72.

47. From 1965 to 1969, for Southeast Asia as a whole, Japan's exports grew by 110.1 percent, while imports grew only 69.4 percent, and the region ended with a $2.07 billion deficit in its trade with Japan (*Asian Almanac*, Vol. 8, No. 3, July 25, 1970, pp. 4080–81).

48. China continues to demand reduced Japanese economic rela-

tions with Korea and Taiwan as a price for further China trade. Japanese trade with Taiwan, however, at $1.2 billion for 1971, is still larger than the $1 billion or so annual trade with China. Symbolic gestures notwithstanding, the Japanese economic interest in Taiwan is not likely to diminish. See *Economist*, March 23, 1972, p. 107.

49. Most attractive to Japan would be a Pacific Free Trade Area, encompassing not only Australia and New Zealand but also Canada and the United States. But little support is likely outside Japan. One set of calculations, made before currency realignments, estimated that in conditions of free trade, Japan's exports to the four countries would rise 56 percent, while their exports to Japan would increase only 14.7 percent. Kiyoshi Kojima, "Japan's Interest in Pacific Trade Expansion," in "Pacific Trade and Development," Japan Economic Research Center, February 1968, cited in G. C. Allen, *Japan's Place in Trade Strategy*, London 1968, p. 42.

50. For a discussion of the Eight Points, see Yasuo Takeyama, "Don't Take Japan for Granted," *Foreign Policy*, No. 5, Winter 1971–1972, pp. 66–87.

51. Talks to establish a joint Ford-Toyo Motor venture in Japan, for example, broke down after three years, as Ford continued to insist on management control. *Japan Economic Journal*, March 14, 1972.

52. See, for example, "Eurojaps Coming?" *Economist*, 26 February, 1972, p. 76.

53. The Japan Economic Research Center, for example, projects that foreign investment in Japan will reach $10 billion by 1980, as compared to $.4 billion in 1968. Japan's own foreign investments, meanwhile, are expected to reach $26 billion by 1980, up from $2.7 billion in 1969 (*Japan Economic Journal*, Jan. 25, 1972).

54. Thus the campaign slogan of Prime Minister Sato in 1970: "The 1960's was an era of no welfare without growth, but we reversed this to no growth without welfare" (*Asian Almanac*, Vol. 9, No. 1, Jan. 9, 1971, p. 4350). As in the United States, however, rhetoric generally exceeds action. Thus, while the Japanese government has set the goal of pollution-free lakes and rivers by 1975 and pollution-free air by 1980, the fine set for violating companies is only $83 for each offense (*Asian Almanac*, Vol. 9, No. 8, February 27, 1971, p. 4438).

Chapter Nine

1. The term "Third World" was made popular by Frantz Fanon in his book, *The Wretched of the Earth*, N. Y., 1968, a moving and polemical description of the poverty and oppression suffered by most of the world's people. The term is, if anything, less precise than even the "Atlantic Community." Generally, the Third World refers to those countries of Asia, Africa and Latin America whose per capita income falls within some broadly accepted norm of what constitutes poverty. A definition of its upper limit is, to be sure, arbitrary. Some include Greece and Turkey, ancient European civilizations like Spain and Portugal, and even Israel, whose per capita income today is in the range of $1300. The style of politics and the range of problems among the 130-odd countries and dependencies of the Third World is almost limitless. In size, they vary from tiny island fragments to whole subcontinents. For some, population is the most pressing problem. Others have an abundance of land and natural resources and are relatively under-populated. For a good essay showing the hazards of generalization about the Third World, see Hla Myint, *Economic Theory and the Under-developed Countries*, London and N. Y., 1971, pp. 3–26. Useful typologies of the Third World may be found in OECD, *Development Assistance, 1971 Review*, Paris, Dec. 1971; also in David Vital, *The Inequality of Small States; A Study of the Small Power in International Relations*, Oxford, 1967.

2. In 1961, President Kennedy invited the General Assembly to designate the sixties as the UN Development Decade (UNDD). General Assembly Resolution 1710 (XVI) (December 19, 1961), aimed for "a minimum annual rate of growth of aggregate national income of 5 percent at the end of the decade," and urged a flow of outside capital and assistance at 1 percent of the combined national incomes of the advanced countries.

3. See for example, Senator Frank Church's speech to the United States Senate "Farewell to Foreign Aid," reprinted in the *Washington Post*, Sunday, November 7, 1971, pp. B1 and B6.

4. For an analysis of the "relatively low estate of the Third World" in the Western world's scale of priorities in the late sixties see

George Liska, "The Third World," in *America and the World,* Baltimore, 1970, pp. 343–423.

5. See the two-part series on Brazil by Everett G. Martin, "Turnabout Nation," *Wall Street Journal,* April 14 and 21, 1972. Over the four-year period 1968–1971, real growth in Brazil has averaged 9.4 percent. At the same time, Everett notes: "The government is a dictatorship that tortures political prisoners. Urban woes proliferate, and millions still live in poverty. Yet on many strictly economic issues, the government has amazed its critics."

6. The World Bank's President observed in 1971:

> We have come to the end of the First United Nations Development Decade (1961–1970), whose target for the developing countries was to achieve an annual rate of economic growth of 5 percent. Although the target has been nearly reached, much of the gain has been eaten away through rapid population increase. Per capita incomes in the developing countries rose little more than 2 percent a year, and their position has deteriorated further vis-à-vis the developed nations, where incomes per head rose nearly twice as rapidly.

> See McNamara "Effects of Trade Policy," *Williams Report,* Papers II, pp. 307ff.

7. See Joseph A. Schumpeter. *Capitalism, Socialism and Democracy,* New York, 1950.

8. On the Andean bloc, see Peter Schleisser, "Restrictions on Foreign Investments in the Andean Common Market," *The International Lawyer,* July 1971, pp. 586–598. See also his "Recent Developments in Latin American Foreign Investment Laws," *The International Lawyer,* January 1972, 64–87.

For an assessment of OPEC, (Organization of Petroleum Exporting Countries), see Walter J. Levy, "Oil Power," *Foreign Affairs,* July 1971, pp. 652–668.

On the "Group of 77" in UNCTAD, see above pp. 222.

9. See McNamara, "Effects of Trade Policy" and Kindleberger, "United States Policy Towards Direct Investment," in *Williams Report,* Papers II, pp. 307–328 and 329–351 respectively.

For a critical view of foreign direct investment in LDC's see Hirschman, "How to Divest in Latin America and Why."

10. For Spanish colonial economic policy, see Jaime Vicens Vives, *An Economic History of Spain,* Frances M. Lopez Morillas, trans.,

Princeton, 1969, especially pp. 566–580. On Britain's early economic relations with her colonies see Knowles, *Economic Developments of the British Overseas Empire*, Vol. I, pp. 1–12, 65–112; also Knorr, *British Colonial Theories*.

11. For a contemporary critique of Spain's colonial economic policy see Mariano Moreno, "Memorial of the Hacendados," in Harold E. Davis, ed. *Latin American Social Thought*. Washington, 1963, pp. 58–77.

12. See Ragnar Nurkse, *Problems of Capital Formation in Underdeveloped Countries and Problems of Trade and Development*, New York, 1967, p. 172.

13. On the other hand, Rául Prebisch, in his famous argument on the deteriorating terms of trade for Third-World exports, noted that the price of commodities relative to the price of manufactures fell steadily "from the 1870's until the Second World War," *The Economic Development of Latin America*, p. 8. For some leading critiques of Prebisch see Chapter 9, note 33.

14. See Platt, *Finance, Trade and Politics*, pp. 333–334.

15. The Union's Northern states did not, and hence struggled to make the United States into a closed regional economy, withdrawn from world interdependence. On the economic struggle between North and South see Charles A. and Mary Beard, *The Rise of American Civilization*, New York, 1928, Vol. II, pp. 3–51.

16. See Charles L. Mowat, *Britain Between the Wars 1918–1940*, London, 1966, pp. 262–267. Others, such as Rául Prebisch, have noted that the decline in a complementary relationship acceptable to industrial and primary-producing countries antedates World War I by several decades. See his *Economic Development of Latin America*.

17. Prebisch describes the period as follows:

With the advent of the great depression, the order that dated back to the nineteenth century, and which the First World War had seriously shaken, now disintegrated. The trends towards agricultural self-sufficiency were encouraged to an extraordinary degree in the industrial countries, which were striving to cut their imports in order to cope with the violent contraction in their exports. Bilateralism and discrimination emerged as the means of mitigating the intensity of this phenomenon. This movement spread throughout the world and forced many developing countries to adopt even more drastic restrictive measures, since the value of primary exports was declining more sharply than that of industrial goods.

"Towards A New Trade Policy," p. 7. For a sympathetic view of autarchy, see Polanyi, *The Great Transformation*, pp. 189–90.

18. For a broader view of the implications and possible benefits of the interior blocs, see Balogh, *Unequal Partners*, Vol. I, p. 113, and especially Amery, *Forward* View, pp. 95–115 and passim.

19. Whereas American support of regional blocs emphasizes their temporary and self-liquidating role, as a stage through which countries pass in strengthening themselves for full participation in a liberal world system, the rhetoric that surrounds such groupings as the Latin American Free Trade Area suggests that the members acquiesce in international cooperation now primarily to gain greater self-sufficiency in the future. See, for example, Prebisch, "Towards a New Trade Policy," p. 15–16.

20. See General Agreements on Tariffs and Trade, *Trends in International Trade*, Geneva, October 1958. The experts were asked to consider the "failure of the trade of the less developed countries to develop as rapidly as that of the industrial countries": and included Roberto de Oliveira Campos, Gottfried Haberler, James Meade, and Jan Tinbergen.

21. In particular, the new articles cited the need for "rapid and sustained expansion of export earnings," both by achieving "stable, equitable and remunerative prices for traditional exports" and by increasing access "in the largest measure possible to markets under favourable conditions for processed and manufactured products currently or potentially of particular interest to the less-developed contracting parties" GATT, Part IV, Article 36. For a discussion of the GATT'S relation with the Third World before 1965, see Patterson, *Discrimination in International Trade*, pp. 323–84.

22. When first offered in 1963, compensatory finance could reach 25 percent of a country's IMF quota, repayable in three to five years. In 1966, borrowers could draw a second 25 percent provided they cooperated closely with IMF policy advice. Bernstein,

"The International Monetary Fund," in Gardner and Millikan, eds., *The Global Partnership*, p. 142.

23. Since, for example, the industrialized countries in 1963 exported about 48 percent by value of the commodities entering world trade (55 percent excluding petroleum), even restricting Third-World exports to commodities would not, in itself, assure complementarity. See Pincus, *Trade, Aid and Development*, pp. 233ff. Harald B. Malmgren, in *Trade for Development* (Washington: Overseas Development Council, 1971, pp. 35–38), classifies products as to their suitability for commodity agreements with the United States. For the period 1963–65, he finds 20 percent of LDC commodities exported to the United States subject to serious competition from substitutes and another 32 percent already facing appreciable trade barriers because of competing domestic producers. For a good summary of commodity agreements and their practical difficulties, see J.W.F. Rowe, *Primary Commodities in International Trade*, Cambridge (England), 1965.

24. Although developing countries continued to export mostly primary goods, trade figures suggested that only the demand for manufactures (or petroleum) could grow enough to assure the foreign exchange needed for sustained development.

Commodity Structure of Exports 1955, 1960, 1965, 1968
(in % of total exports)

| | Developing Market Economies | | Developed Market Economies | | Centrally Planned Economies | |
	COMMODITY CLASS					
		(of which fuels)		(of which fuels)		(of which fuels)
Primary Goods						
1955	87.1	25.2	35.5	5.5	49.9	12.0
1960	85.7	28.0	31.4	4.0	43.1	10.9
1965	82.4	31.2	28.4	3.4	37.8	10.7
1968	78.0	33.7	24.7	3.3	36.3	10.2
Manufactured Goods						
1955	12.9		64.5		50.1	
1965	14.3		68.6		56.9	
1960	17.6		71.6		62.2	
1968	22.0		75.3		63.7	

Source: UNCTAD, *Supplement 1970, Handbook of International Trade and Development Statistics*, New York, 1970, p. 26, Table 4.1.

25. Prebisch, "Towards a New Trade Policy," p. 20.

26. For the opening addresses see *Proceedings of the United Nations Conference on Trade and Development*, Vol. II, Policy Statements, New York, 1964.

27. For a candid American reaction to UNCTAD see Sidney Weintraub, "After the UN Trade Conference: Lessons and Portents," *Foreign Affairs*, Vol. 43, 1964, pp. 37–50.

28. On American expectations before the Conference see Isaiah Frank, "Issues Before the U.N. Conference," *Foreign Affairs*, Vol. 42, 1964, pp. 210–226.

29. See Prebisch, "Towards a New Trade Policy," p. 20.

30. Prebisch, "Towards a New Trade Policy," p. 21.

31. Prebisch, "Towards a New Trade Policy," p. 35.

32. Prebisch, "Towards a New Trade Policy," p. 22.

33. More conventional academic economists often treated Prebisch's doctrines with scorn. For Gottfried Haberler, Prebisch's "attempted explanation of the alleged facts is fallacious, and there is no presumption at all that the alleged unfavorable tendency of the terms of trade will continue in the future." See Werner Baer, "The Economics of Prebisch and the ECLA," *Economic Development and Cultural Change*, Jan. 1962, pp. 169–82. For Jacob Viner, any deterioration in the terms of trade for the Third World would merely reflect differing rates of product improvement. Thus, whereas tractors, tires and automobiles had grown "incomparably superior in quality," primary commodities remained the same. Jacob Viner, *International Trade and Economic Development*, Glencoe, (Illinois) 1952, p. 143. Others explained Prebisch's data, insofar as they did not reject it as grossly insufficient, by pointing to the different methods of customs valuations or the declining costs of ocean transport. Paul T. Ellsworth, "The Terms of Trade between Primary-Producing and Industrial Countries," *Inter-American Economic Affairs*, Summer 1956, pp. 47–65.

Nevertheless, the Prebisch thesis struck a responsive chord among politicians and publicists in the Third World and it thus grew steadily more popular. The explanation Prebisch offered for their economic stagnation was plausible, even if controversial.

Moreover, blaming the rich countries at the industrial center was politically popular.

34. For the "Brasseur Plan," endorsed by France and Belgium, see statement by H. E. Mr. Maurice Brasseur, Minister for External Trade and Technical Assistance of Belgium, 3rd plenary meeting, 24 March, 1964, in *Proceedings of the UNCTAD*, N. Y. 1964, Vol. II, p. 110. Britain endorsed generalized preferences, some claimed primarily as a way of spreading the burden of those preferences she had already granted to Commonwealth countries. See Richard N. Cooper, "Third World Tariff Tangle," *Foreign Policy*, Fall 1971, pp. 35–50.

35. See, for example, Harald Malmgren, *Trade for Development*, Washington, (Overseas Development Council), 1971, p. 43.

36. Ball, "The Open System in North-South Relations," pp. 657–662.

37. Jerome Fried, "How Trade Can Aid," *Foreign Policy*, No. 4, Fall, 1971, p. 52. Mr. Fried was a member of the State Department's Policy Planning Council from 1962–1968.

38. Statement of Under Secretary of State Eugene Rostow before UNCTAD II, New Delhi, *Department of State Bulletin*, Vol. 58, 1968, p. 364.

39. According to the Rome Treaty, other countries no more developed than the Associated African States could also join the EEC's preferential system. Three Commonwealth members—Kenya, Uganda and Tanzania—gained associate status in 1969. Nigeria entered conversations and then withdrew. See William I. Zartman, *The Politics of Trade Negotiations between Africa and the European Economic Community: the Weak Confront the Strong*, Princeton, 1971.

40. In President Nixon's call for "a liberal system of generalized tariff preferences for all developing countries, including Latin America," American determination to dismantle the EC's preferential arrangements seemed thinly veiled by solicitude for Latin America: "We will seek equal access to industrial markets for all developing countries so as to eliminate the discrimination against Latin America that now exists in many countries. We will also urge that such a system eliminate the inequitable 'reverse preferences'

that now discriminate against Western Hemisphere countries." (p. 411) Richard Nixon, "Action for Progress in the Americas" speech to the Inter-American Press Association, Oct. 31, 1969, reprinted in the *Department of State Bulletin*, Nov. 17, 1969, pp. 409–414.

41. As stated in the *Economic Report of the President* and reprinted in *Department of State Bulletin*, March 1, 1971, p. 270, and further clarified in *Department of State Bulletin*, June 7, 1971, p. 752.

Meanwhile, as an earnest of its own good intentions, the United States announced that its own remaining preferential ties with the Philippines would be terminated. *Department of State Bulletin*, October 26, 1970, p. 405.

42. *Journal of Commerce*, March 20, 1972.

43. In early 1972 President Nixon revealed a tougher stance toward the expropriation of American overseas property:

> When a country expropriates a significant United States interest without making reasonable provision for such compensation to United States citizens, we will presume that the United States will not extend new bilateral economic benefits to the expropriating country unless and until it is determined that the country is taking reasonable steps to provide adequate compensation or that there are major factors affecting United States interests which require continuance of all or part of these benefits.
>
> The United States, Nixon continued, could for the same reasons also be expected to withhold its support from loans under consideration in multilateral development banks. *New York Times*, Jan. 20, 1972.

Treasury Secretary Connally's personal views suggested an even tougher posture. When American corporations are threatened with expropriation, he stated, the American government should say: "You don't negotiate just with American business enterprise. You negotiate with the United States Government." *New York Times*, April 19, 1972.

44. See, for example, George Ball, in *Proceedings of the United Nations Conference on Trade and Development*, New York, 1964, Vol. II, p. 395.

45. For the United States government's political risk insurance see, Agency for International Development, "Working With Private Enterprise: 1968 Operations of the Office of Private Resources,"

Washington, 1968, pp. 12–15. See also *OPIC Annual Report, Fiscal 1971*, Washington, 1971, p. 5. For a brief review of the very limited success of multilaterally organized investment protection, see James Greene, "The Search for Common Ground: A Survey of Efforts to Develop Codes of Behavior in International Investment," The Conference Board, Inc., New York, 1971.

46. For the view that the expansion of trade from nonreciprocal preferences to Third-World manufactures will more than offset the costs to developed countries in displacing labor and capital from low-productivity industries, see McNamara, "Effects of Trade," *Williams Report*, Papers II, p. 316. Most American proponents of such LDC preferences also recommend substantial programs of domestic adjustment assistance for industries affected, and reduction of tariffs in phases.

47. *Department of State Bulletin*, Vol. 50, 1964, p. 660.

48. For example, one distinguished American liberal argues: "Membership in the armed forces, control of hierarchical wealth from sources other than land, possession of trade monopolies, even bureaucratic position can all be sources of power over the state. And government in the interest of those who have such power, since they are nonfunctional, will be unrelated and unconducive to economic development," John Kenneth Galbraith, *Economics Peace and Laughter*, Boston, 1971, p. 237.

49. For the classic statement of this view see Frederick J. Turner, *The Frontier in American History.* New York, 1921. For a view which sees the frontier more as escape than resolution of domestic problems see William A. Williams. *The Contours of American History*, Chicago, 1966.

50. For the contemporary British attitudes toward the independence movements in Spanish America, see John Lynch, "British Policy and Spanish America, 1783–1808," *Journal of Latin American Studies*, May 1969, pp. 1–30. For a general view of nineteenth-century British policy toward Latin America see Platt, *Finance, Trade and Politics*, pp. 308–352.

51. For a discussion of Latin America's "feudal" political-economic system, see Glassman, *Political History of Latin America.* For a masterful study of early Latin American leaders, reminiscent in its way of Jacob Burckhardt's *Civilization of the Renaissance in Italy,*

see A. Curtis Wilgus, ed., *South American Dictators During the First Century of Independence*, New York, 1963.

52. Some agricultural production had been used to feed the labor force in the mines, thus forming a nucleus for domestic demand, but in most areas mining was well into decline by independence, and foreign markets for agriculture were thus all the more necessary.

53. For an excellent study of the role of the Latin American state in economic development see Anderson, *Politics and Economic Change in Latin America*, pp. 3–45.

54. In the Depression, Latin American middle and upper income groups suffered far more, relatively, than the traditional poor. Subsistence agricultural sectors, often including a majority of the population, lay beyond the pale of the market economy and remained unaffected by the crisis. Thus, however radical its implications for the future, import-substitution was undertaken initially by and for elite groups to defend their accustomed standard of living. For a discussion of this period, see William P. Glade, *The Latin American Economies: A Study of their Institutional Evolution*, New York 1969, pp. 347–401.

55. See, for example, Jaguaribe. *Economic and Political Development*, pp. 3–93; and his "A Brazilian View," in Raymond Vernon, ed., *How Latin America Views the U.S. Investor*, pp. 67–93. Jaguaribe emphasizes that economic self-sufficiency cannot be pursued by all. For his typology of "nonviable," "less-developed" and "more-developed" Latin American nations, see *Economic and Political Development*, pp. 75–79.

56. World Bank figures reveal that three-fourths among the Third World countries have gross national products of less than $3 billion. Robert S. McNamara, "Effects of Trade Policy," *Williams Report*, Papers II, p. 309. By another estimate only seven have GNP's exceeding the $10 billion annual product enjoyed by the State of Connecticut. Council of Economic Advisors, *Economic Report of the President*, Washington D.C., 1968, p. 192.

57. The Latin American Free Trade Association (LAFTA) provides perhaps the leading example. Tariff cuts stretched out over a dozen years were meant to provide the integrated regional market necessary for efficient industries and greater self-sufficiency. Greater

success may come in the future, but the record to date has not been promising. While by 1968, trade concessions had been negotiated on over 10,000 items, the majority of the items, it seems, are not produced by the granting countries. Nino Maritano, *A Latin American Economic Community: History, Policies and Problems*, Notre Dame, 1970, p. 112. For a brief review of other Third World integration schemes see F. Kahnert et al., *Economic Integration among Developing Countries*, Development Center of the OECD. Paris 1969, pp. 51–99.

Chapter Ten

1. Edmund Burke, *Works*. Boston, 1865, Vol. III, p. 359.

2. Obviously, historical forces can create new nations and national states by amalgamating old, although the process in the past has generally required a good deal of time and coercion. A nation is essentially a psychological reality, an entity that has its primary existence in the minds of its citizens, even if the idea of the nation-state is constantly reinforced by established institutions, habits and symbols. National ideas and the identities which accompany them can, in theory, be changed—although not easily, once they are well-established. For a further discussion of these views, in particular in their relation to the European Communities, see Calleo, *Europe's Future*, chapter 2; and *Coleridge and the Idea of the Modern State*, Conclusion.

3. A second traditional inducement to imperialism by the developed states, the need to gaurantee access to raw materials, seems correspondingly eroded—not only by the increasing substitutibility of many raw materials, but especially by that revival of political will in the Third World which makes colonial domination unlikely and hence ensures a large number of independent and competing suppliers. For the lessons drawn by the Japanese, see chapter 8.

BIBLIOGRAPHY

Acheson, Dean G. *Present at the Creation*. New York, Norton, 1969.

Adams, Brooks. *America's Economic Supremacy*. New York, Macmillan, 1947.

Adams, D. E. *Great Britain and the American Civil War*. New York, 1952.

Adams, Gerald F. and Helen B. Junz. "Effects of the Business Cycle on Trade Flows of the Industrialized Countries," *Journal of Finance*, May 1971.

Adams, Henry. *The Education of Henry Adams*. New York, Modern Library, 1931.

————. *The Degradation of the Democratic Dogma*. Harper Trade Books.

Adams, T. F. M. and N. Kobayashi. *The World of Japanese Business*. Tokyo and Palo Alto, International Publications Service, 1969.

Adler-Karlsson, Gunnar. *Western Economic Warfare, 1947–1967; A Case Study in Foreign Economic Policy*. Stockholm, Humanities Press, 1968.

Adler, Michael. "Specialization in the European Coal and Steel Community," *Journal of Common Market Studies*, March 1970.

Aharoni, Yair. *The Foreign Investment Decision Process*. Boston, Harvard Business School, 1966.

Allen, Kevin and M. C. MacLennan. *Regional Problems and Policies in Italy and France*. London, Sage Publications, 1970.

Amery, Julian. *The Life of Joseph Chamberlain*. Vol. 5, 6. London, St. Martin's Press, 1969. See under Garvin.

Amery, Leo S. *The Forward View*. London, Books for Libraries Press, 1935.

Anderson, Charles W. *Politics and Economic Change in Latin America*. Princeton, Van Nostrand Reinhold Company, 1967.

Asian Almanac.

Bailey, Thomas W. *A Diplomatic History of the American People.* New York, Appleton-Century-Crofts, 1969.

Balakjian, Wabe H. *Legal Aspects of Foreign Investment in the European Economic Communities.* Manchester (England), 1967.

Balassa, Bela. "Whither French Planning," *Quarterly Journal of Economics,* November 1965.

Ball, George. "Cosmocorp: the Importance of Being Stateless," *Atlantic Community Quarterly,* Summer 1968.

———. "The Open System in North-South Relations," *Department of State Bulletin,* Vol. 50, 1964, pp. 657–662, U.S. Govt. Printing Office.

Balogh, Thomas. *Unequal Partners.* Vol. I. Oxford, Fernhill House Ltd., 1963.

The Banker.

Barber, Richard J. *The American Corporation.* New York, Dutton, E.P., 1970.

Beard, Charles A. and Mary. *The Rise of American Civilization.* New York, Macmillan, 1928.

Beaufre, André. *NATO and Europe.* New York, Knopf, 1966.

———. *Deterrence and Strategy.* (R. H. Barry trans.) London, Praeger, 1968.

Beloff, Max. *Imperial Sunset.* New York, Knopf, 1970.

———. *The United States and the Unity of Europe.* New York, Brookings Institution, 1963.

Berle, Adolph and Gardiner C. Means. *The Modern Corporation and Private Property.* New York, Harcourt Brace, 1934.

Blake, Robert. *Disraeli. London,* St. Martin's Press, 1966.

Blum, John M. *From the Morgenthau Diaries: Years of War 1941–1945.* Boston, Houghton-Mifflin, 1967.

Bosanquet, Helen. *Free Trade and Peace in the Nineteenth Century.* Publications de l'Institut Nobel Norvegian. Kristiania (Norway), Putnam, 1924.

Bradley, Gene E., ed. *Building the American-European Market: Planning for the Seventies.* Homewood (Illinois), Dow-Jones-Irwin, Inc., 1967.

Brown, Seyom. *The Faces of Power.* New York, Columbia Univ. Press, 1968.

Brzezinski, Zbigniew. *Between Two Ages: America's Role in the Technotronic Era.* New York, Viking, 1970.

————. *The Fragile Blossom; Crisis and Change in Japan.* New York, Harper and Row, 1972.

Burenstam Linder, Staffan. *An Essay on Trade and Transformation.* New York, Almquist and Wiksells, 1961.

Burke, Edmund. *Works.* Boston, 1865.

Burnie, Arthur. *An Economic History of Europe 1760–1939.* London, 1951.

Cairncross, Alexander K. *Home and Foreign Investment, 1870–1903.* Cambridge, Cambridge Univ. Press, 1953.

Calleo, David P. *The Atlantic Fantasy.* Baltimore, Johns Hopkins Press, 1970.

————. *Britain's Future.* New York, Horizon, 1968.

————. *Coleridge and the Idea of the Modern State.* New Haven, Yale Univ. Press, 1966.

————. *Europe's Future.* New York, Horizon, 1965.

Campbell, Leonard and Robert J. Shupe. "Military Transactions in the United States Balance of Payments," *Survey of Current Business,* United States Govt. Printing Office, February, 1972.

Camps, Miriam. *Britain and the European Community 1955–1963.* Princeton, Princeton Univ. Press, 1964.

————. *European Unification in the Sixties: From the Veto to the Crisis.* New York, McGraw-Hill, 1966.

Carnegie, Andrew. "A Look Ahead," *North American Review,* June 1893.

Church, Senator Frank. "Farewell to Foreign Aid," *Washington Post,* November 7, 1971.

Churchill, Winston S. *Closing the Ring.* Boston, Houghton Mifflin, 1951.

Clairmonte, Frederick. *Economic Liberalism and Underdevelopment: Studies in the Disintegration of an Idea.* London, Asia Publishing House, 1960.

Cleveland, Harold van B. *The Atlantic Idea and Its European Rivals.* New York, McGraw-Hill, 1966.

————. "How the Dollar Standard Died," *Foreign Policy,* No. 5, 1971–72.

Cohen, Jerome B. *Japan's Economy in War and Reconstruction.* Minneapolis, Univ. Minnesota Press, 1949.

————. *Japan's Postwar Economy.* Bloomington, Ind., Indiana Univ. Press, 1958.

Cohen, Stephan D. *International Monetary Reform 1964–1969: The Political Dimension.* New York, Praeger, 1970.

Cohen, Stephen S. *Modern Capitalist Planning: the French Model.* Cambridge, Harvard Univ. Press, 1969.

Commission of the European Economic Community.
Ninth General Report on the Activities of the Community: 1 April 1965 – 31 March 1966. Brussels, 1966.
Proposed Statute for the European Company. Brussels, 1970.

Committee on Economic Development.
Non-Tariff Distortions of Trade. New York, 1969.
The United States and the European Community: Policies for a Changing World Economy. Washington, November 1971.

Connally, John B., Secretary of the Treasury, Remarks at the International Banking Conference of the American Bankers Association. Munich, May 28, 1971.

Coombes, Charles A. "Treasury and Federal Reserve Foreign Exchange Operations," *Federal Reserve Bulletin,* United States Govt. Printing Office, October 1971.

Cooper, Richard N. *The Economics of Interdependence.* New York, McGraw-Hill, 1968.

Coudenhove-Kalergi, Richard. *Paneuropa: 1922–1966.* Wieu, München, Herold, 1966.

Couve de Murville, Maurice. *Une Politique Étrangère.* Paris, Plon, 1971.

Curzon, Gerald. *Multilateral Commercial Diplomacy.* New York, Praeger, 1966.

Dahrendorf, Ralf. *Society and Democracy in Germany.* New York, Doubleday, 1967.

Dam, Kenneth W. *The GATT: Law and International Organization.* Chicago, Univ. of Chicago Press, 1970.

Debré, Michel. "Statement by the Governor of the Bank for France," *Summary Proceedings Annual IMF Meeting 1967.*

De Gaulle, Charles. *Major Addresses, Statements and Press Conferences.* Paris, 1963.
————. *Memoirs of Hope; Renewal 1958–62; Endeavor 1962.* London, 1971.
————. *Press Conference.* February 4, 1965.

Devlin, David and Kruer, George. "The International Investment Position of the United States: Developments in 1969," *Survey of Current Business,* United States Govt. Printing Office, October 1970.

Devlin, David T. "The United States Balance of Payments: Revised Presentation," *Survey of Current Business,* United States Govt. Printing Office, June 1971.

Dilke, Sir Charles. *Greater Britain: A Record of Travel in English-Speaking Countries.* New York, Fertig Howard, 1869.

Dunning, John H. and Rowan, D. C. "Inter-firm Efficiency Comparisons: United States and U.K Manufacturing Enterprises in Britain," in Dunning, ed. *Studies in International Investment,* London, Humanities Press, 1970.

Economic Planning Agency, Government of Japan. *New Economic and Social Development Plan.* May 1970.

The Economist.

Einzig, Paul. *The Euro-Bond Market.* London, St. Martin's Press, 1969.

Epstein, Leon D. *Britain—Uneasy Ally.* Chicago, Univ. Chicago Press, 1954.

"The Euro-Dollar Market: Some First Principles," *Morgan Guaranty Survey,* October 1969.

European Community. "Economic and Monetary Union," March 1971.

European Communities Press Release, "A Review of the Commercial and Monetary Relations between the United States and the European Community." Washington, 1971.

Fanon, Frantz. *The Wretched of the Earth.* New York, Grove Press, 1968.

Fischer, Fritz. *Germany's Aims in the First World War.* New York, Norton, 1967.

——. *Krieg der Illusionen.* Düsseldorf, 1969.

Ford, Worthington C., ed. *Letters of Henry Adams 1892–1918.* Boston, Kraus Reprint Corp., 1938.

——. *A Cycle of Adams Letters, 1819–1865.* Boston, Kraus Reprint Corp., 1921.

Frank, Isaiah. "Issues Before the U.N. Conference," *Foreign Affairs,* Vol. 42, 1964.

Friedrich, Carl J. *Europe an Emergent Nation.* New York, Harper Trade Books, 1969.

Galbraith, John K. *The Affluent Society.* Boston, Houghton-Mifflin, 1958.

——. *Economics, Peace and Laughter.* Boston, Houghton-Mifflin, 1971.

——. *The New Industrial State.* 2nd edition, revised. Boston, Houghton-Mifflin, 1971.

Gardner, Lloyd C. *Economic Aspects of New Deal Diplomacy.* Madison, Beacon, 1964.

Gardner, Richard N. *Sterling-Dollar Diplomacy.* Oxford, Clarendon Press, 1956.

Gardner, Richard N. and Max N. Millikan, eds. *The Global Partnership.* New York, Praeger, 1968.

Garraty, John A. *Henry Cabot Lodge, A Biography.* New York, Knopf, 1968.

Garvin, J. L. *The Life of Joseph Chamberlain.* 3 Vols. London, St. Martin's Press, 1932. See under Amery, J.

General Agreements on Tariffs and Trade. *Trends in International Trade: A Report by a Panel of Experts.* Geneva, 1958.

Gilbert, Joseph. *Designing the Industrial State.* Chicago, 1972.

Gilpin, Robert. "The Politics of Transnational Economic Relations," *International Organization,* Summer 1971.

Giscard d'Estaing, Valery. Speech at the *U.S.-EEC Businessmen's Conference.* March 1972.

Glade, William P. *The Latin American Economies: A Study of Their Institutional Evolution.* New York, Van Nostrand Reinhold, 1969.

Gladstone, William E. "Kin Beyond Sea," *North American Review,* Vol. 127, 1878.

Glassman, Ronald M. *Political History of Latin America.* New York, Funk and Wagnalls, 1964.

Gordon Walker, Patrick. *The Commonwealth.* London, 1962.

Grattan, Clinton H. *The United States and the Southwest Pacific.* Cambridge, Harvard University Press, 1961.

Halévy, Élie. *The Growth of Philosophical Radicalism.* London, Kelley, 1949.

Hanrieder, Wolfram F. *The Stable Crisis.* New York, Harper Trade Books, 1970.

Heimann, Eduard. *History of Economic Doctrines.* New York, Oxford Univ. Press, 1964.

Hellmann, Rainer. *The Challenge to U.S. Dominance of the International Corporation.* New York, Dunellen, 1970.

Herring, George C. "The U.S. and British Bankruptcy," *Political Science Quarterly,* June 1971.

Hettlage, Robert. *Die Veränderungen in den Handelsbilanzen der EWG-Länder zwischen 1958 und 1967.* Munich, 1967.

Hirsch, Seev. *Location of Industry and International Competitiveness.* Oxford, Oxford University Press, 1967.

Hirschman, Albert O. "How to Divest in Latin America and Why," *Princeton Essays in International Finance No. 76,* 1969.

Hobsbawm, Eric J. *Industry and Empire: Economic History of Britain Since 1750.* London, Penguin, 1968.

Hobson, John A. *Imperialism, a Study.* 3rd ed. revised. Ann Arbor, Univ. Michigan Press, 1938.

Hoffmann, Stanley. "Rousseau on War and Peace," in Hoffmann *The State of War: Essays on the Theory and Practise of International Politics,* New York, 1965.

Houthakker, Hendrik and Magee, Stephen. "Income and Price Elasticities in World Trade," *The Review of Economics and Statistics,* May 1969.

Hufbauer, Gary C. and Adler, F. M. *Overseas Manufacturing Investments and the Balance of Payments.* Washington, 1968.

Hull, Cordell. *Memoirs.* 2 Vols. New York, Macmillan, 1948.

Hunt, K. "NATO Without France: The Military Implications," *Adelphi Papers No. 32,* London, 1966.

Hymer, Stephen and Rowthorn, Robert. "Multinational Corporations and International Oligopoly: the Non-American Challenge," in Charles P. Kindleberger, ed. *The International Corporation.* Cambridge (Mass.), MIT Press, 1970.

International Monetary Fund.
  Direction of Trade Annual 5 and 7, 1963–1970.
  International Financial Statistics. 1971.

Iriye, Akira. *Across the Pacific: An Inner History of American-East Asian Relations.* New York, Harcourt Brace, 1967.

James, Robert. *Rosebery.* New York, Macmillan, 1963.

Japan Economic Journal, International Weekly.

Jaquaribe, Helio. *Economic and Political Development.* Cambridge, 1968.

Journal of Commerce.

Kahn, Herman. *The Emerging Japanese Superstate.* Englewood Cliffs, (N.J.), Prentice-Hall, 1970.

Kahnert, F. et. al. *Economic Integration among Developing Countries.* OECD. Paris, 1969.

Keegan, William. "Six Protest at U.S. Plan," *Financial Times.* September 16, 1971.

Kindleberger, Charles P. *American Business Abroad.* New Haven, Yale Univ. Press, 1969.

———. *Foreign Trade and the National Economy.* New Haven, Yale Univ. Press, 1962.

————. *The International Corporation.* Cambridge (Mass.), MIT Press, 1970.

Klopstock, Fred H. "Money Creation in the Euro-Dollar Market —A Note on Professor Friedman's Views," *Federal Reserve Bank of New York, Monthly Review,* United States Govt. Printing Office, January, 1970.

Knowles, Lilian C. A. *Economic Development of The Overseas Empire.* London, Kelley, 1928.

Kohl, Wilfred L. *French Nuclear Diplomacy.* Princeton, Princeton Univ. Press, 1971.

Kolko, Gabriel. *The Politics of War.* New York, Random House, 1968.

————. *The Roots of American Foreign Policy.* Boston, Beacon Press, 1969.

Krause, Lawrence B. "A Passive Balance of Payments Strategy," *Brookings Papers on Economic Activity, No. 3,* The Brookings Institution, Washington, 1970.

————. "Trade Policy for the Seventies," *Columbia Journal of World Business,* January/February 1971.

Layton, Christopher. *Transatlantic Investments.* New York, International Publications Service, 1970.

Lenin, Vladimir I. *Imperialism, the Highest Stage of Capitalism: a Popular Outline.* New York, China Books, 1939.

Lessing, Lawrence. "Why the U.S. Laggs in Technology," *Fortune,* April 1972.

Levin, Gordon N., Jr. *Woodrow Wilson and World Politics.* New York, 1968.

Lichtheim, George. *Imperialism.* New York, Praeger, 1971.

Liska, George. *Europe Ascendant: The International Politics of Unification.* Baltimore, Johns Hopkins Univ. Press, 1964.

————. "The Third World," in Robert E. Osgood, *et al., America and the World.* Baltimore, Johns Hopkins Univ. Press, 1970.

List, Friedrich. *The National System of Political Economy.* London, Kelley, 1885.

Little, Jane S. "The Euro-dollar Market: its Nature and Impact," *New England Economic Review,* May-June 1969.

Lockwood, William. "The Socialist Society, India and Japan," *Foreign Affairs,* October, 1958.

London Times.

MacArthur, John H. and Bruce R. Scott. *Industrial Planning in France.* Boston, Harvard Business School, 1970.

Maddison, Angus. *The Economic Growth of the West.* New York, Norton, 1964.

Maffry, August. "Bretton Woods—and Foreign Trade," *Foreign Commerce Weekly,* October 7, 1944.

Magdoff, Harry. *The Age of Imperialism.* New York, Monthly Reviews Press, 1969.

Mahan, Alfred T. *The Interest of America in Sea Power, Present and Future.* Boston, Kennikat, 1918.

Malmgren, Harald B. *Trade Wars or Trade Negotiations? Non-Tariff Barriers and Economic Peacekeeping.* Washington, Overseas Development Council, 1970.

Manser, W. A. P. "U.K. and the EEC: The Prospects for Finance," *National Westminister Quarterly Review,* February 1972.

Maritano, Nino. *A Latin American Economic Community: History, Policies and Problems.* Notre Dame, Univ. of Notre Dame Press, 1970.

Martin, Everett G. "Turnabout Nation," *Wall Street Journal,* April 1972.

Marx, Karl and Engels, Frederick. *Manifesto of the Communist Party.* New York, Penguin, 1932.

May, Ernest R. *American Imperialism: A Speculative Essay.* New York, Atheneum, 1968.

Mayne, Richard. *The Community of Europe.* London, Norton Press, 1962.

———. *The Recovery of Europe from Devastation to Unity.* New York, Harper and Row, 1970.

McKinnon, Ronald. "Optimum World Monetary Arrangements and the Dual Currency System," *Banca Nazionale de Lavoro, Quarterly Review,* December 1963.

Meade, James E. "Japan and the General Agreements on Tariffs and Trade," *Three Banks Review,* London, 1957.

———. *The Theory of International Economic Policy.* London, Oxford Univ. Press, 1955.

Meyer, Henry C. *Mitteleuropa in German Thought and Action, 1815–1945.* Hague, Nighoff, 1955.

Monypenny, William F. and Buckle, Charles E. *The Life of Benjamin Disraeli, Earl of Beaconsfield.* London, Russell, 1912.

Mumford, Lewis. *The Pentagon of Power.* New York, 1967–1970.

Muth, Hanns P. *French Agriculture and the Political Integration of Western Europe.* Leyden, Humanities Press, 1970.

Nath, Stephen K. *A Reappraisal of Welfare Economics.* London, Kelley, 1969.

Nevins, Allan. *The War for the Union.* New York, Scribner, 1959.

Northedge, F. S. *British Foreign Policy.* London, Praeger, 1962.

New York Times

Officer, Lawrence H. and Lawrence B. Smith, "The Canadian-American Reciprocity Agreement of 1855 to 1866," *Journal of Economic History,* December 1968.

Organization for Economic Cooperation and Development. *Development Assistance, 1971 Review.* Paris, 1971.

Economic Survey, Japan. Paris, 1964.

Gaps in Technology. Paris, 1968.

Liberalization of International Capital: Japan. Paris, 1968.

National Accounts of OECD Countries, 1953–1969. Paris, 1970.

Osgood, Robert E. *NATO the Entangling Alliance.* Chicago, Univ. Chicago Press, 1962.

Parrish, Evelyn M. "The United States Balance of Payments: Fourth Quarter and Year 1970," *Survey of Current Business,* United States Govt. Printing Office, March 1971.

Patterson, Gardner. *Discrimination in International Trade, The Policy Issues: 1945–1965.* Princeton, Princeton Univ. Press, 1966.

Pincus, John. *Trade, Aid and Development.* New York, McGraw-Hill, 1967.

Platt, Desmond C. M. *Finance, Trade, and Politics in British Foreign Policy, 1815–1914.* Oxford, Oxford Univ. Press, 1968.

Polanyi, Karl. *The Great Transformation.* Boston, Beacon Press, 1957.

Polk, Judd. "The New World Economy," *Columbia Journal of World Business,* January/February 1968.

Polk, Judd et al. *United States Production Abroad and the Balance of Payments.* New York, National Industrial Conference Board, 1966.

Pompidou, Georges. *Presidential Press Conference.* September 13, 1971.

Prebisch, Rául. *The Economic Development of Latin America and Its Principal Problems.* New York, Praeger, 1950.

———. "Towards a New Trade Policy for Development," *Proceedings of the United Nations Conference on Trade and Development,* Vol. II, New York, 1964.

Preeg, Ernest. *Traders and Diplomats.* Washington, Brookings Inst., 1970.

Pryke, Richard. *Public Enterprise in Practice.* London, MacGibbon and Kee, 1971.

Raymond, E. T. *The Man of Promise: Lord Rosebery.* London, 1923.

Reddaway, William B. *Effects of U. K. Direct Investment Overseas.* London, Cambridge Univ. Press, 1968.

Ricardo, David. *The Principles of Political Economy and Taxation.* London, Penguin, 1911.

Robinson, Edward A. G. ed. *Economic Consequences of the Size of Nations.* London, Macmillan, 1963.

Rolfe, Sidney. *The International Corporation.* Paris, International Chamber of Commerce, 1969.

Rolfe, Sidney and Walter Darum, eds. *The Multinational Corporation in the World Economy.* New York, Praeger, 1970.

Rousseau, Jean-Jacques. *Political Writings.* C. E. Vaughn, ed. New York, Franklin, Bart, 1962.

Rowan, Hobart. "Understanding the Functions of Benign Neglect Policy," *Washington Post,* May 23, 1971.

Rueff, Jacques. *The Monetary Sin of the West.* New York, Macmillan, 1972.

Salant, Walter. "Does the International Monetary System Need Reform?," Washington, Brookings Inst., 1964.

Samuels, Ernest. *Henry Adams: The Major Phase.* Cambridge (Mass.), Harvard Univ. Press, 1964.

Sansom, George B. *The Western World and Japan.* New York, Knopf, 1950.

Schlesinger, Arthur, Jr. *The Coming of the New Deal.* Boston, 1958.

Schumpeter, Joseph A. *Capitalism, Socialism and Democracy.* New York, Harper and Row, 1950.

Scitovsky, Tibor. *Welfare and Competition: The Economics of a Fully Employed Economy.* London, Irwin, 1964.

Seeley, J. R. *The Expansion of England.* London, Univ. Chicago Press, 1898.

Semmel, Bernard. *The Rise of Free Trade Imperialism.* Cambridge, Cambridge Univ. Press, 1970.

Servan-Schreiber, Jean-J. *The American Challenge.* New York, Atheneum, 1967.

————. *The Spirit of May.* New York, McGraw-Hill, 1968.

Shonfield, Andrew. *Modern Capitalism: The Changing Balance of Public and Private Power.* New York, Oxford Univ. Press, 1965.

Siekman, Philip. "Europe's Love Affair with Bigness," *Fortune,* March 1970.

Skidelsky, Robert. *Politicians and the Slump*. London, Humanities, 1967.

Snyder, Louis L., ed. *The Imperialism Reader*. Princeton, Van Nostrand, 1962.

Starke, Joseph G. *The ANZUS Treaty Alliance*. Melbourne, International School Book Service, 1965.

Statistical Office of the European Communities. *Foreign Trade Monthly Statistics*. Luxemburg, 1964–1972.

Statistical Office of the European Communities. *National Accounts, 1960–1970*. Luxemburg, 1971.

Stevens, Robert W. "Wishful Thinking on the Balance of Payments," *Harvard Business Review*, November-December, 1966.

Strange, Susan. *Sterling and British Policy*. London, Oxford Univ. Press, 1971.

Streit, Clarence K. *Union Now*. New York, Harper, 1939.

Swann, Dennis. *The Economics of the Common Market*. Harmondsworth (England), Penguin, 1970.

Takeyama, Yasua. "Don't Take Japan for Granted," *Foreign Policy*, No. 5, Winter 1971–1972.

Taylor, Alan J. P. *The Origins of the Second World War*. Greenwich (Conn.), Atheneum, 1961.

Temple, Henry W. "William H. Seward," in Samuel F. Bemis, ed., *American Secretaries of State and Their Diplomacy*. New York, Cooper Square Publishers, 1928.

Tocqueville, Alexis de. *Democracy in America*. Vol. I. New York, Oxford Univ. Press, 1954.

Torrens, Robert. *The Budget*. London, Kelley, 1844.

Triffin, Robert. *Gold and the Dollar Crisis*. New Haven, Yale Univ. Press, 1960.

————. "The International Monetary System," in *International Monetary Problems*. London, 1966.

————. *The World Money Maze*. New Haven, Yale Univ. Press, 1966.

Tugendhat, Christopher. *The Multinationals*. London, Eyre and Spottiswoode, 1971.

United Nations Conference on Trade and Development. *Supplement 1970, Handbook of International Trade and Development Statistics*. New York, 1970.

United Nations.
    Monthly Bulletin of Statistics. New York, 1971 and 1972.
    Yearbook of International Trade and Statistics 1969. New York, 1971.

United States Agency for International Development. "Working with Private Enterprise: 1968 Operations of the Office of Private Resources," Washington, United States Govt. Printing Office, 1968.

United States Board of Governors of the Federal Reserve System. *The Federal Reserve System: Purpose and Function.* Washington, United States Govt. Printing Office, 1963.

United States Bureau of the Census.

> *Highlights of the United States Export and Import Trade.* Report FT 990. Washington, United States Govt. Printing Office, December 1971.

> *Statistical Abstract of the United States 1971.* Washington, United States Govt. Printing Office, 1971.

> *Statistical Abstract of the United States 1969.* Washington, 1969.

United States Congress, House, Subcommittee on Foreign Economic Policy of the Committee on Foreign Affairs. "New Realities and New Directions in United States Foreign Economic Policy," United States Govt. Printing Office, February, 1972.

United States Department of Commerce.

> *Business Statistics 1969.* Washington, United States Govt. Printing Office, 1969.

> *Overseas Business Reports 71–009.* February 1971.

> *Policy Aspects of Foreign Investment by United States Multinational Corporations.* Washington, January 1972.

> *Survey of Current Business,* Monthly.

> *United States Multinational Enterprise and the United States Economy.* Washington, January 1972.

> Office of Business Economics. *United States Direct Investments Abroad 1966, Part I: Balance of Payments Data.* Washington, 1971.

"United States Economic Measures Alarm EC," *European Community,* September, 1967.

Van Alstyne, Richard W. *The Rising American Empire.* Oxford, Quadrangle, 1960.

Vernon, Raymond. "Future of the Multinational Enterprise," in Charles P. Kindleberger, ed. *The International Corporation.* Cambridge (Mass.), MIT Press, 1970.

——. "Multinational Enterprise and National Sovereignty," *Harvard Business Review,* March/April 1967.

Vernon, Raymond, ed. *How Latin America Views the United States Investor.* New York, Praeger, 1966.

Viner, Jacob. *International Trade and Economic Development.* Glencoe (Illinois), Free Press, 1952.

Vital, David. *The Inequality of Small States: A Study of the Small Power in International Relations.* Oxford, Oxford Univ. Press, 1967.

Vives, Jaime V. *An Economic History of Spain.* Princeton, Princeton Univ. Press, 1969.

Wilgus, A. Curtis, ed. *South American Dictators During the First Century of Independence.* New York, Russell, 1963.

Wilkins, Mira. *The Emergence of Multilateral Enterprise.* Cambridge (Mass.), Harvard Univ. Press, 1970.

Williams, John. *Postwar Monetary Plans and Other Essays.* New York, 1945.

Williams, Philip M. *French Politicians and Elections, 1951–1969.* Cambridge, Cambridge Univ. Press, 1970.

"Williams Report." Commission on International Trade and Investment Policy. *United States International Economic Policy in an Interdependent World.* Washington, 1971, compendium and 2 volumes: United States Govt. Printing Office.

    Abegglan, James C. "Dynamics of Japanese Competition," *Papers II.*

    Fooks, Marvin M. "Trade Adjustment Assistance," *Papers I.*

    Houthakker, Hendrik. "The United States Balance of Payments—A Look Ahead," *Papers I.*

    Kindleberger, Charles P. "United States Policy Towards Direct Investment with Special Reference to the Less Developed Countries," *Papers II.*

    Krause, Lawrence B. "The Balance of Payments of the United States and Other Countries: An Equilibrium View," *Papers I.*

    Kravis, Irving. "The Current Case for Import Limitations," *Papers I.*

    McNamara, Robert S. "Effects of Trade Policy on Economic Development," *Papers II.*

    Metzger, Stanley D. "Adjustment Assistance," *Papers I.*

    Pizer, Samuel. "Capital Restraint Programs," *Papers I.*

    Rosovsky, Henry. "The Economic Position of Japan: Past, Present and Future," *Papers II.*

Trezise, Philip H. "United States-Japan Economic Relations," *Papers II.*

United States Department of State, "United States Trade and Investment Policy in an Interdependent World," *Papers I.*

Welch, Henry W. "United States-Canada Automotive Trade Agreements," *Papers I.*

Williams, William A. *The Contours of American History.* Chicago, Quadrangle, 1966.

————. *The Tragedy of American Diplomacy.* New York, Dell, 1962.

Willis, F. Roy. *France, Germany and the New Europe.* Stanford, Stanford Univ. Press, 1968.

Winch, Donald. *Economics and Policy.* London, International Publishing Service, 1969.

Woodham-Smith, Cecil. *The Great Hunger: Ireland 1845–1849.* London, Harper-Row, 1962.

Yanaga, Chitoshi. *Big Business in Japanese Politics.* New Haven, Yale Univ. Press, 1968.

————. *Japanese People and Politics.* New York, Wiley, 1956.

INDEX

Acheson, Dean: Atlanticism and, 87; mentioned, 87, 282n, 303n

Adams, Brooks: Atlanticism and, 47; pessimism of, 48; economic theories, 50; as federalist, 70; imperialism of, 77; on U.S. power, 273n; mentioned, 61

Adams, Henry: religion and, 18; Atlanticism and, 47; on second law of thermodynamics, 48; pessimism of, 48; World War I and, 51; as federalist, 70; on Theodore Roosevelt, 273n; on father, 274n; mentioned, 272n

Adams, John Quincy: nationalism, 69

Adjustment Assistance Programs: preferences and, 343n; mentioned, 305n, 307n

Africa: EEC trade with, 124; Kenya, 341n; Tanzania, 341n; Uganda, 341n. See also Association of African States

Agriculture: Franco-German entente and, 127; in Latin America, 344n. See also Common Agricultural Policy

Alaskan boundary dispute: Lodge and, 52

America: See United States

American selling price: Kennedy Round and, 307n

Amery, Sir Julian: Joseph Chamberlain and, 260n, 265n

Andean Pact: investment code of, 222; mentioned, 335n

Anglo-French Commercial Treaty (1860): 262n

Anglo-Japanese Payments Union: U.S. and, 327n: mentioned, 303, 326n

Anti-dumping laws: Japan and, 332n

Anti-Trust Policies: 175

ANZUS Treaty: 325n

Argentina: British ties with, 29

Asia. See Southeast Asia, Vietnam War and country headings

Asian Currency Union: Japan and, 332n

Asquith, Herbert: 265n

Associated African States: EEC and, 341n; mentioned, 236

Atlantic Community: formation of, 43; stability of, 64; danger to, 65; U.S. threat to, 66; John Kennedy on, 82; decline of, 84; economic crisis in, 85; members of, 305n; as trading community, 305n, 306n; mentioned, 59

Atlanticism: description of, 16–17; to America, 16; free trade and, 20, 186; Communism and, 43; Europeanism, 62, 277n; mentioned, 19, 47, 278n

Attlee, Clement: opposed to U.S., 42; mentioned, 202, 267n

Australia: as British Dominion, 30; Pacific Free Trade Association and, 333n; mentioned, 325n

Autarchy: Third World and, 223, 225, 226, 227; mentioned, 12, 337

Balance of payments: British surplus in, 28; U.S. deficit in, 85, 88, 89, 90, 96, 284n; adjustment of, 88, 110; "Benign Neglect" theory of, 90, 91, 286n, 287n; devaluation and, 101; evolution of in U.S., 104; measures of, 290n; investment and, 314n; mentioned, 291n. See also basic balance, current account, liquidity balance

Ball, George: on nuclear weapons, 278; on Third World, 234; liberalism and, 240; mentioned, 236, 237, 240, 248

Basic balance: definition of, 96; U.S. deficit in, 97, 98, mentioned, 290n

Battle Act: 227n, 326n

Beaufre, André: on France, 272n; on nuclear weapons, 278n

Belgium: Brasseur Plan and, 241n

Bentham, Jeremy: on self-determination, 188; mentioned, 35

Bergson, Henri: effect on Adamses, 48; theory of evolution and, 272n

Bethmann-Hollweg, Theobald von: 275n

Beveridge, Sir William: Report of, 267n

Birth Control: urged by Ricardo, 21

Bismarck, Otto von: on mercantilism, 27; public authority and, 185; influence on Japan, 205; state socialism, 263n

Boer War: 31

Bosanquet, Bernard: 262n

Brasseur Plan: 341n

Bretton Woods Agreement: significance of, 40, 116; U.S. attitude toward, 40; as gold-dollar system, 88; convertibility in, 89, 117; effect on national economies, 89; fixed exchange rates in, 89; breakdown of, 90; liquidity and, 105; debate on, 282n; mentioned, 40, 81, 88, 268n

Briand, Aristide: De Gaulle and, 79

Britain: See Great Britain

British Empire: Labour Party and, 267n; mentioned, 224, 280n

Brussels: See EEC

Burma: withdrawal from Commonwealth, 280n

Bundy, McGeorge: on nuclear weapons, 278n

Burke-Hartke Bill: Foreign Trade and Investment Act, 304n; arguments against, 320n

Burke, Edmund: opposition to Atlantic unity, 57; idea of state and, 136, 137, 254; mentioned, 313n, 346n

Calleo, David: on Coleridge, 260n; on De Gaulle, 272n; on Britain, 272n, 283n, 306n; balance of payments, 284n; mentioned, 277n, 281n, 287n, 346n

Canada: hurt by timber quota, 26; relations with Britain, 30, 31, 32; U.S. and, 70, 120, 296n; economic growth of, 261n

Capital Controls: interest equalization tax, 99; U.S. and, 99, 292n, 293n, 316n

Carey, Henry: 26, 40

Caribbean: U.S. interest in, 33; economic growth of, 261n; mentioned, 246

Carnegie, Andrew: proposed Anglo-American partnership, 52

Ceylon: independence of, 280n

Chamberlain, Joseph: imperial preferences, 31, 57; attitude toward India, 32; Anglo-German relations, 54; mentioned, 43, 265n

Chiang Kai-shek: 201

Chile: British ties with, 29

China: People's Republic of, 12, 201, 214, 215, 326n; Nationalist, 200

Church, Frank: on U.S. foreign aid, 334n

Churchill, Sir Winston: Stalin and, 38; Iron Curtain speech of, 45, 269n; on Lend-Lease, 268n, 269n; mentioned, 267n

Clay, Henry: on mercantilism, 266n
Clayton, Will: 269n
Cobden, Richard: opposed to British Empire, 25, 30; economic ideals of, 45, 261n; mentioned, 60, 189
Cobbett, William: against free trade, 23
Cold War: duopoly of, 4, 8; Atlanticism and, 19; Russia during, 42; United Nations, 42; ebbing of, 43; effect on U.S., 61, 63; Europe and, 80; Asia during, 200; mentioned, 43
Coleridge, Samuel T.: political ideals of, 23; and Marx, 24
Colonialism: as economic imperialism, 11; and investments, 30; U.S. attitude on, 33; European extension of, 33. See also imperialism
Commodity agreements: Third World and, 229
Common Agricultural Policy (CAP): hurts U.S. exports, 81; re-distribution of resources and, 115; Franco-German entente, 127; De Gaulle, 127, 308n; problems with, 93, 127, 307n, 308n; devaluation and, 289n; trade negotiations, 306n; mentioned, 289n, 294n
Common External Tariff: trade negotiations and, 306n
Common Market: See EEC
Commonwealth: See Great Britain and country headings
Communism: effect on U.S., 42; Atlanticism and, 43; Europe and, 44
Comparative Advantage: concept of, 20; 21–22; weakness of theory, 129
Compensatory Financing: 337n
Comte, Auguste: 279n
Concert of Europe: as plural system, 9
Confederalism: aspect of federalism, 9; EEC and, 10, 184; multinational corporations and, 190

Connally, John B.: on U.S. military expenditures, 99; and expropriation, 342n; mentioned, 292n, 294n, 302n
Co-Prosperity Sphere: 206, 325n
Consumption indifference curve: definition of, 132; mentioned, 309n, 310n
Convertibility: in liberal system, 13; Britain and, 41; period of, 88, 89, 208; and Bretton Woods, 89; threatened, 107; of dollar, 286n; Pompidou on, 288n; mentioned, 284n
Consumer sovereignty: 134
Corporation: role in U.S. economy, 318, 319n. See also international corporations
Corporatism: and liberalism, 189; mercantilism, 189; de Lamennais and, 279n
Coudenhove-Kalergi: Paneuropa and, 79–80; opposed to U.S., 80; De Gaulle and, 125; mentioned, 80, 281n
Couve de Murville, Maurice: on Fouchet Plan, 281n; mentioned, 308n
Croly, Herbert: 319n, 323n
Curzon, George N.: 267n
Customs Union: organization of, 14

Dahrendorf, Ralf: criticism of U.S., 302n
Dalton, Hugh: 267n
Declaration of Independence: 20, 77
Deflation: effect of, 100
De Gaulle, Charles: Atlanticism and, 16; U.S. respect for, 77; support of gold, 92, 287n; C. Streit and, 127; victories of, 127–128; mentioned, 83, 117, 279n, 281n, 283n
–on Europe: British entry into EEC, 75, 125, 281n; conflict with Monnet, 75; and EEC, 75, 81, 125; Coudenhove-Kalergi and, 79–80,

De Gaulle, Charles—*Cont.*
125; force de frappe, 80; Germany, 80; CAP negotiations, 127, 308n
—opposition to U.S.: hegemony, 19, 38, 76, 80; Criticism of NATO, 45, 75, 272n; involvement in Vietnam War, 80, 92; monetary hegemony, 81, 92; withdrawal from NATO, 82; U.S. corporations, 92; U.S. deficits, 92; European inflation, 92
Department of State: opposed to Britain, 39
Department of Treasury: and Britain, 39
Depression: Third World and, 225, Latin America and, 344n
Détente: in Cold War, 64, between U.S. and Russia, 80
Development gap: 221
Dilke, Charles: Anglo-Saxon relation, 56
Dillon, Douglas: trade negotiations, 307n
Diminishing returns: principle of, 21
"Diplomatic Currency": 281n
Dirty floats: and dollar crisis, 107
Dodge Stabilization Plan: Japan and, 325n
Disraeli, Benjamin: agricultural protection and, 24; Robert Peel and, 24; repeal of Corn Laws, 24; Crystal Palace Speech, 54
Dollar: 1971 crisis of, 83, 85, 90, 93, 294n; weakness of, 83, 89, 90, 106, 107, 121, 284n, 285n; as liquidity supply, 89, 105; devaluation of, 85, 90, 101, 102, 104, 106, 121, 285n; as reserve currency, 88, 101, 105, 109; foreign holdings of, 89, 90, 91, 96, 101, 103, 106, 107, 209; support for, 90, 91; European attitude toward, 90, 94; floating of, 103; mentioned, 283
"Draper Report": on Japan, 325n
Dulles, John F.: geopolitics and, 43

Eastern Europe: economic isolation of, 277n
Economic Commission for Latin America (ECLA): 233
Economic efficiency: concept of, 130; limits of, 138; and technology efficiency, 312n
Economic growth: importance of, 21; ideal of, 129; problems with, 140
Economic imperialism: definition of, 11–12; Britain and, 29
Economic integration: nationalism and, 4
Economic liberalism: U.S. attitude toward, 3. See also liberalism
EEC: British membership in, 81, 272n, 306n; and monetary system, 93, 106; Commission of, 110; Japan and, 123; trade of, 112, 135, 167, 300n; agriculture and, 127; Confederalism, 184, 190; Third World and, 226, 236, 237; Fouchet Plan, 281n; self-sufficiency of, 301n; Kennedy and, 317n, mentioned, 112
European Free Trade Association (EFTA): need for control of, 13; Japan and, 123
European integration: U.S. support of, 73
European Monetary Bloc: trade in, 42; fixed exchange rates and, 113; mentioned, 116
European Monetary Union: development of, 93, 115, 289n, 290n; currency of, 113; problems with, 114, 115; mentioned, 297
European parliament: agriculture and, 308n
European Payments Union (EPU): U.S. and, 44, 62; end of, 64, 88; Marshall Plan and, 87
Everett, Edward: Mercantilism and, 266n
External economies: 309n

Fabians: 185
Factor Mobility: 136, 187, 188
Federalism: U.S. and, 9, 19, 67–69;

Federalism—*Cont.*
tradition of, 47; problems with, 10, 48; Europe and, 67; laissez-faire and, 188; Britain, 280n; mentioned, 9–10, 70, 279, 280
Federalist Papers: 280n
Federal Reserve System: 302n
Fischer, Fritz: on Germany, 275n
Fixed exchange rates: Bretton Woods and, 89; description of, 111; EEC and, 112
Flexible exchange rates: favored by U.S., 112
Floating currencies: 103, 287n
Force de frappe: De Gaulle and, 80
Foreign aid: U.S. to Europe. See also Marshall Plan
Foreign Assistance Act: 277n
Foreign exchange: troop costs and, 99
Foreign Investors Tax Act (1966): 294n
Ford Motor Company: in Japan, 333n
Fouchet Plan: 281n
Fowler, Henry M.: 296n
Franc (French): devaluation of, 93, 283n
France: free trade and, 26; relations with U.S., 45, 103, 287n; Indo-China War, 45, 283n; Germany and, 53, 102, 112; British entry into EEC, 125; importance of agriculture to, 127, 128, 308n; Brasseur Plan, 341n; mentioned, 93, 272n, 283n
Free Trade: problems of, 4, 103, 134, 310n; hegemony and, 12, 19; Britain and, 12, 19, 20, 25, 37; U.S. and, 20, 35, 139, 140, 186; benefits of, 133–134, 311n; Ricardo on, 261n; mentioned, 11, 14, 22, 26, 43, 262n, 319n
French planning: 289n
Friedman, Milton: 290n
Fulbright, J. William: on U.S. imperialism, 78
Functionalists: 279n

Galbraith, John K.: multinational corporations and, 173
Gaullism: conflict with Europeanism, 74. See also De Gaulle
General Agreement on Tariffs and Trade (GATT): effect on tariffs, 13, 64, 168; U.S. and, 64, 104; Third World and, 228, 337n; Japan and, 201, 202, 203, 326n, 327n; mentioned, 65, 75, 141, 142
General Motors: 138
General Will: Burke and, 136; Rousseau on, 136
Genoa Conference (1922): 287n
Germany: mercantilism, 12, 27; and Britain, 27, 53, 54, 55, 56, 61; free trade and, 26; military power of, 30, 61; Europe and, 53; and France, 55, 80, 102, 112; colonies of, 54; liberalism in, 75, 262n; monetary policies of, 101, 102; Ostpolitik, 115, CAP and, 127
Giscard d'Estaing, Valéry: 283n, 297n
Gladstone, William: on U.S., 53; on British Empire, 54; liberalism of, 54; Cobden Treaty and, 262n
Gold: in Europe, 13; Britain and, 32; Bretton Woods and, 88; U.S. supply of, 89, 90, 283n; dollar convertibility to, 89, 90; De Gaulle on, 92, 287n; mentioned, 13, 60, 91, 266n
Grand Design: 82, 124, 238, 239, 317n
Great Britain: Asia and, 29, 45, 201, 326; during 1930's, 56; collective security, 45
—Commonwealth: as colonial power, 11, 25, 30, 31, 336n, 343n; U.S. inheritance of empire, 19; decline of, 26, 30, 41, 280n; Canada and, 26, 30, 31; mentioned, 10, 45, 125, 200, 201, 202, 225, 236, 272n, 280n, 306n, 326n, 327n, 341n
—military position: 12, 30, 45
—free trade: 12, 19, 20, 25

Great Britain—*Cont.*
—nineteenth century: 22, 314n; farming of, 22; middle class during, 22; trade during, 22, 23, 264n; investment during, 264n, 265n
—decline: 28, 30, 40, 41, 46
—United States: in conflict with, 37–38; hegemony over Britain, 40–41, 45, 57–58; special relationship and, 45, 52, 56
—Labour: policies of, 38; government of, 38; preferences, 39; movement of, 164
—economy: exports and, 39; strength of, 41; growth of, 56–57; investments of, 164; post-World War II, 283n
—Germany: 53, 54, 56, 61, 93
Grew, John: 206
Gross National Product (GNP): 101, 313n
Group of 77: 222, 230

Haberler, Gottfried: 228, 231, 286n
Halévy, Elie: 266n
Halifax, Edward F.: 280n
Hallstein, Walter: De Gaulle and, 75
Hamilton, Alexander: 27, 69, 70, 71, 262n, 279n
Hay, John: 47, 273n
Hay-Pauncefort Treaty: 52
Hegel, Friedrich: 188
Hegemony: U.S. federalism and, 71, 72, 108. See also U.S.
Herter, Christian: 82
Hickenlooper Amendment: 326n
Hitler, Adolf: 256
Hobsbawm, E. J.: 264n, 265n, 314n
Holland: See Netherlands
Hoover, Herbert: 266n, 277n, 319n
Hoover, J. Edgar: 50
House, Edward M.: 276n
Houthakker, Hendrik: 294n
Hull, Cordell: free trade and, 33, 37, 43, 118, 329n; use of Lend-Lease, 40; on Japan, 325n; mentioned, 35, 36, 42, 43, 60, 62, 63, 64–65, 82, 83, 87, 88, 104, 105,

Hull, Cordell—*Cont.*
120, 226, 236n, 240n, 248n, 266n, 267n

Imperialism: U.S. and, 7, 34, 47; Spanish Empire, 224, 335n, 336n; mentioned, 50, 172, 318n, 346n
Imperial System: definition of, 8
Import-substitution: 12
Inconvertibility: 90
India: Britain and, 28–29, 30, 265n, 267n; independence of, 280n
Inflation: 304n
Interdependence: 65, 71, 82, 118
Interest equalization tax: 99, 292n, 293n
International Business Machines: 138
International corporations: feeling against, 4, 21, 165, 291n, 317n, 323n, 335n; investments of by U.S., 34, 75, 83, 87, 91, 96, 107, 121, 167, 175, 176, 179, 182, 286, 294n, 316n, 320n; European, 165, 183, 184, 286n, 321n, 322n; ideals of, 170, 186, 187; mentioned, 187, 190, 289n, 314n, 315n, 318n
International Monetary Fund (IMF): liquidity and, 13, 105, 110, 116; convertibility and, 37; development of, 40, 42, 110, 282n; Cold War, 42, 87; relation to NATO, 62, 64; EEC and, 93; Third World, 228, 337n; mentioned, 65, 87, 88, 116, 278n, 285n, 288n, 297n, 303n
International Monetary System: 85, 87, 89, 108
International Trade Organization (ITO): 37, 40, 41
Ireland: 26, 280n
Irwin, John: at UNCTAD, 237
Isolationism: in U.S., 47
Italian City States: 9
Italy: 9, 26, 262n
Ivan the Terrible: 78

Jackson, Andrew: 48, 266n
Japan: strength of, 14, 196, 200,

Japan—*Cont.*
201, 203, 205, 325n, 328n, 329n, 332n, 333n; U.S. and, 14, 107, 120, 197, 198, 199, 200, 213, 327n; relations with West and, 54, 196, 197, 198, 199, 208, 217; Britain and, 55, 200, 201, 202, 212, 326n, 327n, 328n; revaluation and, 201, 210, 332; economy, 199, 207, 324n, 332n, 333n; and Europe, 200, 203, 204, 209, 210, 212; domestic situation, 204, 205, 206, 207, 210, 216, 328n, 329n, 333n; trade and, 204, 205, 208, 327n, 332n, 333n; China and, 214, 215, 326n, 327n; mentioned, 198, 206, 214, 236n–237n, 327n, 332n

Japanese Peace Treaty: 325n, 326n

Jefferson, Thomas: 77

Johnson, Lyndon B.: 82, 99, 119

Kahn, Herman: 207

Kautsky, Karl: 318n

Kennedy, John F.: and France, 81; Atlantic Community and, 82, 317n; on trade, 119, 307n

Kennedy Round: U.S. and, 104, 127, 307n; agricultural aspects, 125, 126, 306; mentioned, 83, 104, 119, 122, 124, 125, 126, 141, 239, 303n, 305n, 306n, 307n

Key Currency: 283n

Keynes, John M.: 39, 40, 41, 105, 174, 282n

Kindleberger, Charles P.: 186

Korean War: 44, 201, 202, 325n

Krause, Lawrence: 286n, 287n

Lamennais, Félicité Robert de: 279n

Latin America: Britain and, 29, 30, 31; development of, 243, 244, 245, 246, 247, 248; U.S. and, 33, 36, 341n

Latin America Free Trade Association (LAFTA): 337n, 344n, 345n

League of Nations: 9, 58

Lend-Lease: Britain and, 37, 40; mentioned, 267n, 268n, 269n

Lenin, Vladimir I.: 51, 318n

Legitimacy: 9

Liberalism: 171, 224, 225. See also Free Trade; Hull

Lincoln, Abraham: 69

Liquidity: U.S. and, 89, 91, 105, 106; supply of, 89, 91, 92; discussion of, 104–106; SDRs and, 105; crisis in Britain, 283n

Liquidity Balance: 95, 290n

Liska, George: 335n

List, Friederich: 26, 27, 205, 262n

Lloyd, George D.: 55

Lodge, Henry Cabot: U.S. Navy and, 49, 273n; on immigration, 49, 272n, 273n; imperialism of, 49, 77, 277n; mentioned, 47, 49, 51, 58, 70, 274n

London: 31, 32

London Economic Conference: 36

MacArthur, Gen. Douglas: 199

McNamara, Robert: 278n

Maddison, Angus: 263n

Madison, James: expansion and, 34; universal view, 70; federalist principles of, 68–69; mentioned, 280n

Madisonian system: limitation of, 70; Third World and, 242

Mahan, Alfred T.: geopolitics of, 43; Atlanticism and, 47, 51; on Eastern threat, 49; imperialism of, 77; mentioned, 49, 52, 61, 66, 197, 274n, 276n

Malthus, Robert: effect of Ricardo, 21; mentioned, 221, 243, 261n

Mao Tse-tung: 42

Mark: fluctuation of, 93

Market mechanism: theory of, 130; shortcomings of, 136

Marshall Plan: importance of, 44; effects of, 44, 62, 64, 77, 88, 96; EPU and, 87

Marx, Karl: 24, 189, 202, 260n

Marxism: Atlanticism and, 18; Ricardo and, 20; America and, 34; international corporations and, 172, 187; mentioned, 172–173

"Master currency": 282n

"May events": 285n
Meiji restoration: 205
Mercantilism: as cause of World
  War II, 3; definition of, 13; Brit-
  ain and, 23, 26, 28, 32; America
  and, 26, 36; recent, 129, 141,
  254; European tradition of, 185,
  266n; trade and, 141; Third
  World, 224
Mestizo population: 244
Mexico: 70
Middle East: 124
Military expenditure: See Foreign
  exchange; United States
Mitteleuropa: 27, 54, 275n
Moley, Raymond: Roosevelt and,
  35; on protectionism, 266n
Monnet, Jean: De Gaulle and, 75;
  Europe and, 80
Mounier, Emmanuel: 279n
Monopoly: 131, 308n
Montevideo Conference: 36
Morgenthau, Henry: liberalism of,
  37, 43; on Bretton Woods Sys-
  tem, 87, 282n; mentioned, 42,
  88, 268n
Morgenthau Plan: 268n
Most-favored-nation principle: 232,
  234, 238. See also Japan
Multilateral nuclear force (MLF):
  81

Nationalism: decline of, 3–5; reviv-
  al, 5, 67; and Third World, 242
Nationalist China: 326n
Nation State: evolution of, 5;
  strength of, 6; "minimal," 11–12;
  free trade and, 20; durability of,
  67–68; in Europe, 73; clash with
  corporations, 189; vs. federalism,
  189; Burke on, 137, 254; men-
  tioned, 253, 254, 255, 346n
Naumann, Friedrich: 275n
Netherlands: 247, 281n
"Neutral currency": 283n
New Deal: 319n
New Zealand: 333n
Nietzsche, Friedrich: 48
Nigeria: civil war, 10; EEC and,
  341n

Nixon, Richard M.: economic policy of, 83, 99, 100, 106, 119, 236,
  302n, 341n; U.S. troops and, 103;
  on expropriation, 237, 342n; Pompidou and, 285n; mentioned 291n
Non-tariff barriers: 303n
North Atlantic Treaty Organization
  (NATO): development of, 42,
  45, 46, 65; liberalism and, 43;
  Brussels Treaty and, 45; Britain
  and, 45, 46; France and, 45, 75,
  82, 272n, 281n; U.S. and, 46, 61,
  63, 71, 82, 87; détente and, 61,
  82, 305n; mentioned, 88, 119
Norstad, Gen. Lauris: on Atlantic
  Community, 186–188
Nuclear: 87. See also Multilateral
  Nuclear Force; and country headings

Offset agreements: 291n, 292n
Open-door policy: 33, 77
Organization for Economic Cooperation and Development (OECD):
  13, 82, 305n
Organization for European Economic Cooperation (OEEC): 42,
  87
Organization of Petroleum Exporting Countries (OPEC): 222,
  335n
Overseas Private Investment Corporation (OPIC): 342n, 343n
Osgood, Robert E.: 272n
Ostpolitik: 115
Output Consumption Equilibrium:
  133

Pacific Free Trade Area: 333n
Pakistan: 10, 280n
"Paretian optimum": 310n
Peek, George: 35, 266n
"Personalism": 279n
Philippines: 342n
Physiocrats: 261n
Pluralism: 4, 6, 8–9, 13, 108, 116
Polk, Judd: 187, 188
Pollution: 121
Pompidou, Georges: 285n, 288n

Population Growth: 20. See also Malthus
Pound: 283n
Prebisch, Rául: 230, 231, 232, 233, 234, 245
Preferences: 232, 238, 239, 341, 342
"Product Cycle" Theory: 318n
Production possibility curve: 131–132, 309n
Protectionism: U.S. and, 26, 42, 85, 86, 103, 104, 116, 119, 120, 122, 125, 126, 305n; mentioned, 12, 103, 121, 304n, 320n
Proudhon, Joseph: 279n

Rathenau, Walter: 275n
Raymond, Daniel: 27
Regional policy: 223, 225, 226, 301n, 337n
Revaluation: 101, 103. See also Germany and Japan
Reuss, Henry: 287n
Revisionism: 92, 318n. See also De Gaulle
Ricardo, David: pessimism of, 34; economic ideals of, 129, 171; free market and, 174, 261n; diminishing returns, 260n, 261n; mentioned, 25, 31, 163, 187, 189, 314n
Rio de Janeiro Agreement: 296n
Rogers, William: 330n
Roman Empire: 8, 46
Roosa bonds: 284n
Roosevelt, Franklin D.: 35, 37, 118
Roosevelt, Theodore: 47, 50, 70, 266n, 319n, 323n
Rosebery, Lord: 265n
Rostow, Eugene V.: 235, 236, 237, 278n
Rousseau, Jean Jacques: 136, 137, 313n
Rueff, Jacques: 284n, 287n
Russia: See U.S.S.R.

SACEUR: 71
Saint-Simon, Henri de: 5, 279n
Sato, Eisaku: 216, 333n
"Scarce currency clause": 282n

Schiller, Karl: 302n
Schlesinger, Arthur: 266
Schumann, Maurice: 302n
Schumpeter, Joseph: 222
Seeley, J. R.: 56, 57, 69, 70, 276n
Semmel, Bernard: 261n, 262n
Servan-Schreiber, J. J.: 288n
Shonfield, Andrew: 139
Silvermaster group: 270n
Smith, Adam: 20, 171, 187, 189
Smithsonian Agreement: 285n, 304n
Southeast Asia: 214, 215
Spanish-American War: 33
Spanish Empire: 224, 335n, 336n
Special drawing rights: U.S. and, 105, 106, 298n; liquidity and, 105, 296n; EEC on, 106; nature of, 106, 297n; France and, 296n; mentioned, 285n, 287n, 288n, 289n
Special Relationship: 50–52, 53, 54, 55, 57, 283n
Speculation: 92, 93, 101, 289n
Stalin, Joseph: 38, 42
States' rights: 280n
Sterling bloc: 41, 278n
Stimson, Henry: 277n
"Stop-Go" policy: 283n
Strange, Susan: 282n
Streit, Clarence: Atlantic Alliance and, 59; concept of world state, 60, 70; Europe and, 80; mentioned, 63, 69, 277n
Supranationalism: 9, 10
Supreme Command for Allied Powers (SCAP): 204, 329n
"Swap agreements": 284n
Switzerland: 247

Tariffs: Europe and, 13, 32; mentioned, 82, 107, 311n
Taylor, A. J. P.: 276n
Technology: effect of, 4, 5, 35, 133; abundance of, 137, 172; mentioned, 131, 171, 312n, 318n, 320n, 321n, 323n
Third World: U.S. position on, 234, 235, 236, 237, 238, 241, 242, 334n; trade of, 336n, 338n, 340n; preferences, 338n, 343n; prob-

Third World—*Cont.*
lems in, 43, 344n; mentioned, 228, 241, 334n; 336n, 337n
Tocqueville, Alexis de: democracy, 18; on U.S., 274n; federalism and, 279n
"Top currency": 281n
Torrens, Robert: 261n, 265n
Tourism: 98, 100
Trade: Agreements Act, 36, 125, 266n, 267n, 305n, 307n; restrictions to, 64, 124, 232, 311n; U.S. balance of, 85, 88, 100, 101, 102, 104, 118, 120, 121, 294n, 295n, 303n, 304n, 314n; liberalization of, 104, 307n; EEC, 123; U.S., 123; regionalization, 123, 124; mentioned, 89, 107, 118, 119, 122, 124, 130, 133, 231. See also balance of payments, current account, free trade
Treaty of Rome: 341n. See also EEC
Treaty of Versailles: 59
Triffin, Robert: 89, 203, 283n
Truman Doctrine: 43
Truman, Harry: 42, 268n
Turner, Frederich J.: 280n
Two-tier gold market: 284n
Two-tier most favored nation system: 235

Unemployment: 100. See also Dollar
Union of Soviet Socialist Republics (U.S.S.R.): relations with U.S., 38, 53, 63; Europe and, 45, 53, 61, 63, mentioned, 8, 12, 231
United Nations: 37, 42, 87
United Nations Conference on Trade and Development: 222, 230, 235, 236, 237, 340n
United Nations Development Decade: 334n, 335n
United Nations Economic Commission on Asia and the Far East (ECAFE): 332n
United Nations Relief and Recovery Administration (UNRRA): 268n
United States: Cold war and, 8, 61, 63, 80, 200; Latin America and,

United States—*Cont.*
33, 341; Asia, 33; U.S.S.R., 70, 120, 296; foreign policy, 277n, 326n, 330n
—Civil War: federalism and, 10; reconstruction after, 48–49, 53, 69, 336n
—military: decline of, 4; hegemony of, 14, 30, 65; expenditures for, 47, 85, 98, 103, 292n
—Europe: hegemony over, 35, 42, 43; generosity for, 44, 77; mentioned, 19, 38, 80, 81, 92, 126, 302n
—protection: 12, 26, 33, 42, 85, 86, 99, 104, 116, 119, 292n, 293n, 316n
—economy: 27–28, 33, 42, 47, 53, 70, 100, 112, 121, 266n, 280n
—and Britain: 28, 29, 31, 32, 33, 39, 40–41, 45, 47, 52, 53, 54, 57–58, 121, 275n
—decline: 39, 83, 88, 90, 95, 96, 102, 103, 105, 107, 108, 109, 116
—corporations: 59, 83, 85, 163, 164, 165, 166, 167, 171, 172
—as nation-state: 67–69, 70, 77
—monetary policies: 88, 89, 94, 139, 142
Uruguay: 29
Utopianism: 130

Vatican City: 108
Venezuelan boundary dispute: 52
Vietnam War: 80, 82, 92, 120
"Virtuous circle" theory: of growth, 313n

Wakefield, Edward G.: 261n, 265n
Warsaw Pact: 8
Washington Disarmament Conference: 55
Welfare State: 138, 140, 257
White, Harry Dexter: 37, 40, 42, 43, 268n, 270n, 282n
Wilhelm II: 275n
Williams, W. Appleman: 206n
Wilkie, Wendell: 61
Wilson, Harold: 326n

Wilson, T. Woodrow: world view of, 3, 58, 78, 87; mentioned, 58, 77–78, 239n, 247–248, 276n
World War I: 32, 34, 51, 55
World War II: 61

Yalta: 80
Yen: 107
"Yoshida letter": 326n

Zollverein: 202n